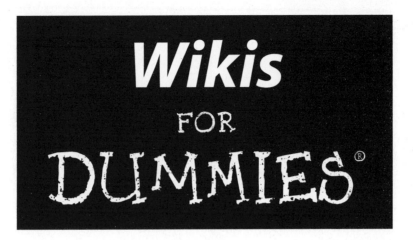

Wikis FOR DUMMIES®

by Dan Woods and Peter Thoeny

Foreword by Ward Cunningham
Inventor of wikis

Wiley Publishing, Inc.

Wikis For Dummies®

Published by
Wiley Publishing, Inc.
111 River Street
Hoboken, NJ 07030-5774
www.wiley.com

Copyright © 2007 by Wiley Publishing, Inc., Indianapolis, Indiana

Published by Wiley Publishing, Inc., Indianapolis, Indiana

Published simultaneously in Canada

WILEY

Wikis For Dummies®

Wiki Markup

Although each wiki engine markup is slightly different, they're all easy to use. This table highlights the differences between markup for the MediaWiki and TWiki wiki engines.

To Create This	MediaWiki Markup	TWiki Markup

Headings 1 through 3	`== Level 1 ==`
	`=== Level 2 ===`
	`==== Level 3 ====`
		`---+ Level 1`
		`---++ Level 2`
		`---+++ Level 3`

Bullets (add asterisks to make sub-bullets)	`* bullet`
	`** second-level bullet`
	`*** third-level bullet`
		`*`
		`*`
		`*`
		(3, 6, 9 spaces; asterisk; space)

1. 2. 3.	`#` `#` `#`	`1.` `1.` `1.`
italic	`''italic''`	`_italic_`
bold	`'''bold'''`	`*bold*`
bold italic	`'''''bold italic'''''`	`__bold italic__`

Wiki Linking

Here are different ways to create links in MediaWiki and TWiki. Chapter 7 covers wiki linking.

MediaWiki	TWiki	Type of Link
`[[Name of page]]`	`NameOfPage` Wiki words create automatic links.	Internal.

`[[name of page|`
`display text]]`
	`[[Name of Page]]`
	`[[Name of Page]`
	`[display text]]`
		Aliased internal. In MediaWiki, you can use a pipe (|) to give an internal link a different name. In TWiki, you use nested square brackets.

`http://www.wiley.com`	`http://www.wiley.com` `[[http://www.wiley.com]]`	Automatic external; links automatically and displays link on page.
`[http://www.wiley.com` `Wiley home page]`	`[[http://www.wiley.com` `Wiley home page]]`	Aliased external. Name of link is displayed instead of link.

Wiki Management Tasks

Keep your wiki clean and up to date. Decide what to delete by checking these six items:

- ✔ **Data retention policy:** Do you have to keep it or archive it?
- ✔ **The author:** Is the author keeping the page up to date?
- ✔ **The date:** Is the page old and out of date?
- ✔ **The content:** Does this page overlap with other pages?
- ✔ **The links:** Could the content be linked to other pages?
- ✔ **The word count:** Is the page short and its contents suitable to be incorporated on another page? Is the page overly long? Should it be split into multiple pages?

Wikis For Dummies®

Cheat Sheet

Wiki Design Tips

Chapter 8 provides hints about how to design an effective wiki; here's a 30-second flyover of that chapter:

- Find the right structure and taxonomy to use: whole, parts, subparts; organizational chart; actions in a sequence; alphabetical list; timeline; order of importance; geography.

- Make navigation easy and obvious.

- Use templates to give pages a common structure and make using the wiki more intuitive.

- View design as a research problem. Find a design that works and use it as a basis for your own design.

- Name pages descriptively (because page names usually become links).

- Divide your wiki into sections and create categories.

- Add supporting pages such as a site map, list of users, page with templates, or Frequently Asked Question (FAQ) page.

- Use color and images to help make the wiki attractive and to communicate content and navigation information.

- Consider incorporating themes if you're using a hosted wiki.

- Change the look of your wiki with skins — if you host your own wiki.

Routine Management Checklist

Daily	Monthly	Annually
Set up users; reset passwords; delete users.	Check the structure of each area.	Evaluate whether the wiki is achieving its purpose.
Create groups and permissions for them.	Assess whether the wiki needs to change to reflect organizational changes.	Create a list of best practices.
Review changes to the wiki, and roll them back if there are problems (such as inappropriate postings or active pages being used as a sandbox for practice).	Look for pages with lots of changes or pages that grow and grow. Trim as necessary.	Reassess the wiki's management systems; for example, is there an easier way to do backups?
Try out the structure of the front page of the wiki to make sure links are active and working.	Like cells, sometimes wikis need to divide. If a new project has been grafted onto an existing wiki, make a new web for it.	Celebrate the wiki and recap what it contributes to your organization.
Look for obsolete pages.	Look for obsolete pages and delete them or repurpose the content.	
Back up the wiki or make sure it is backed up.	Send an e-mail newsletter to promote the wiki and encourage use.	

For Dummies: Bestselling Book Series for Beginners

About the Authors

Dan Woods has a background in technology and journalism. He has a BA in Computer Science from the University of Michigan. He was CTO of both TheStreet.com and CapitalThinking, led development at Time Inc.'s Pathfinder, and created applications for NandO.net, one of the first newspaper Web sites. Dan has a MS from Columbia University Graduate School of Journalism. He covered banking for three years at *The Record of Hackensack;* was Database Editor for three years at the *Raleigh News & Observer;* and has written more than ten books on various technology topics, in addition to numerous white papers and magazine articles. Dan Woods founded the Evolved Media Network to offer services in technology communications using the Communication by Design methodology.

Peter Thoeny is the founder of *TWiki,* the leading wiki for corporate collaboration and knowledge management. Managing the open source project for the last seven years, Peter invented the concept of *structured wikis,* where free-form wiki content can be structured with tailored wiki applications. He is a recognized thought-leader in wikis and social software, featured in numerous articles and technology conferences including LinuxWorld, *Business Week, The Wall Street Journal,* and more. A software developer with more than 20 years of experience, Peter specializes in software architecture, user interface design, and Web technology. He graduated from the Swiss Federal Institute of Technology in Zurich, lived in Japan for eight years working as an engineering manager for Denso building CASE tools, and managed the Knowledge Engineering group at Wind River for several years. With StructuredWikis.com and TWiki.net, Peter is now offering services, support, and training for enterprise wiki deployments.

Dedication

The authors dedicate this book to Ward Cunningham, whose vision for what wikis could be and generous spirit in sharing his invention have made the world a better place to live.

Co-author Peter Thoeny is dedicating this book to all contributors of the open source TWiki over the past eight years who, with their hard work, helped propel wikis into the workplace.

Authors' Acknowledgments

The authors would like to thank Ward Cunningham for inventing wikis and for his generosity in sharing the concept with the world. Ward helped us write the book by providing his thoughts in several interviews and writing a wonderful foreword. What the world needs now is not only more wikis, but more Wards as well.

This book was written using the Communication by Design methodology of Evolved Media Network in which a group of people, using a wiki of course, creates this book using a division of labor. Dan Woods and Peter Thoeny played the role of editor/analysts who designed the book, performed the research, and invented and captured the content. The writing team included Dan Woods, Peter Thoeny, Noah Robischon, Deb Cameron, Deb Gabriel, John Biggs, and Erin Schulte. We offer our sincere thanks to them all.

This book would never have happened without the support and *For Dummies* wisdom of Katie Feltman, Nicole Sholly, Teresa Artman (all of Wiley), and Keith Underdahl, who was brought in to help us. We authors bow and tip our hats to you.

Many people in the wiki world were interviewed for this book or contributed content in various ways, including interviews and e-mail. We thank them for their enthusiasm and positive attitude. This generous group of people includes: Jimmy Donal Wales, founder of Wikipedia; Adam Frey and James Beyers of WikiSpaces; Joe Kraus of Google/JotSpot; Ramit Sethi of PBwiki; Ken Tyler of seedwiki; Matt Wiseley of EditMe; Sam Obio of BluWiki; Steven Marder of Swicki; and several others who chose not to be named.

Many, many wikis are described in this book, but many great wikis are not. Given that hundreds of thousands (if not millions) of wikis thrive on the Web, covering them all would be impossible. We attempted to capture a representative sample, but no doubt we have failed. For example, because of the deadline for this book, we weren't able to include screenshots from Google's JotSpot, which will no doubt change the world of wikis when it officially launches as part of Google's application toolset. We tried to include wikis in each of the broad categories we defined: content-focused, process-focused, community, and ease-of-use wikis. We are certain, though, that more categories will emerge, and perhaps the ones that we have defined will morph into new ones. If you know about good wikis that deserve attention or have comments on the book, we do want to keep the conversation that resulted in this book going in any way we can. Peter Thoeny would love to hear from you at www.structuredwikis.com and Twiki.net and would be overjoyed to help you build a wiki of your own. Dan Woods will be continuing research and reporting on wikis at www.evolvedtechnologist.com. Please visit us in either place to share your thoughts.

Publisher's Acknowledgments

We're proud of this book; please send us your comments through our online registration form located at www.dummies.com/register/.

Some of the people who helped bring this book to market include the following:

Acquisitions, Editorial, and Media Development

Project Editor: Nicole Sholly

Senior Acquisitions Editor: Katie Feltman

Senior Copy Editor: Teresa Artman

Technical Editor: Lee Musick

Editorial Manager: Kevin Kirschner

Media Development and Quality Assurance: Angela Denny, Kate Jenkins, Steven Kudirka, Kit Malone

Media Development Coordinator: Jenny Swisher

Media Project Supervisor: Laura Moss-Hollister

Editorial Assistant: Amanda Foxworth

Senior Editorial Assistant: Cherie Case

Cartoons: Rich Tennant (www.the5thwave.com)

Composition Services

Project Coordinator: Lynsey Osborn

Layout and Graphics: Claudia Bell, Carl Byers, Carrie A. Foster, Shane Johnson, Stephanie D. Jumper, Jennifer Mayberry, Alicia B. South, Julie Trippetti, Christine Williams

Proofreaders: Aptara, Jessica Kramer, Susan Moritz, Charles Spencer

Indexer: Aptara

Anniversary Logo Design: Richard Pacifico

Publishing and Editorial for Technology Dummies

   Richard Swadley, Vice President and Executive Group Publisher

   Andy Cummings, Vice President and Publisher

   Mary Bednarek, Executive Acquisitions Director

   Mary C. Corder, Editorial Director

Publishing for Consumer Dummies

   Diane Graves Steele, Vice President and Publisher

   Joyce Pepple, Acquisitions Director

Composition Services

   Gerry Fahey, Vice President of Production Services

   Debbie Stailey, Director of Composition Services

Table of Contents

Foreword

Foreword by Ward Cunningham

You have a thought. You want to write it down. You're thinking your computer might be pretty good for that, but, surprise — it's not.

You need two things when you want to write. You need the words to say what you are thinking, and you need a place to put them.

Before wikis, computer writing was all about the words. The computer could help you type them, spell them, hyphenate them, size them, shape them, and align them. But when it came to developing your thought, well, you were on your own.

Now, with wikis, you have a place to write. A wiki is a place to write in the same way that a party is a place to talk. There are thoughts all around you. Some are interesting, some less so. At a party or on a wiki, a word or two will be your trigger. Ideas start flowing. Talking or writing, you're among friends, the stage is set, you say your piece, it fits in, your words trigger the next thought: conversation.

A wiki is like a party that doesn't have to stop. It's a party that doesn't get crowded because new rooms appear when needed. It's a timeless party where you can try each conversation over and over until you get it right.

You might be wondering how a page becomes a party. Maybe you've typed pages and pages before, and it never seemed like fun. "Where do words go if not on the page?" you might be thinking.

That's what this book explains. It shows you in plain English and with many examples just how powerful your computer becomes when you're at a wiki. Dan and Peter show you big ones, little ones, noisy ones, and quiet ones. They show you wikis that are for work and wikis at play. You're going to love this book. Party on.

Ward Cunningham
Portland, Oregon
2007

Introduction

*W*ikis, born in 1995, had a quiet childhood. Now, as wikis approach their teens, they are having a heck of a coming-out party as they are used absolutely everywhere for everything imaginable. *Wikipedia,* an online encyclopedia created by using a wiki, is one of the most-used reference works on the planet. United States (U.S.) federal intelligence agencies — the CIA, the NSA, the Defense Department, and others — use a wiki to help gather, share, and analyze information. Google, IBM, Motorola, SAP, Sun, Yahoo!, and tens of thousands of other companies run important parts of their businesses with wikis. Hundreds of thousands of families, clubs, schools, and scientists use wikis for every sort of task. We even wrote this book with the help of a wiki. All these examples are just the tip of the iceberg when it comes to prominent use of wikis.

The number of ways how wikis are being offered and hosted is also exploding. In October 2006, Google (the famous search engine company) purchased *JotSpot,* a commercially developed wiki, which will be added to Google's core offerings of mail, calendar, and shared documents sometime in 2007. WikiSpaces, wetpaint, Wikidot, Wikia, XWiki, BluWiki, seedwiki, PBwiki, Riters, StikiPad, Central Desktop, and others offer free, hosted wikis that are ready to use over the Internet. Companies such as Socialtext and Atlassian offer wikis that can either be installed or hosted. By far, the largest number of wiki sites are run by open source wiki engines, such as TWiki, MoinMoin, MediaWiki, and a number of others.

Boggles the mind a bit, doesn't it? You're probably looking at this book because you heard about wikis and wonder whether they can help you get where you want to go. They *can* help you, and the *how* is really quite easy. We wrote this book because wikis changed our lives and how we work. With just a bit of effort, we suspect that wikis will do the same for you, just like they have for millions of other people. So read on.

About This Book

In *Wikis For Dummies,* you will find a top-to-bottom guide to understanding what wikis are and how to use them. Unlike many other types of technology you might encounter, you need to realize that wikis aren't a product or a brand or a company. Rather, *wikis* are collections of Web pages that anyone can edit — a style of Web site invented by Ward Cunningham. This book introduces you to the basics of the style and shows how they're implemented with minor variations in specific products. The sorts of skills and knowledge that you can acquire with this book include how to

- ✔ Edit wiki pages by using wiki markup or WYSIWYG (What You See Is What You Get) editors.
- ✔ Format the information on a wiki page.
- ✔ Link wiki pages.
- ✔ Organize the pages in your wiki so people can find them.
- ✔ Choose the right home for your wiki.
- ✔ Attract users to your wiki.
- ✔ Manage your wiki.

Foolish Assumptions

In *Wikis For Dummies,* we don't assume any prior knowledge of HTML (Web markup language), wiki markup, programming languages, or system administration skills. However, we do assume that you have surfed the Web. We also assume that you have a working knowledge of personal computers and have used browsers to go to Web sites. If you've used a Web mail system such as Yahoo! Mail, Gmail, or Hotmail, you'll find that editing a wiki page is just about the same as writing and sending an e-mail.

Conventions Used in This Book

By *conventions,* we simply mean a set of rules that we employ in this book to present information to you consistently. When you see a term *italicized,* look for its definition, which is included so that you know what things mean in the context of wiki creation and maintenance. Web site addresses and e-mail addresses appear in `monofont` so that they stand out from regular text. Wiki markup and HTML appear in a separate font, set off from the rest of the text, like this:

```
---+ My First Wiki Page
```

What You Don't Have to Read

We structured this book *modularly* — that is, it's designed so that you can easily find just the information you need — so you don't have to read whatever doesn't pertain to your task at hand. We include sidebars here and there throughout the book that contain interesting information that isn't necessarily integral to the discussion at hand; feel free to skip over these. You also don't have to read the paragraphs marked with Technical Stuff icons, which parse out uber-techy tidbits (which might not be your cup of tea).

How This Book Is Organized

Wikis For Dummies is split into four parts. You don't have to read it sequentially, you don't have to look at every part, you don't have to review each chapter, and you don't even have to read all the sections in any particular chapter. (Of course, you can if you want to; it's a good read.) And the Table of Contents and the index can help you quickly find whatever information you need. In this section, we briefly describe what each part contains.

Part 1: Introducing Wikis

Part I shows you what wikis are and what they are not. You can read the history of how Ward Cunningham created the idea of wikis and how wikis slowly propagated from engineering departments to the mainstream. You get your feet wet by seeing the basics of creating and adding content to a page. We then take you on a tour through examples of what wikis are used for and show you the most famous wiki of all — Wikipedia.

Part II: Making Your Own Wiki

Part II assumes that you've gotten the bug and are ready to dive into the detailed mechanics of designing and creating wiki pages. No matter which choice you make for creating your wiki, by putting content on a wiki, you enter a new world. It all begins with your first page. Usually, people get started by going to one of the many hosted wikis described in this part. Read along there to follow the instructions on setting up your new wiki — there it is! A blank wiki page! In this part, we also give you the details of formatting wiki pages, linking them, and the principles of wiki design.

Part III: Promoting, Managing, and Improving Your Wiki

Part III focuses on meeting the challenges of promoting a wiki as well as choosing and installing your own wiki engine if that's what makes sense for you. You can read how to manage and protect your wiki as well as the possibilities for adding advanced functionality by using the structured wikis concept. (*Structured wikis* add advanced features to make wikis work like spreadsheets, databases, or automated tools for managing complex step-by-step processes.)

Part IV: The Part of Tens

The Part of Tens covers wiki attitudes and roles as well as ways how wikis are used at the office. This part also provides a list of innovative and exotic wikis that are worth a look.

Icons Used in This Book

For Dummies books are known for those helpful icons that point you in the direction of really great information. This section briefly describes each icon used in this book.

Tip icons point out helpful information or key techniques that save you time and effort.

Remember icons are used to note particularly important things in the text to greatly help you understand the technology.

The Warning icon is synonymous with, "Hey, you! Be careful!" When you see this icon, pay attention and proceed with caution.

This icon denotes that techie stuff lurks nearby. If you're not feeling very techie, you can skip this info.

Where to Go from Here

If you're new to wikis, read Chapter 1 to get your bearings and Chapters 3 and 4 to get an idea of what can be done with wikis. If you want to get your feet wet right away, go to Chapter 2, which gets you started creating wiki pages.

If you're pretty familiar with wikis and want to deepen your skills, start with the chapters in Part II. If you're running a wiki and want more advanced advice, Part III will be the best first stop, and you can reach back to the other chapters as needed.

Part I
Introducing Wikis

The 5th Wave   By Rich Tennant

"It was supposed to be a simple sleep potion. That's why you can't always trust the information you get off of 'Wiccapedia.'"

In this part . . .

In this part, we show you the world of wikis in all its beauty and complexity. In Chapter 1, we explain that wikis are not just one product but a style of product that has many exemplars. You can see how and why Ward Cunningham invented wikis. And you can read how wikis are not blogs, forums, or other styles of Web sites.

Chapter 2 is where newbies can get their hands wet and type an initial wiki page. Chapter 3 shows how wikis are used for all sorts of reasons. Chapter 4 surveys *Wikipedia,* the most famous wiki in the world. We wish you good wiki-ing.

Chapter 1

Understanding Wikis: From Ward's Brain to Your Browser

In This Chapter

▶ Finding your way to wikis

▶ Understanding what makes a wiki a wiki

▶ Comparing wikis with blogs and other Web sites

▶ Examining the history and future of wikis

▶ How to start using wikis

*W*hen Ward Cunningham started programming the first wiki engine in 1994 and then released it on the Internet in 1995, he set forth a simple set of rules for creating Web sites that pushed all the technical gobbledygook into the background and made creating and sharing content as easy as possible.

Ward's vision was simple: Create the simplest possible online database that could work. And his attitude was generous; he put the idea out there to let the world run with it. The results were incredible. Ward's inventiveness and leadership had been long established by the role he played in senior engineering jobs, promoting design patterns, and helping develop the concept of Extreme Programming. That a novel idea like the wiki flowed from his mind onto the Internet was no surprise to those who knew him.

The wiki concept turned out to have amazing properties. When content is in a shared space and is easy to create and connect, it can be collectively owned. The community of owners can range from just a few people up into the thousands, as in the case of the online wiki encyclopedia, Wikipedia.

This chapter introduces you to the wonderful world of wikis by showing you what a wiki is (or can be), how to find and use wikis for fun and profit, and how to get started with a wiki of your own. We even take a brief look at some possible futures for wikis.

Finding Your Way to Wikis

How does one usually enter the wiki world? So much is made of the community-enabling aspects of wikis that the everyday value of wikis can get lost. You don't have to be on a mission to create the best encyclopedia in the world, build a winning startup, or organize the ideas of thousands of people for wikis to be useful. Wikis are amazingly helpful for simple tasks. Say you want to set up a carpool schedule for your hockey team, or arrange a food chain for a sick friend, or share ideas about the latest fashions in opening moves from members of your chess club. For all these scenarios, wikis are frequently the fastest way to do it. Part II of this book focuses on the mechanics of getting a wiki up and running, creating and linking pages, and organizing information — all the techniques and skills to serve the needs of individuals.

And you can't predict what happens when a wiki hits a group of people. Whatever happens, though, those groups are generally never the same again because wikis rarely start as a top-down decision. Wikis succeed because someone found his way to a wiki, created some pages, and let the world know. A few people get the idea and start changing and adding pages. Usually, many others use the information on the wiki. For every one person who writes content on a wiki, tens or even hundreds read it. For large public wikis, that ratio might be more like 1:100,000.

Wikis invade organizations when one team starts using them and then other teams find out about it and learn how to solve their problems with wikis. Pretty soon, the whole company is using wikis. Part III of this book focuses on the special challenges encountered when using wikis in businesses and other large organizations, or when a wiki created for any purpose becomes popular and used by thousands of people.

No matter who you are, finding your way to wikis and figuring out how they can help you doesn't come by overanalyzing the subject. To get value from wikis, you must start putting up pages with information you want to share with others. Relax; making a wiki successful is not a problem that you must solve by yourself. Everyone you invite to use your wiki will help you get it right.

What makes a wiki a wiki

Perhaps the simplest definition of a wiki that accurately captures its essence is the following:

> A *wiki* is a collection of Web pages that anyone can edit.

Several questions then follow naturally: What's on those pages? Who is included in the community of *anyone?* What will those folks be doing when they edit the pages? Are there any rules for how the ownership of the content is shared?

And those very questions lead to the definition of a specific wiki. A precise general definition of a wiki is hard to come by for two reasons:

- ✔ **When Ward Cunningham developed the wiki concept, he set down the basic ideas and let the world run with it.** The world then ran in many directions, so each wiki *engine* (the program that runs a wiki; see Chapter 10 for more on wiki engines) works a little differently. There is no wiki academy that decides whether a wiki engine or a wiki is worthy to carry the name.

- ✔ **The mechanisms of wikis are so simple that they make people wonder how such a basic set of workings can be such a big deal.** The hidden factor is that much of the value of wikis derives not from the mechanisms but instead from the culture that seems to naturally form around a wiki in the people who use it.

Ward Cunningham was interested in solving problems and sharing his ideas, so he didn't rush to the patent office. Rather, he put his ideas on the Portland Pattern Repository (`http://c2.com/ppr`) for others to find and even improve. (c2 stands for Cunningham and Cunningham, Inc., which is Ward's company.) The brilliance (not to mention generosity) of this approach is that it allowed scores of wiki engines to bloom. Almost all are *open source* (software distributed for free, along with guaranteed access to the source code), and others are commercial software. From Ward's basic foundation, the idea of wikis quickly evolved, largely because of the culture of cooperative innovation.

To clarify just what wikis are, we reach into our vast metaphorical toolbox for the best image to help you understand the mechanisms that have created so much excitement. Hmm, what might work? A note pad? No, that's not general enough. The HyperCard program? (See "The History and Future of Wikis" later in this chapter for more on HyperCard.) Close, but too complicated. PostIt notes? Nah, too sticky and too small. A pack of index cards? That's it!

To get going with wikis, imagine that a wiki is just a container that can hold a pack of index cards.

What can you do with an index card container? You can

- ✔ Add new cards.
- ✔ Write information on the cards.
- ✔ Link one card to another.
- ✔ Sort the cards and search through them.
- ✔ Copy the cards.
- ✔ Keep track of the changes that you make to them.

The information on each card can be plain text or text with formatting (such as bold, underlining, italics, or headings). You can put bullet points on cards as well as tables of information.

The pages of a wiki are like the index cards in our container. Instead of physical objects, they're electronic virtual objects created by the wiki engine. Figure 1-1 shows a wiki page that we used to keep track of this book while it was being written.

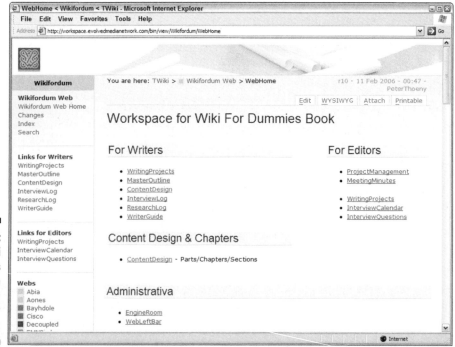

Figure 1-1:
This wiki page was used while writing *Wikis For Dummies.*

One of the most important aspects of wiki index cards is that they can be linked. One card (or page, or whatever you want to call it) can easily refer to another. To jump to a linked card, you simply click a link, just like you move through any other Web site. Cards can even be linked to other cards that don't yet exist. When you click a link to a card that doesn't exist, the wiki engine creates it; then, you can add whatever you like and save it.

The ability to handle partially completed content by putting in links to topics (covered later) is one of the most powerful aspects of wikis. It allows your thoughts to flow and to easily keep placeholders for issues to which you want to return.

If you think of all these cards in a central place where anyone can go and look at them and (this is the important part!) *change them to add their two cents,* then you are on to the secret sauce of wikis and are ready to begin using and contributing to wikis yourself. A whole new culture is created as people work together to build and improve a wiki. This value of shared content ownership is quite powerful. It allows people to use their special knowledge to correct each other and to complete thoughts and ideas started by others.

But wait, you must be thinking, there must be more to it. A simple little Microsoft Access or MySQL database can do all those index card things. Yes, there is more to it — or actually, less to it. The reason why wikis are as popular as they are is that creating and editing content on a wiki is easy, easy, easy. That's why wikis have succeeded. The idea of a shared online database is not unique, but the quest for an easy-to-use computer program is rarely realized. An easy-to-edit, shared online database of pages that really works? That's a wiki.

Comparing wikis and other communication tools

One of the fastest ways to improve your understanding of wikis is to see how wikis are different from many other tools for Internet-based communication such as e-mail, blogs, bulletin boards, forums, content management systems, and Web publishing systems.

Wikis are toolkits for creating pages. The pages created can work in many different ways. This is key to understanding the differences between a wiki and other forms of Web sites and tools for collaboration.

✔ **Wikis are not e-mail.** Individual e-mails share some wiki properties — they are easy to create, they can be quickly formatted, and almost anyone can create an e-mail. And, e-mail can also be used for one-to-one or many-to-many communication by sending mail to many people or by using mailing lists. However, e-mail lacks a central place where everyone can work at once. And e-mail also doesn't allow many authors to work on the same page or for pages to be linked. E-mails are also usually short whereas wiki pages can be as long as needed.

✔ **Wikis are not blogs.** A *blog* is a set of pages on which short entries are posted, usually appearing in a list with the most recent entries on top. Comments can appear attached to each posting. RSS (*really simple syndication,* a format for live online data feeds) feeds allow people to be notified when new blog content appears. (Note that RSS feeds can apply to any sort of content, but they seem to be wildly popular with blogs.)

Wiki pages can be made to look like blog pages, but they don't come out of the box with all the pages needed to automatically write and publish blog entries. Blogs are usually focused on one-to-many communication, but wikis are more oriented to many-to-many communication about shared content.

✔ **Wikis are not bulletin boards or forums.** *Bulletin boards* (sometimes called *forums*) are Web pages where you can ask a question, make a comment, or put forth a proposition to which others can respond. The list of comments about a topic appears in a long list of entries, which sometimes branches into subtopics.

Bulletin boards are more focused on many-to-many communication than blogs but in a way that is more structured than wikis. Wiki pages can be used like bulletin boards in a style called *thread mode,* in which new comments are added to the bottom of a wiki page, but this is a style (not a structure) that is enforced by the wiki. In bulletin boards, the structure of the pages and the communication are always the same and cannot be changed by the people using the board.

✔ **Wikis are not content management or Web publishing systems.** Content management and Web publishing systems are general purpose engines for creating all sorts of Web sites. Like wikis, content management systems are toolkits; unlike wikis, though, they aren't governed by the rules that Ward Cunningham set down for what wikis are.

Almost any kind of Web site, blog, bulletin board system, and wiki can be built by a content management system. Many content management systems have extensions to allow wikis to be included in the Web sites that are built. Usually, content management systems can only be used by expert programmers, but wikis can be used right away by almost anyone.

The (almost) formal definition of a wiki

In the preceding section, we determine that wikis aren't e-mail, blogs, bulletin boards, or Web publishing systems. So what *are* wikis, exactly?

One of the reasons why wiki engines went off in many different directions is that Ward Cunningham didn't define wikis too tightly, and he set nothing in stone. However, the first wiki that he created at the Portland Pattern Repository had a bunch of features that have become so widely imitated that they became the *de facto* definition of wiki. In our opinion, for a wiki to be a wiki, it must have the following characteristics:

- **The pages must be stored in a central, shared repository.** The wiki should be located in one place to make it easy to share.

- **Anyone should be able to edit pages.** Wikis are flexible, which means the organization of the information on each page can be changed as needed and not just by an expert or an administrator.

- **Editing should be easy and accessible and not require special tools.** The wiki should be simple, making getting started easy. Wikis are easy to master, which allows other people to join in and create pages.

- **Formatting information pages should be much simpler than using HTML.** Table 1-1 shows how much simpler it is to create links (see the following bullet) and bullets in a typical wiki than in *HTML,* the language used to program most Web pages.

  Linking one page to another should use WikiWords or use a technique that is just as easy. See Chapter 7 for more on WikiWords and creating links in wikis.

- **A list of recently changed pages should be available.**

Table 1-1	Wiki Markup versus HTML	
	TWiki.org	*HTML*
Creating links	ThisIsALink	`<A HREF="ThisIsALink.HTML">` `ThisIsALink</A>`

Creating bullets	`* A bullet`
	`    * A sub-bullet`
		`<ul>`
		`<li>A bullet</li>`
		`<ul>`
		`<li>A sub-bullet</li>`
		`</ul>`
		`</ul>`

No formal standard for wikis exists like the standards that are used for HTML. HTML (HyperText Markup Language) is controlled by an official standards body that changes the standards for HTML according to a public, collaborative process that is governed by a set of rules. Lots of people have said that creating a standard for wikis would be a good idea, and many proposals have been made for standardizing various aspects of wikis, but none have taken hold. Given the fact that the idea of wikis is not controlled by anyone, a standard is not likely to emerge any time soon. The definition of wikis used in this chapter represents the true spirit of wikis, although like with any community in which a thousand anythings have bloomed, some people are sure to disagree. No doubt they will say so on their wiki — or more likely, on their blog.

Having no set standards for wikis doesn't mean that wikis haven't evolved. Several innovations created since the first days of wikis have become part of almost every wiki engine:

- **Versioning:** Saving a version of each wiki page so that previous versions can be referred to or restored
- **Attaching files:** Allowing files to be attached to wiki pages
- **Backlinks:** Allowing easy browsing of all pages that link to a certain page
- **Notification of changes:** Alerts sent when a page has been changed
- **Searching:** Offering some way to enter words to search for in wiki pages
- **Printable pages:** Creating a printable version of a page that takes out the navigation

It is only fair to point out that printable pages were not invented by wiki developers. This innovation occurred in many different types of sites, but it is now a standard feature of almost every wiki engine.

You, Too, Can Wiki

So, you must be thinking, "Let me have at a wiki! I want to see what it's all about. How can I get started?" But another part of you must be thinking, "If wikis are so great, why don't more people know about them? Why aren't more people using wikis?" It turns out that understanding the second question is key to making progress with the first.

Starting your wiki engines

The growth of wikis was severely limited up until 2006. Before then, the only way you could use a wiki was to first set up a wiki engine on a server. This meant that to use a wiki, you had to have access to a server that was available through the Internet as well as the skills to set up and run a wiki engine.

For most people, these barriers were insurmountable. And even if someone had the skills, he had to have access to a server connected to the Internet. In engineering organizations, this is almost always no problem. Servers and skills to set them up abound. That is one reason why wikis have been so popular in engineering organizations and generally scarce everywhere else.

But from 2004 to 2006, something dramatic changed. Entrepreneurs noticed the market opportunity for providing *hosted wikis* (also known as *wiki farms*) that allowed people to create wikis without needing their own server or special skills. With a hosted wiki, anyone can get started right away. All you need to know is how to create and edit wiki pages, which is much easer than setting up a wiki engine.

JotSpot, WikiSpaces, Wikia, PBwiki, XWiki, BluWiki, and Fluxent (to name just a few) all offer hosted wikis, mostly based on open source software. Google's entry into the field with its purchase of JotSpot will dramatically widen the awareness of wikis.

The great thing about hosted wikis is that you just have to sign up to start working. What sometimes bothers people about hosted wikis is that you have to sign up for an account, which means keeping track of yet another login and password. To make money, hosted wikis usually either have on-page advertising, or they have some sort of per-user charge that hides advertising and/or gives access to premium services.

Creating your first wiki page

The best way to start wiki-ing is to find an existing wiki (that is, a hosted wiki) and start adding to it. To start creating your first wiki page, you can go to any of the wikis in this list:

- ✔ http://wikisfordummies.pbwiki.com
- ✔ http://wikisfordummies.wikispaces.com
- ✔ http://wikisfordummies.xwiki.com
- ✔ http://wikisfordummies.wetpaint.com
- ✔ http://wikis-for-dummies-swicki.eurekster.com

Each of these wikis was set up at a different hosted wiki provider to allow readers of this book quick access to page creation. Go to any of these Web sites, and you will see a prominent link to a sandbox page of the sort shown in Figure 1-2, which shows the page on http://wikisfordummies.pbwiki.com. A *sandbox* is a practice page on a wiki where you can go to play around and become familiar with the ways of the wiki. Click the Sandbox link to go to a page that looks something like Figure 1-3.

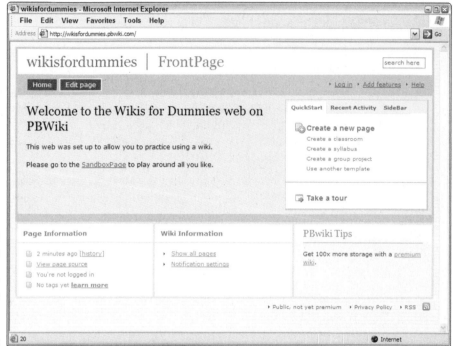

Figure 1-2:
This is the
*Wikis for
Dummies*
home page
on PBwiki.

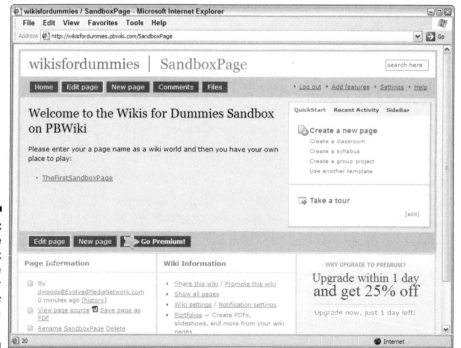

Figure 1-3:
Here's the
Sandbox
page on the
*Wikis for
Dummies*
web on
PBwiki.

A generic sandbox page allows you to create your first wiki page. To create a page at PBwiki, follow these steps:

1. **Click the Edit Page button.**

2. **Enter the PBwiki password, which is** wikis4dummies.

   After you enter the password, you see a page that looks like Figure 1-4. If it doesn't look like Figure 1-4, click the Switch to Classic Mode link in the upper right of the window.

3. **At the end of the list, enter a name for your reader page in camel case, something like** TestPage.

   Camel case is a way to capitalize words, using capital letters in the middle of a word, to indicate that the word is a link to a page. MyTestPage, ThisTestPage, and a TestPage are all camel case and would be recognized as links by most wikis. For more on using camel case, see Chapter 7.

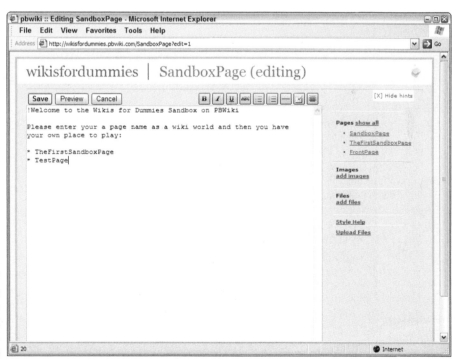

Figure 1-4:
Editing the
Sandbox
page.

4. Click Save.

You see a link that reads `TestPage`. The name is underlined with red dashes to indicate that it has not yet been created. When you click `TestPage`, a page appears asking whether you want to apply a template or change the name of your page. Don't change its name. (And for now, skip the template — come back later and be adventurous.)

5. Click Create New Page.

You see a new page into which you can enter text. This is your first wiki page. Play around, have fun. Don't worry. You can't break anything.

In other wikis, pages that are inserted as links but have not yet been created are indicated in other ways. One common method places a question mark at the end of the name of the page like this: `TestPage?`

If you feel ready, you can create an account on any of the hosted wikis listed here and start creating your wiki right away. Chapter 5 explains how to find a home for your wiki. Chapters 6, 7, and 8 cover how to create content, link pages, and design your wiki.

Wabi-sabi: The beauty of unfinished content

Wabi-sabi is one of the most important attitudes to embrace as you start entering the world of wikis. Most of us are nervous about putting incomplete work in a public place. For wikis to work, though, this has to happen. One of the cultural aspects that wikis embrace is the value of unfinished or half-finished content. One of the reasons why ideas can flow so quickly when creating content in a wiki is that links to wiki pages can serve as placeholders for later thinking. When you move through capturing an idea, you can write about the idea you have; when a complex problem comes up, you can just put a link to a wiki page that you plan on creating and continue with the flow of your thoughts. Then, you or someone you're working with can then use that link to the new page as a way to build on the initial ideas. In wikis, the idea of one author is shattered. Because of this, unfinished content ends up being encouraged because it provides the opportunity for other authors to come in and help finish the job.

Wabi-sabi is a Japanese expression that roughly translates to the "beauty of things imperfect, impermanent, and incomplete." It is the beauty of things modest and humble. It is the beauty of things unconventional. Observe a ceramic cup for a tea ceremony, for example. It might have rough edges, an irregular shape, and glazing that covers only half of the cup. This cup represents the content you initially put on a page, in rough shape, without finishing touches. Unlike a tea cup though, a wiki page may and will change over time. Share content often and early, and people will participate and help improve the content.

Putting Wikis to Work

After you have a home for your wiki, the fun begins. Wikis reward action and participation. Here's the wrong approach: Spend huge amounts of time planning what will be on your wiki and deciding how people will use it. The right approach: Get content up on the wiki and show people how they can change and improve it. Hand them this book, for example. What happens then is that the nerds come out. You will know them by their sense of excitement and by how much they write on the wiki.

Of course, certain patterns and structures work really well on wikis. And wikis can and should be designed for certain purposes. *Content-focused wikis* are all about a subject or many subjects. For example, Wikipedia is a content-focused wiki. *Process-focused wikis* are wikis that are focused on getting something done, like managing a project or writing a book. *Community wikis* bring a group of people together based on a shared interest. And *ease-of-use wikis* are for people who just want to put up a Web site the easy way: for example, to share family photos or create a quick brochure. In Chapter 3, we cover all these types of wikis. The type of wiki should influence the wiki's design. We cover many different design ideas in Chapter 8. The most important thing is to get people on the wiki. We explain the tricks and techniques for that in Chapter 9.

Who are wiki people?

To make wikis successful, you need to understand the conditions under which wikis thrive and the sorts of people who use them.

It is no accident that wikis had early success among engineers, and then next among the sort of writers/editors who make Wikipedia happen. Wikis are about sharing knowledge; to do so, you have to have enough passion to actually sit down and communicate your ideas. Writing is one barrier, and putting your ideas out there for others to see can also be scary. Who does this sort of thing?

Knowledge nerds, that's who — nerds whose passion for knowledge overcomes most everything else (like taste in clothes, for example). There are engineering nerds and word nerds, law nerds and math nerds, medical nerds and music nerds. You get the idea. Nerds know things and want to spread the message. So, a wiki won't work unless you have passionate nerds somewhere in your organization who want to get their knowledge out.

For those who think we're kidding or that we're a few cards short of a full deck, we're not. In most wiki environments, the key thing that happens is that some- one really wants to share information or get everyone on the same page — and that they are willing to spend time to make it happen. That person is the *wiki champion,* and he or she eventually becomes the wiki coach. (See Chapter 16 for descriptions of the various roles people play in wikis.) After that person makes a stand and gets a wiki engine going, a committed group of others needs to join in and start creating and sharing knowledge, or else the wiki withers and dies. The reason why wikis are such a big deal is that they uncover the nerds in an organization who want to make a difference; by sharing knowledge, they can make that difference.

Everyone need not be a nerd for wikis to succeed. There just needs to be enough nerds to make the wiki useful. For every nerd, 20, 40, or perhaps 60 other people benefit from the information just by clicking through the wiki and seeing what's there.

The first things to ask yourself when you set out to introduce a wiki into an environment are: Who will join me in sharing knowledge on the wiki? Who has the passion? Do we really have enough wiki people to make this work?

The lifecycle of wiki people

The natural lifecycle of the wiki person is another useful thing to keep in mind as you discover how to make wikis a part of your life. How fast you move through this lifecycle when you encounter a wiki is usually a good indi- cator of how important a wiki is to you. Some knowledge nerds go from a reader to a champion in a matter of days, and the wiki concept makes their brain rage with possibilities.

The first way how most folks start using a wiki is as a *reader.* You go to a wiki, see the content, and enjoy it. That might just be enough. Many people who regularly use Wikipedia have no idea that it is a community-created resource that they could get involved with if they wished.

The big first step for most wiki users is to actually reach into a wiki and change some content to improve it. You see something incorrect, and you want to fix it. When you do this, you have become an *editor.* Although this sounds like a simple act, it has an unusually large emotional effect. After you change content, it no longer belongs to all those other people: It becomes partially yours. As every writer knows, the pleasure and pride of authorship is a satisfying reward.

After you join the community of authors of a wiki, it doesn't take long for your imagination to lead you to ways to extend the wiki by creating content that covers new areas. You have progressed to become a *contributor* of a whole new chunk of content that may be corrected by others.

Although many wikis start out as self-organizing communities where everyone just takes care of what needs to be done, certain roles and processes naturally develop. As you participate and lead these activities, you become a *manager* of a wiki. (Chapter 12 covers the typical wiki management tasks.)

The final step in the lifecycle of a wiki user is recognizing that a new wiki is needed to meet your needs or the needs of a community to which you belong. By starting a new wiki, you become a wiki *champion* and bring the benefit of wikis to others.

Herding a small group with wikis

The first thing that generally happens with a wiki is that a small group starts using it for project management or to jointly create some sort of content. For project management, the wiki becomes a repository of lists, notes, schedules, and documents, all keeping the state of the project up to date. As an example, this book was written using a wiki to coordinate the activities of everyone who worked on it. Content creation can encompass documenting requirements for a software program, writing a policy-and-procedure manual, or collecting and posting research. It could be anything.

The first project on the wiki leads to the second and the third, and the group of wiki users starts growing. As the user base grows, you have to be more methodical about running your wiki. You then need a more structured, wide-body wiki.

Wide-body wikis for your company

If a small-scale wiki works for you, pass Go, collect $200, and roll it out company-wide. If you're not just creating an interesting collaboration environment for a few folks but changing the entire culture of your company, however, that requires more planning. It's not that the use of the wiki becomes restricted, but the support activities must be planned for. The idea is not to force a specific wiki solution on people but to teach them to put wikis to work by themselves. Wiki coaches must be trained so that each group using the wiki has someone to turn to. System administrators must be trained to perform tasks such as setting up new webs, managing user accounts, and archiving old content when necessary. Chapter 13 of this book covers all these issues related to the care and feeding of wikis.

After a company has become wiki-wise, the more advanced uses of structured wiki applications might make sense. Structured wikis are described in Chapter 14. Although the fundamental transformation of the workplace occurs through basic wiki functionality, structured wiki applications can be a huge boost to productivity. Structured wiki applications help track and automate flexible processes that combine both structured and unstructured elements.

Going public with your wiki

In the first years of wikis, much of the action in wikis took place within corporations and other large organizations. The rise of Wikipedia and hosted wikis shows that wikis can organize large groups of people quite effectively outside of an organizational context. Some companies try to use wikis to communicate with customers. Activists use wikis to organize people for social change or to create special kinds of content. In Chapter 9, we cover wiki evangelism and explain the different ways how people carry the message of wikis to new domains.

The History and Future of Wikis

So far, the idea of wikis has been explained from the general to the specific: from the outside-in, is one way to say it. To better understand the essence of wikis, understanding wikis from the inside-out is also useful. How did the idea originate? What was Ward Cunningham's mission when he developed the wiki concept? What were the false starts? How did the idea of a wiki flower into being? The following sections explore some of the history behind wikis as well as the directions in which they might go.

HyperCard and other wiki precursors

You can find many wiki-like things in the past. For example, Tornado Notes, which became InfoSelect, was a database of free-form notes. And FolioViews made it easy to link between pages. Of all the precursors, HyperCard is probably the most wiki-like thing that existed before wikis. HyperCard was a program created by Bill Atkinson for organizing information; when it came out in 1987, it was distributed with every Macintosh computer sold.

HyperCard used the metaphor of index cards and stacks of cards. On each card, fields of information could be stored, text could be entered, and cards could be linked. Boy, this sounds a lot like a wiki. What wasn't wiki-like about HyperCard was that it was not on the Web. In their first incarnation, HyperCard stacks could be used on a single computer or a bunch of computers sharing a file system where a common stack could be accessed. Still, HyperCard stacks weren't created to allow anyone on the Internet to be able to access them through a browser. This is a big difference from wikis.

The other thing about HyperCard was that it was sort of a programmer's tool. It was easy to use, but when you wanted to link one card to another, you had to go through some rigamarole, like starting at the card to which you were linking, jumping to the card from which you were linking, and then planting the link there. The rest of HyperCard was a pretty cool programming environment, but it wasn't very easy for normal people to use. This is another big difference from wikis.

Of course, the biggest and most influential predecessor of wikis is the World Wide Web. Without Web sites and browsers to provide easy, universal accessibility, wikis could not exist. The World Wide Web introduced the linking and browsing paradigms now found in wikis.

Ward's challenge

The unusual aspect of the development of wikis is that Ward Cunningham didn't set out to create wikis. Ward's goal was to share information. In 1995, he was deeply involved in the consulting firm Cunningham and Cunningham, Inc., working with other people on developing the idea of Extreme Programming (a radical restructuring of the process of creating software), and also developing the concept of reusable patterns in software development.

The itch that Ward wanted to scratch was to create a repository of patterns that other people could see and modify as well as supplement with their own patterns. The idea was to create a shared space that allowed people to communicate and collaborate about this nifty idea of patterns.

Ward's solution

As Ward Cunningham pondered the challenge of easily sharing information, the stars started to align. As an accomplished programmer, Ward knew how to write programs for the Web. As a seasoned developer and as someone who really wanted to get others interested in patterns, Ward was suspicious of the idea that just writing any old script that imitated traditional approaches would actually solve his communication problem. He knew that his solution had to be easy to use and accessible to everyone without much effort.

So, by using the Perl scripting language, Ward at first created a system that was a database of pages. Then he figured out a way to edit those pages in a browser window. Web browsers were spreading like wildfire, and making editing happen through a browser window meant that everyone could use his repository without much effort.

But then he had to figure out how to make the information on the pages look good, convey information, and (most of all) link to other pages that were related. Again, Ward felt that all this had to be much easier than existing alternatives like HTML, which is why the simple markup language was invented.

After Ward got his ideas working, he went back to his work of creating pages about patterns. It was like falling downhill. What took two hours or longer in HyperCard could be done in 10 or 20 minutes or even faster. In about three hours, Ward had 15 or 20 pages done.

The only thing left was the naming. Ward first considered using the word Quick. A product called Quick Basic already existed (an easy-to-use form of the BASIC language), and Ward considered using the name QuickWeb. That seemed about as exciting as cold oatmeal. Ward then remembered that *wiki wiki* means *quick* in Hawaiian, and he called his invention the *WikiWikiWeb,* which eventually got shortened to *wiki.*

The not-so-overnight success of wikis

Wikis gradually took hold over the 11 years following Ward Cunningham's development of his first wiki engine, called WikiBase. During that time, the concept was expanded by the open source community. Wikis became popular with one group, then another, and eventually began invading the mainstream.

It didn't take too long for wikis to be noticed by developers in the open source community. What happened was that many people discovered — surprise, surprise — that Ward hadn't thought of everything. This, of course, was no surprise to Ward, who assumed that he hadn't thought of everything and was eager to see what other people would think of.

If you ever go to the Portland Pattern Repository front page (http://c2.com/cgi/wiki), you might be surprised at how bare-bones it is compared with other wiki sites you may have visited, such as www.wikipedia.org. What Ward created was the dune buggy of wikis. Some features added by the open source community include

✔ **Version control:** The ability to save every version of a page and go back to previous versions as needed. This is important because so many people might change a page; see Chapter 13 for details.

✔ **Access control:** The ability to control who accesses the wiki and what they can do; also covered in Chapter 13.

✔ **Plug-ins for added functionality:** The ability to add in any other kind of functionality that might be needed. See Chapter 14 for some great examples of plug-ins.

Wikis lurk in the realm of the engineers

As the number of wiki engines grew, the concept became extremely popular in engineering, technology, and software development companies. Here are some reasons why:

✔ Engineers are early adopters of anything cool.

✔ To get a wiki running in the early days, you had to have access to a server and know how to set up a wiki engine. Engineers had these skills.

✔ Even though wikis were easy for anyone to use, engineers found them ultra-simple. Some aspects of a wiki, like the simple markup, never presented a problem for engineers even though they could seem somewhat scary to newcomers.

✔ Wikis were incredibly flexible in how they could represent different ways to organize information. Engineers love *taxonomies,* which are different structures of information. (We discuss taxonomies in Chapter 8.) That a wiki could organize information many different ways at the same time seemed cool to an engineer.

The open source roots of wikis

Almost all early implementations of wikis were open source, which is one of the reasons why so much experimentation took place about the right way to build a wiki engine. Wikis have succeeded because in many ways, they bring the open source values of shared ownership and rapid-fire experimentation to the world of collaboration, content creation, and knowledge management. The fact that so many early wikis were open source eased the way for the propagation of wikis in so many different kinds of organizations. After the ideas of wikis were in tens of thousands of brains, ideas like Wikipedia and other innovative uses sprang up. Now that the idea of wikis has become so popular, entrepreneurs have created commercial versions of wikis with special features that are not shared. Although some resent this commercialization as a form of robbery of ideas that were in the public domain, others (including us) see the emergence of commercial wikis as confirmation that wikis are here to stay. It is clear, though, that the road to this success could not have happened without the structures and values of open source showing the way.

So, at many of the biggest companies in the world — such as Sun Microsystems, the German software maker SAP, and Motorola — and at many other companies all over the world, wikis became the central nervous system, all the while lurking in relative obscurity.

Wikis grow beyond engineering

The next wave of wiki expansion occurred as awareness of wikis grew organically inside companies. An engineer would show someone from marketing the requirements for a new system on the wiki. They would discuss it, the engineer would just edit the page to change the requirements, and perhaps an e-mail would be automatically sent out notifying everyone on the team that something had changed.

The marketing person would look at this and say, "Dude, this is pretty darn useful. How can I get one of these for my projects?"

In this way, the marketing department and eventually other departments overcame the technical barriers that stopped them from using a wiki by themselves. They couldn't set up a wiki engine. They had no skills to do so. They had no servers on which to put a wiki engine. But the engineers did.

Many an engineer became an unofficial wiki champion, leading the way in the use of wikis. They would set one wiki up for one team, and that team would use it with another, who would want their own, and then the cycle would repeat until lots of people were using this really easy project management tool without ever knowing that it was a wiki.

The other way awareness of wikis expanded was the growing momentum behind Wikipedia, which was founded by Jimmy Donal Wales (who had started an earlier version of an online encyclopedia, Nupedia). Nupedia (which used a different, non-wiki technology) didn't catch on, but as soon as the project was switched to a wiki, a new culture took hold. Thousands of people starting working on Wikipedia and also spreading the word about wikis.

Wikis go commercial

The growth of wikis certainly didn't happen in a vacuum. The technology press paid attention as did a few academics. As in the open source and engineering communities, there was much activity. New wiki engines were created every year, and still are. (Dan's current favorite newcomer is TiddlyWiki, a wiki created by using JavaScript, that is contained within an HTML page.) Wikis were created for special purposes: DokuWiki is an excellent wiki engine created for writing and publishing documentation. Microsoft created a wiki engine called FlexWiki as an open source project built by using .NET technology.

The commercial use of wikis expanded rapidly through the many, many open source wiki engines that were available. Peter Thoeny, creator of TWiki (and co-author of this book), created a huge wiki at Wind River dedicated to product support. Google has revealed that it is a major user of wikis and has one of the largest internal wikis in terms of the number of pages. Yahoo!, Amazon, and hundreds of other companies have jumped on the wiki bandwagon as well.

Recognizing that the basic concepts of wikis were quite powerful, and that a large segment of the information technology world (the world of corporate computer users) was nervous about the support and maintenance burdens of open source technology, a number of entrepreneurs stepped in and built on the ideas that were developed in the open source wiki engines. Some of these include

- ✔ **Socialtext (www.socialtext.com):** Ross Mayfield created Socialtext, which built a product to deliver the benefits of many of the technologies used in social networking as an integrated product. Socialtext combines blogs, wikis, and other features to create an environment to help groups communicate and do work.

- ✔ **JotSpot (www.jot.com):** JotSpot, founded in 2004 by Joe Kraus and Graham Spencer, calls itself an *application wiki*. JotSpot offers a wiki with many features, such as e-mail integration and database-like functionality, which allow it to create wikis that are applications but also wikis. JotSpot was purchased by Google in October, 2006.

- ✔ **Atlassian (www.atlassian.com):** Atlassian, an Australian company, created Confluence, what it calls an *enterprise wiki* that complements the company's first product, JIRA (a bug-tracking database). Confluence is one of the more popular wikis in corporate environments.

Hosted wikis open the door to everyone

Other companies such as WikiSpaces, PBwiki, wetpaint, Wikia, BluWiki, XWiki, and more offer free wiki hosting, which we discuss in greater detail in Chapter 5. These companies frequently put advertising on pages but also offer premium versions of wikis with advanced features. Each of these companies helped promote the use of wikis in environments that were previously unfriendly to open source or that wanted the special features in each of these products.

The process of wiki propagation didn't stop inside companies. After wikis spread from engineering to other parts of firms, those who dealt with customers realized that wikis could be an excellent way to harvest information and build communities.

Amazon.com was the most prominent company to put wikis on its site. At the end of many Amazon.com pages is a ProductWiki section, where visitors to the site can add their thoughts on the products. Other companies are following suit, and the number of wikis facing consumers grows every month.

Where wikis will go

We have a long way to go before wikis are part of everyday life. Most people still don't know the term, let alone the cultural changes that wikis entail and the benefits they can bring. We can take a quick look into the wiki future and make some predictions, though.

Wikis become your desktop, your Web site, your intranet

What has happened for Dan (the other co-author of this book) is that wikis have taken the place of his desktop. His day starts at his e-mail inbox and on the home page of his wiki. He doesn't store files on his personal computer but stores them on the wiki. When he writes a project management note, he writes it in the wiki first and then sends a link to the wiki page to others who are working on the project, or he copies from the wiki into an e-mail. The first step in a new project for Dan? Creating a wiki to manage it.

Wikis will invade other applications

Wikis will come to most people over the next ten years through hosted wikis and wikis embedded in other applications. Many wikis that are now being developed are being added to existing environments. Large software companies have yet to get serious about incorporating wikis into their products, but this will all change as Google's incorporation of JotSpot puts wikis into the hands of millions of people who cannot get over the current barriers to using wikis. Software manufacturers will then take notice, and you will find wiki functionality as part of enterprise applications and desktop productivity suites.

Wikis will disappear

After wikis have conquered, they will disappear and become part of the landscape. Our grandchildren will wonder why anyone ever worked without them. Perhaps, they won't be called wikis. They will just be the way things are done, just like how WYSIWYG (What You See Is What You Get) editing is no longer an innovation for word processors but is instead just the way they are assumed to work.

Chapter 2

Contributing Content to a Wiki

. . . .

In This Chapter

▶ Introducing the basic skills needed to use wikis

▶ Navigating wikis

▶ Editing text on a wiki page

▶ Creating links to wiki pages

▶ Attaching files to wiki pages

▶ Printing wiki pages

▶ Playing it safe with wiki pages versions

▶ Using the Changes link to see what's up with a wiki

. . . .

*I*n the world of wikis, the fundamental act — the source of all value, the golden spike, the first cause, the chicken before the egg — is creating a page. Your journey to mastery of this skill of terrifying power begins right now.

If you imagine these words spoken from a mountaintop with lightning flashing all around, take comfort in knowing that finding your way around wikis and creating wiki pages isn't terrifying at all. After understanding a few simple rules and ideas, almost anyone can create a wiki page. And that, my friend, is a big reason why wikis have become the sensation they are.

Millions of wiki pages have been created by average Joes and Josephines all over the world. Wikis have been used to create encyclopedias, manage projects, document technology, and even write books (like this one, for example). The knowledge carried on wiki pages has been used and improved by millions of other people. However, the whole ball can't start rolling until someone creates a page on a wiki, and someone else takes a look.

In this chapter, you explore the knobs, dials, and steering wheels of a wiki. You see how to navigate within a wiki; create, link, print, and organize pages; and format text. By the end of this chapter, you'll be able to go to a wiki and add your own two cents.

Basic Wiki Skills

Every act that you perform requires some basic skills. Dribbling is a basic skill that you must learn before playing basketball. You have to know how to boil water to cook pasta. Wikis are no different. The basic wiki skills are

- ✔ **Navigating wiki pages:** Finding your way from here to there and back again
- ✔ **Creating and editing pages:** Creating and formatting your own content by using wiki markup
- ✔ **Linking pages:** Adding vital links, which is much easier than using HTML (Web markup language)

Mastering these basic wiki skills will take you back to when you started to learn how to use a word processor or a spreadsheet. At first, the structure of the page seemed strange. Then you started to understand all the moving parts and how to make changes. Pretty soon, everything lost its strangeness, and a sense of excitement emerged about what you could do with this new-found power. Getting started with wikis will remind you of that transformation and prepare you to use a tool that can change your life and the way you work — forever.

Navigating wiki webs

The goal of this chapter is to help you master basic wiki skills by using the wiki that you can find at `http://twiki.org`. With this wiki (TWiki), you can find your way around and then create a page of your own in the *sandbox*. (A *sandbox* is a practice area where you can do all things wiki with no worries because the pages aren't live.) Along the way, we point out those elements common to most wiki pages. *Hint:* You will quickly notice that many elements repeat themselves over and over on each page of a wiki.

However, getting around wikis can be a bit tricky because each wiki is a little bit different. Numerous wiki engines exist, each of which has its own style. (A *wiki engine* is the software that drives the wiki, whether TWiki, Confluence, or MediaWiki [the wiki engine used by Wikipedia]. See Chapter 10 for details.) And, each wiki engine usually allows you to customize the structure of each page, moving some elements around. The good news is that wikis aren't that different: If you master how to navigate one wiki, you'll know how to navigate another, similar to how you browse Web sites with different navigational layouts without really thinking twice about it.

Exploring the structure of a basic wiki page

The first stop is `http://twiki.org`, which is the site for the community organized around *TWiki,* one of the most popular wiki engines in the world. When you go to `http://twiki.org`, the first thing that you see is a page like the one in Figure 2-1. Open this site in a Web browser if you haven't yet.

The TWiki.org home page (as shown in Figure 2-1) reflects the general structure of a wiki page, which usually has

> ✔ **A page body that displays the content of the page:** For example, everything under the headline *TWiki — An Enterprise Collaboration Platform* is the page body.
>
> ✔ **Navigation between webs on the wiki and between parts of the web that you might be on:** On the left side of the page, under the heading Site Map, is a list of links, some of which are webs.
>
> A *web* is a group of wiki pages. Read more about them in the upcoming section, "Walking through webs."
>
> ✔ **A list of tools for editing and doing other things to change the content of the page you're viewing:** The TWiki.org home page doesn't have the list of editing tools because it is an introduction page. This is a theme that you might find to be true in many wikis. The first set of navigation pages doesn't emphasize editing and content creation. Instead, the first set focuses on helping you find your way around the wiki.

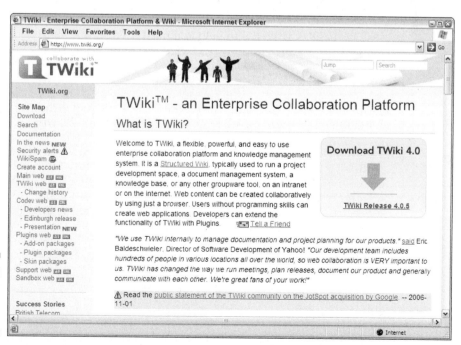

Figure 2-1:
Start at the TWiki.org home page.

To create a page, move from the home page to the page with all the editing tools. To do this, first study a bit about how to get around your wiki town, which is known in dull computer science circles as *wiki navigation.*

Most wikis have lots of webs, which have pages that link to groups of pages and lots of pages that link to each other. Some pages play a navigational role; others contain content; and many do both. The beauty of wikis is that the way everything is organized is up for grabs and can be crafted to meet the needs at hand. For that reason, there is no widely applicable set of rules about wiki navigation — just a few simple ones.

Walking through webs

Most wikis are organized into many different webs. All webs — no, we're not talking about the World Wide Web here — are simply different groups of wiki pages. *Webs* are the highest level of organization of a wiki. Here's an example: If Amazon.com were a wiki, it would have one web for books, another for DVDs, another for electronics, and so on. (Although Amazon.com is not a wiki, the company is making innovative use of wikis to capture information from consumers, as you can find out in Chapter 3.)

As we mention in Chapter 1, you can think of a wiki as a collection of index cards. Imagine two containers in your wiki: one with index cards about U.S. presidents and another with index cards about U.S. senators. These would be two different webs. Lyndon Johnson would have an index card in each web because he was both a Senator and a President. However, even though the cards have the same name, they would be different cards.

Each web has its own set of names for cards. The nerdy name for a set of names is a *namespace.* Most wikis have a way for information on one web to link to another, so it is likely that the page in the presidential web would link to the senatorial web, and vice versa.

You can read in Chapter 8 — where we discuss how to design a wiki — how to figure out how many webs you need and what should be in them.

One of the newest ideas in wikis is the *sub-wiki,* which is a web that is underneath another web. Sub-wikis were created as the number of pages in a web grew and grew and became difficult to manage. In essence, sub-wikis allow a wiki web to have a directory structure. For example, you could have the Wikibook web, the Wikibook/Chapter1 web, the Wikibook/Chapter2 web, and so on. The chapters in the book are the sub-wikis.

Finding your way around: Links are on the left, Luke

At http://twiki.org (visit this site if you're not there already), you can see that one of the webs listed on the left is named *Sandbox web.* (Ignore the link to download the latest version of TWiki; that's for wiki administrators, not for wiki users.) In a wiki sandbox, you can play around without worrying that you are going to break anything. Click the Sandbox web link to go to the Sandbox page shown in Figure 2-2.

One thing that is almost always true of wikis (and many other Web sites) is that the navigation is on the left. The Sandbox web section has links to important pages:

- ✔ **Sandbox web home:** This page goes back to the home page of the web (the one shown in Figure 2-2), which can be a handy link to have when you want to migrate from deep in a wiki back to the beginning.

- ✔ **Changes:** This link shows a list of pages that have recently been changed. This can be a great way to find pages you have been working on or to see what others have been up to recently. See the upcoming section, "Tracking Versions and Changes," in this chapter for details.

- ✔ **Index:** This is just a list of all wiki pages. TWiki calls pages *topics*. As you read more about different wikis, you'll find that one of the problems with the fact that a thousand wiki flowers have bloomed is that different wikis have different names for the same thing. In other words, although most wikis have a topic list on the left, they might use different names, such as Index or Contents.

- ✔ **Search:** This link goes to a page that allows searching.

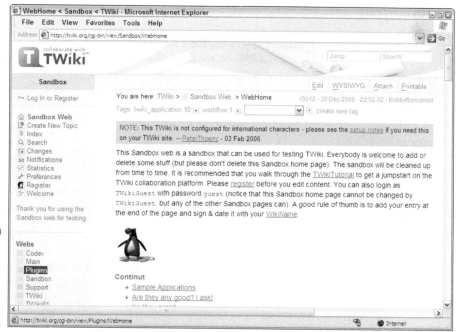

Figure 2-2:
Practice
navigation
in a
sandbox.

These are the basic navigation tools that allow you to get around within a web. Some people call this *local navigation,* but you don't have to call it anything. Just use it to get where you want to go.

Jumping around in webs

In addition to the basic navigation tools listed in the preceding section, wikis usually include ways to jump from web to web, or to a specific page. Choose from these techniques to jump around in wiki webs:

- ✔ **From web to web:** Underneath the local navigation for the Sandbox page shown in Figure 2-2 is a list labeled *Webs,* which shows the webs on the wiki. Because webs represent major content areas, this is the main way to get from one big section of a wiki to another. When working with a wiki, it's not at all uncommon to have several Web browser windows open, each pointing to different webs on a wiki. The list of webs is how you find your way around a wiki, just like how you browse through directories when you open a file from a word processing or spreadsheet program.

- ✔ **To a page:** If you look at the upper-right corner of the page shown in Figure 2-2, you can see a Jump field. Enter the name of a page in the Jump field and then press Enter to be transported directly to the page you're interested in. In TWiki, if you enter the name of a different web, a period, and then the name of the page in the different web, you can jump right there. For example, type **Main.WebPreferences** in the Jump box and press Enter to go right to the page in the main web. Although not every wiki engine has a Jump field, many do.

Following a trail of bread crumbs

A *bread crumb* is a listing of pages — such as TWiki⇨Sandbox⇨WebHome — that you can travel through to get to a page. As you jump around inside wikis and wiki webs, remembering where you've been and where you are might become difficult. In this situation, bread crumbs come in handy. Because most wikis make liberal use of links, you click and click, winding your way through all sorts of webs and pages before you land on just the right page. When you do land on that page, you want to know where the heck you are. Usually, there are many ways to know that, such as looking at the local web navigation (in the address bar of your Web browser program), which usually says the name of the web. However, that tells you only the web — not how deep the page you are on is in the web and how to get there. Bread crumbs give you this information.

At the top of Figure 2-2, the line that reads `You are here: TWiki > Sandbox Web > WebHome` is a bread crumb. In TWiki.org, the first part of the bread crumb is the name of the web you're in. The second part is a list of pages that you could travel through to get to that page.

In TWiki.org, bread crumbs don't tell you how you got to a page, which could be through many different links. Instead, they tell you how you could get back to the page you are on starting from the main page of the web in which the page is located. Bread crumbs at TWiki.org and many other wiki engines express a hierarchy of pages that are linked to one another. Think of a hierarchy of pages sort of like folders on your hard drive.

Another sort of bread crumb used on other wikis (like DokuWiki) shows the exact set of pages you clicked to get to the page you're on. This sort of bread crumb changes each time you take a different route to a page. This type of bread crumb tracks where you have been, not which page owns which other page.

Searching a wiki

Another popular way to get around a wiki is to search it just as if you were in Yahoo! or Google. If you click the Search link in the local navigation of the Sandbox web at `http://twiki.org`, you get a page that looks like Figure 2-3.

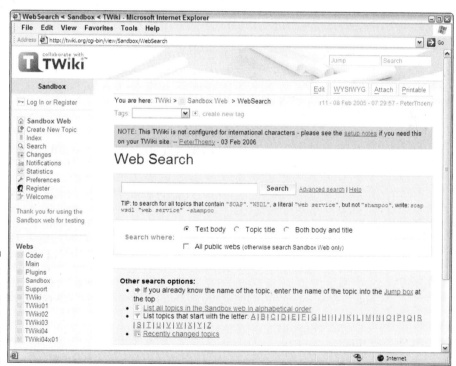

Figure 2-3: Search a wiki like any other search engine.

To search the wiki, just type the keywords that you're looking for and then press Enter; a list of pages that have those words displays. Try a sample search at `http://twiki.org`. As you can see from the choices under the search box, TWiki allows the search to be controlled. For example, you can search in the text of a page, the title, or both. Most wikis now have some way to search through pages.

Note: Although most wikis have some sort of search capability, they frequently don't work very well. (Confluence, a commercial wiki engine, is one exception to the rule.) For simple searches, they usually work fine. When you want to search with multiple keywords or in any fancier way, though, you might be disappointed. After a wiki becomes large scale, usually a top-flight search engine needs to be added.

Editing and creating wiki pages

Knowing how to find pages is useless if there are no pages to find. After you get navigation skills under your belt, you can start editing pages. (Editing pages is a little easier than creating them, so we start with editing.) One of the things that you might have noticed about wiki pages is that they can be pretty long. The Sandbox page at `http://twiki.org` is one of the longest. This page changes a lot, but the first three links are pretty constant:

- **Sample Applications:** These show advanced functions of TWiki.org.

- **Generic Sandbox Topics:** Some generic pages were created in advance for users to play with.

- **Create Your Own Sandbox Page:** Here, people create their own pages to play with.

The easiest way to start editing a wiki page is to edit one of the Generic Sandbox pages at TWiki.org. To do this, click Generic Sandbox Topics, and then click any sandbox topic, such as Sandbox45. You will find that almost all the pages have something in them. Worry not; these pages were made to be edited and re-edited, so just find a page that you want to change and click it. You see something like Figure 2-4.

Look at the top right of the page body area to see four links that provide tools:

- **Edit:** This link allows the page to be edited in basic text editor format, with wiki markup showing, which we cover later in this section.

- **WYSIWYG:** This link allows you to edit in WYSIWYG mode. *WYSIWYG —* What You See Is What You Get — means that when you change something on a page to make it a heading, you see the text change to become that heading. We cover WYSIWYG editing later in this section, too.

✔ **Attach:** This link allows files to be attached to the page. For more about this topic, see the later section, "Attaching Documents to Wiki Pages."

✔ **Printable:** This link displays just the page body, without the navigation, which is a nice format for printing. More about printing appears later in the chapter. (See the upcoming "Printing Wiki Pages" section.)

All wiki engines have these functions, but the links might be in a slightly different place. For example, MediaWiki and Confluence use tabs at the top of the page instead of links.

Editing text

To begin editing, click the Edit link on the sandbox page you selected. You will then be asked to enter a login name and password. If you enter **TWikiGuest** (this is case-sensitive, so type it as it's shown here) as the login name and **guest** as the password, you will be allowed to edit the page. After you enter the login and password, you see a page like Figure 2-5.

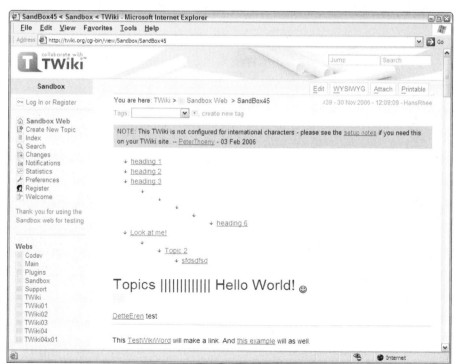

Figure 2-4:
Start to edit
a generic
sandbox
page.

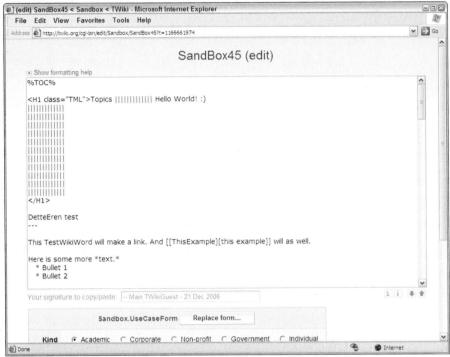

Figure 2-5:
Edit a page
in text
mode.

Figure 2-5 shows what it's like to edit a page in *text mode,* which is the most common way to edit wiki pages. Text mode is sort of old-fashioned because it's not like most modern word processing programs that operate in WYSI-WYG mode. See the following section for more on WYSIWYG editing.

This is called text mode because you enter simple text in a formatting language; what you see when the page is saved and displayed, though, is much more attractive. When you click the Edit button, the Web browser that you're using asks the wiki engine to reach into the database and grab the text that represents the page you were just looking at, putting that text in a form that can be edited in the Web browser.

If you look at the edit page, you see funny things like ---+++ preceding lines of text. You also see spaces followed by * in front of words and sentences. You are looking at *wiki markup.* In wiki text-mode editing, wiki markup consists of simple patterns of characters that tell the wiki engine to make the page look a certain way. For example, using ---+ at the beginning of a line tells the wiki engine to make the rest of the text on that line a *Level 1 heading,* which is the largest heading. Using the same text but with two plus signs makes the rest of the text a *Level 2 heading,* which is slightly smaller than Level 1.

To see how to use wiki markup to edit a wiki in text mode, follow these steps:

1. **Delete everything in the *text box* (the white box in the middle of the page) by selecting its contents with the mouse (or by pressing Ctrl+A) and then pressing Delete (on your keyboard).**

   This wipes out the contents of that window. Now it's a blank slate, just waiting for you. (Bask for a moment in the feeling of power this gives you.)

2. **Type the first line:**

   ```
   ---+ My First Wiki Page
   ```

3. **Type the second line:**

   ```
   ---++ Level 2 Headings are Smaller than Level 1 Headings
   ```

4. **Type the third line:**

   ```
   ---+++ Level 3 Headings are even smaller
   ```

5. **Type the fourth line:**

   ```
   ----
   ```

6. **Type the fifth line:**

   ```
   Isn't it nice how horizontal rules break up a page
   ```

7. **Type the sixth line:**

   ```
      * Bullets do as well
   ```

   You just typed in wiki markup text that will display in a way that looks much better when the edits are saved and the final page is displayed.

After you enter the text, TWiki allows you to do one of several things. You can scroll down to see buttons that allow you to

- ✔ **Save the page.** Clicking the Save button puts the changes you just made into the database, and then redisplays the page.

- ✔ **Preview the page.** Clicking the Preview button lets you first see whether the page looks the way you like, and then either go back and edit some more or save it.

- ✔ **Cancel your edit.** Clicking the Cancel button discards your changes. Your changes are discarded.

The names of these basic buttons might differ from one wiki engine to another, but all wikis offer these basic functions.

If you save the page you just entered, you see a page like Figure 2-6.

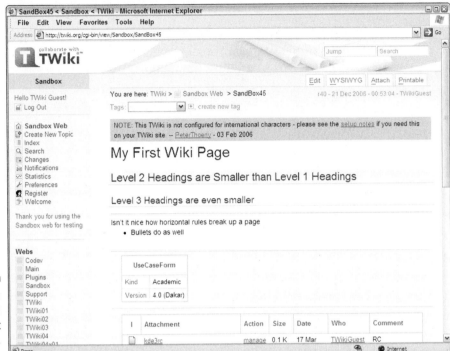

Figure 2-6:
You created
your first
wiki page.

Remember, if this markup seems strange and difficult, compare it with the HTML version shown in Chapter 1, which is even stranger and more difficult. Despite its apparent weirdness, using wiki markup in text mode is pretty easy to get used to. Millions of people have learned it, and it has the advantage of being able to work with the basic capabilities of any Web browser. Editing in text mode is one thing that every browser does and does well.

Using WYSIWYG editing

As we mention earlier, some advanced wikis offer WYSIWYG editors. With these, instead of using wiki markup and the text box, you use an editor that's almost like the word processors you're likely accustomed to.

Look in the list of tools in Figure 2-6 to see the WYSIWYG link. If you click that link, you see the page shown in Figure 2-7.

WYSIWYG editing of a TWiki page relies on DHTML (Dynamic HTML) code that's sent to the browser to allow editing of pages. You type in your text. To format it, you select the text and then click the appropriate toolbar button to set the text as a heading, a bullet, or a specific text style.

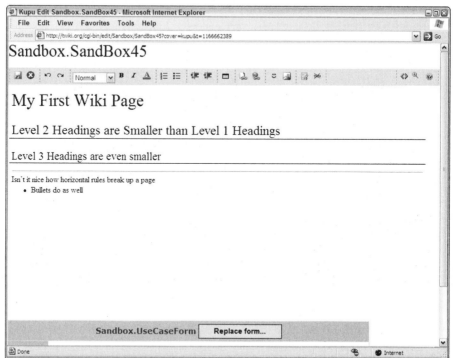

Figure 2-7:
You can do WYSIWYG editing in a wiki.

When it works correctly, WYSIWYG editing can be quick and easy, and using it prevents you from having to learn markup. The great thing about WYSIWYG editing tools for wikis is that they open up the ability to create and change pages to an even larger group because people who can't or don't want to learn wiki markup can still participate.

A problem with WYSIWYG editing is that it doesn't work consistently — or not at all — depending on the browser and the wiki engine you're using. Although using the WYSIWYG editor can help you create pages or edit text, most frequent users of wikis use wiki markup. As time goes by, fans of wikis all hope and expect that this situation will get better and that WYSIWYG editing will be the way we all work. But until then, it is always a good idea to use the preview feature to make sure your WYS is actually WYG.

The headings, horizontal rules, and bullets we have shown you are by far the most common ways that wiki pages are formatted. There are many more tricks to using wiki pages, and we explain them all in Chapter 6.

Linking wiki pages

As the earlier discussion of editing pages shows, making things as easy as possible is a really wiki thing to do. The way that wiki links are created is perhaps the most clever innovation of wikis. As you can read in the comparison of wiki links and HTML in Chapter 1, you end up typing a lot less to create a wiki link than an HTML link. What we don't explain in Chapter 1, though, is how exactly a wiki engine knows that the funny-looking text `ThisIsALink` is actually a link to a new page. Now, grasshopper, you will discover the ways of wiki linking.

Less is more: Creating a link

The key to understanding wiki links in most wikis is the idea of *camel case*. Camel case describes a string of letters, beginning with an uppercase letter, that doesn't contain any blanks, and that has uppercase letters between the first and last characters. So to make a word camel case you need a string that has at least two uppercase letters separated by at least one lowercase characters. Camel case words used for wiki links are *WikiWords*. Here are some comparative examples:

- ThisIsCamelCase
- Thisisnot
- thisisnoT
- thisIsNot
- THisisnot
- ThisIs
- SoisthiS

One property of camel case linking deserves a special mention: WikiWords create links by removing characters from a word instead of adding them. For example, the words *Wikis For Dummies* become a link by taking out the spaces: WikisForDummies. For most other forms of linking, such as creating HTML links, lots and lots of characters must be added.

If you haven't done so already, open a wiki page for editing at `http://twiki.org`, as described earlier in this chapter. Click the Edit link on a page you edited and then add this line to the end of what you already have:

```
MyFirstWikiLink
```

The page should look similar to Figure 2-8.

Figure 2-8:
Create a
camel case
link in text
edit mode.

When you're done typing the link and save the page, the result should resemble Figure 2-9.

The novel feature of the page shown in Figure 2-9 is that a question mark — which is actually a link — has been added after the word in camel case (the WikiWord). The question mark is an indication that the word is a wiki link that leads to a page that doesn't yet exist.

Keep in mind that using camel case is just one strategy for making links easy. The original wiki created by Ward Cunningham, TWiki, and many other wikis use camel case for links, but we explain other approaches in Chapter 7. In fact, for some people, camel case links are confusing, and other methods work better. The important thing is that creating wiki links must be easy.

More is more: Creating a new page

Okay, you can have a link to a page that doesn't exist. So, how does the new page get created? Quite simply, actually. All you have to do is click the question mark that appears at the end of the link. (See the previous section on creating links.) The browser window takes you to text mode, where you can add the content of the page, as shown in Figure 2-10.

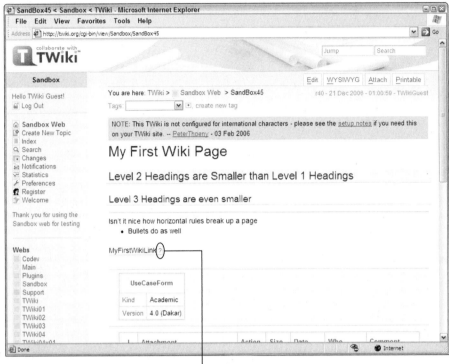

Figure 2-9:
Links to a
nonexistent
page bear a
question
mark.

Indicates this is a link to a page that doesn't exist yet.

After you add content and then save the page, the link no longer shows up with a question mark. Instead, it is a link to the page that you just created and shows up underlined in a special color (or however links are identified in your browser).

One implication of using WikiWords for links is that all the pages are going to be named as WikiWords as well. In other words, WikiWords are both names of links and names of pages. The same WikiWord is used for both the link and the name of the page, and the link is created automatically. This is a good thing because it leaves no room for confusion. This type of simplification is just so full of wiki-ness it makes your SpineTingle.

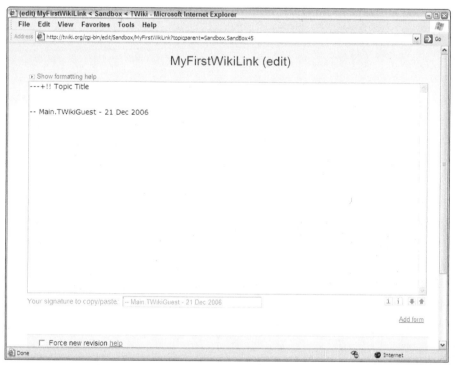

Figure 2-10:
Now you
can edit
your newly
created
page.

Identifying page parents

Earlier in this chapter, we show how bread crumbs help you identify the position of a page in a wiki's hierarchy. Suppose that on your first wiki page, you enter this text:

```
---+ My First Wiki Page
```

After you click Save, you see the page shown in Figure 2-11. One thing to notice is that the bread crumbs now reflect that you created the new page as a link from your test page. The bread crumbs show the TWiki page, then the Sandbox web, then the test page, and finally the new page that you just created. The test page — which in Figure 2-11 is called SandBox45 — is considered the *parent page* of your newly created page. This path from one page to another is created when the pages are created. If the link structure is changed so that now the Sandbox web also links directly to the page that you created, the bread crumbs won't be changed unless you use some of the advanced tools that we explain in Chapter 13.

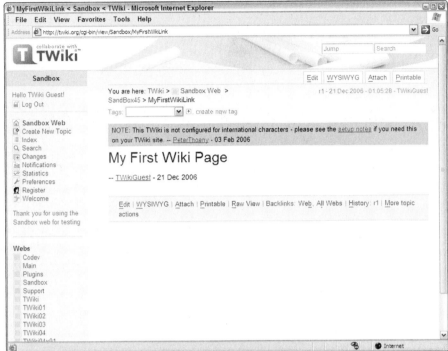

Figure 2-11:
Your first
wiki page
has been
saved.

Parent pages are also important when creating pages other ways. In TWiki, you can add a page by clicking the Create New Topic link on the left side of the page and specifying a parent page. In other wikis, you'll see an Add Page or Add Child Page link. When you create pages this way, you'll have an option to specify what the parent page should be. When you add a link and click it to create a new page (as you did earlier), the new page is automatically a child of the page on which you added the link. If only managing children were this easy in the real world!

Finding lost pages

One thing that can happen to a page is that all the links to it can be deleted. If this happens, the page can be potentially lost. If the page that links to the page is deleted or edited to remove the link, the page is now an orphan or lost.

However, you can always go to lost pages by using one of two methods:

- ✔ **Use Jump navigation.** Type the name of the lost page in the Jump field, as we mention earlier in this chapter.

- ✔ **List all topics in the web.** To list all topics in a web, click the Index link in the left navigation section.

Although it's possible to "lose" a page by erasing the links to it, with wikis, you never have to worry about broken links within your wiki. If you rename a wiki page (which you can do in TWiki by selecting More Topic Actions, and then Rename/Move Topic), the wiki itself will change the name of the page's link on every page in the wiki. It's another wiki miracle.

Attaching Documents to Wiki Pages

Attaching documents is a feature that emerged as wikis started to be used more and more often in the corporate world. In the view of some wiki purists, all information on a wiki should be captured on a wiki page. However, this isn't practical in a world where so much information is stored in word processing and spreadsheet files.

TWiki.org solves this problem through the Attach link. When you click the Attach link, an Attach page like the one shown in Figure 2-12 is displayed. Click Browse to select a file to attach.

Figure 2-12:
Attach a file
to a wiki
page.

The Attach page allows word processing files, spreadsheets, JPEGs, GIFs, or PDF files to be attached to a page. When images (JPEG or GIF files) are attached, they appear in the list at the end of the file, but they can also be displayed in the body of the page by adding an image link. When the file is uploaded, select the Create a Link to the Attached File check box to create either a link to the file (if it is not an image) or an HTML image tag that refers to the file stored at the end of the page using a special variable. Here's what the HTML might look like:

```
* Little Pebbles T-Shirt: <br />
  <img src="%ATTACHURLPATH%/littlepebblesBW.jpg"
       alt="littlepebblesBW.jpg" width="549"
       height="779" />
```

The string %ATTACHURLPATH% is a TWiki variable that is filled in with the directory in which the image file is stored so that it can be displayed on the page. You can read much more about variables and how they can be used to customize and control links in Chapter 7 and wikis in general in Chapter 13. If you attach an image file and choose to have it show up on the page, the result looks like Figure 2-13.

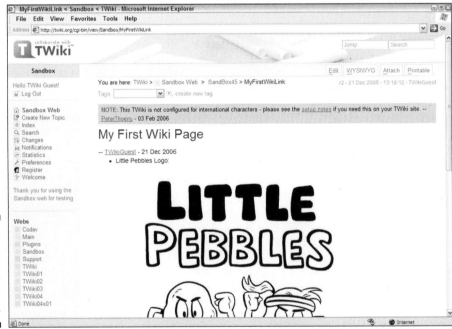

Figure 2-13:
You can display an attached image in a wiki page.

This simple file-attaching functionality is quite powerful and enhances your ability to create wiki pages that are attractive and serve as a shareable repository for documents. Crack! Another bolt of the simplifying lightning of wikis has struck.

Printing Wiki Pages

Printing from a wiki is as simple as printing any other Web page in a browser. To preview how a printed page will appear, choose File⇨Print in your Web browser. If you preview a regular wiki page, you'll probably see navigation links and tools that you don't really need on the printed copy. To pretty things up, most wikis offer a Printable link on each page. Click the Printable link to display a version of the page formatted in an attractive way for printing.

Tracking Versions and Changes

One of the challenges of collective ownership of wiki content is that one person can change a page in a way that others might not like. On Wikipedia, the multilanguage encyclopedia covered in Chapter 4, this happens all the time. Pages are changed back and forth in an Internet-era form of a slow-motion argument. In the early days of wikis, this was a huge problem because there was no record or version of each page. If someone wiped out a page, it was gone unless someone had saved a copy.

In a sizable wiki, having a large number of authors can also create the challenge of not knowing what has been updated. Version tracking and the ability to see a list of recent changes attack both of these problems head on.

How versions keep wikis safe

Versioning is the idea of keeping track of every change made to a page. TWiki recognized the versioning problem quite early and was one of the first wikis to introduce the idea of capturing every version of a page so that previous versions could be referenced and restored, and also so that an audit trail of who changed what could be maintained.

Look at the bottom of the page shown in Figure 2-14 to see a portion of the footer with this text:

```
History: r2 < r1
```

Figure 2-14:
Wiki pages
show
version
history.

The page version numbers start with 1 and increment from there. Each version is referred to by its version number and the letter r. r1 is the first version of the page, r2 is the second, and so on. If you click the less-than sign between r2 and r1, for example, you see the differences between those two pages. If you click r1, you see the earlier version of the page. TWiki also maintains versions of attachments to pages.

With versioning, a lot of the fear of letting multiple authors loose on a set of content disappears.

Tracking changes in a Wiki

One of the most valuable but least used parts of most wikis — largely because most people don't know what it is — is the Changes link. The *Changes link* shows a list of the pages that have been recently changed, when they were changed or created, and who changed them. Figure 2-15 shows what TWiki presents when the Change link is pressed.

The Changes report provides a quick summary of what's happening on a web as well as allowing you a quick way back to the pages you've been working on.

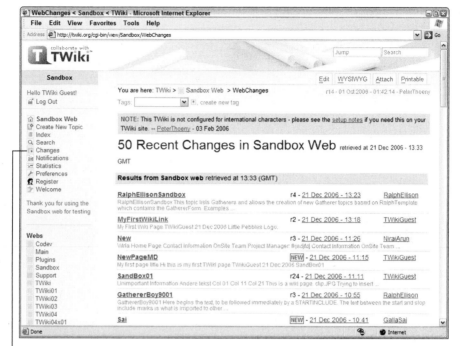

Figure 2-15:
You can see
a report of
changes to
wiki pages
on a web.

The Changes link

Chapter 3

The Thousand Problem-Solving Faces of Wikis

*T*he universal applicability of wikis represents a challenge to the beginner. Wikis can help almost any group of people do almost anything, which can make it difficult to figure out how to get started. This chapter takes you through all sorts of examples of wikis ranging from the biggest — with hundreds of thousands of pages, used by thousands of people all over the world — to the smallest, which exist to help just a few people.

In taking this tour, you'll probably find wikis so valuable that they become part of your everyday life. You are also likely to find wikis that seem so useless you cannot understand why anyone would ever visit.

Almost every wiki has ten readers for each person who actively adds content. If you really get lucky, you might find a wiki so exciting that you join the core content-creating team and start shoveling your ideas and thoughts into it by the bucketful.

The main goal of this chapter is to make the idea of what wikis can do much more specific. By the end of this chapter, you will have many ideas for new wikis that can help you (or others you know) get where you want to go.

The Many Categories of Wikis

We categorize wikis in this chapter by the nature of their content or the reason why people use them. Sometimes, the content is the star of the show. Other times, the group creating the content or the goal of the people who created the wiki takes precedence when categorizing the wiki. Wiki categories include

- ✔ **Content-focused wikis:** These wikis focus on a specific kind of content, such as reference material, hobbyist content, travel information, or documentation on a certain technology.

- ✔ **Process-focused wikis:** Some wikis are devoted to the study and advancement of processes. A productivity wiki might be used to encourage collaboration and project management within a company. Other common types of process-focused wikis include task-oriented wikis, advocacy wikis, and educational wikis.

- ✔ **Community wikis:** Most communities can benefit from wikis. Community wikis might serve location-specific communities or virtual communities built around a shared interest or need.

- ✔ **Ease-of-use wikis:** Wikis are easy to use, so it's only natural that they are used to make challenging tasks easier. For example, small businesses frequently create online brochure Web sites with wikis because they're easy to create and manage. Family wikis are used to share news, photos, and other information. And personal wikis are used to easily share information about themselves.

Keep a few things in mind as you read about the wikis in this chapter:

- ✔ **Not all the wikis mentioned here are public.** You won't be able to visit the Goowiki that Google uses to help run its company, or the internal wikis at SAP, or the Intellipedia used by the United States government.

- ✔ **The four listed categories are not hard and fast.** Some content-focused wikis also could be considered process-focused wikis. For example, a wiki on Marvel comics could be seen as both an entertainment wiki and a productivity wiki.

- ✔ **Don't be surprised when you stumble upon unfinished wikis.** You might come across pages that are half finished or discover that you're looking for content that hasn't been created yet. The quality of every wiki varies by the intensity of the community's interest in it.

Content-Focused Wikis: The Goldmine of Shared Content

When exploring the world of wikis, you'll find that content-focused wikis are by far the largest wiki category. *Content-focused wikis* use the shared-ownership and easy editing aspects of wikis to bring together a large group of people to create some content.

In a way, every wiki is about the content on the pages, but sometimes that content is just a means to an end. For a book project, a wiki might hold the outline and notes. This is not the case in a content-focused wiki. Instead, the content on the pages is the end unto itself, and much time is spent creating, correcting, massaging, improving, and debating those pages. (Using our book analogy, a content-focused wiki would contain a living version of the book that could continue to be changed and expanded.)

Most folks use content-focused wikis, such as Wikipedia, when looking for an answer or to learn about a topic. When you encounter pages on a content-focused wiki, you might not even know that a wiki is being used to publish them.

Doing research with reference wikis

If imitation is the sincerest form of flattery, Wikipedia must feel mightily flattered. Wikis created to provide reference and encyclopedic information are the most active areas of wiki creation, with many of the wikis named *wiki*-this or that-*pedia* (in honor, no doubt, of Wikipedia).

Reference wikis vary in quality, but they can quite frequently be time-saving godsends when you're doing something like trying to track down the difference between a brouhaha and a donnybrook. If you want to create your own reference wiki, visit the following wikis to see how they work.

Wiktionary

```
http://en.wiktionary.org
```

Wiktionary — a collaborative online dictionary with more than 300,000 entries in nearly 400 languages — is to a Webster's dictionary what Wikipedia is to *Encyclopaedia Brittanica*. The English version was launched in 2002 and includes definitions, etymologies, pronunciations, sample uses, synonyms, antonyms, and translations. The Wiktionary front page features links to a Word of the Day, different languages, categories, topics, rhymes, and a thesaurus.

The Wikimedia Foundation

Wiktionary and Wikiquote operate under the umbrella of the Wikimedia Foundation, which runs Wikipedia and many other sites. Most of the Wikimedia wikis are reference wikis with a well-developed set of pages that explain what the wiki is intended to do, how to get involved, the proper form for entries, and what is allowed and not allowed. Anyone creating their own reference wiki would do well to imitate all these aspects of the Wikimedia sites.

Wikiquote

```
http://en.wikiquote.org
```

When you're looking for a famous quote from a movie, book, or historical figure, try Wikiquote. Wikiquote is a free, searchable database of quotes from people and creative works. The site, launched in July 2003, has blossomed quickly. Pages are available in nearly 90 languages, and the English version of Wikiquote — the largest, followed by German — has nearly 9,000 pages. Translations of non-English quotes also are available. Users of Wikiquote can search by names, literary works, films, TV shows, themes (such as art or love), or categories like Last Words or Tongue Twisters.

BibleWiki

```
http://bible.tmtm.com
```

BibleWiki has a page for each chapter of the Christian Bible, and the wiki's goal is to provide free, scholarly commentary for the entire text, including different translations and original Hebrew or Greek texts for some verses. The site aspires to skirt "disputes over religious doctrine" by sticking to explanation of the text and avoiding interpretation.

This site has an elegant design that allows you to locate any verse in the Bible with just a few clicks. The community portal offers a list of wanted pages, pages that don't exist but are linked to from at least two pages, and other suggestions for how to add short articles. You must register to add content.

Baseball Reference Bullpen

```
www.baseball-reference.com/bullpen
```

Figure 3-1 shows the main page of the Baseball Reference Bullpen wiki. A collaborative encyclopedia of all-things baseball with more than 38,000 articles on subjects ranging from statistics, ballparks, Hall of Fame players, the Negro League, and even Little League, Baseball Reference Bullpen aims to "collect and organize the vastness of baseball knowledge."

Figure 3-1:
The
Baseball
Reference
Bullpen is
a great
resource
covering
America's
pastime.

The Baseball Reference Bullpen goes beyond other reference wikis by providing a detailed description of what must be included in an article as well as step-by-step instructions for creating and editing pages.

CosmeticsWiki

```
http://cosmeticswiki.com
```

CosmeticsWiki (as shown in Figure 3-2) has more than 35,000 pages on beauty, skin care, hair products, and other cosmetics, including information on ingredients, prices, testimonials, and beauty tips.

CosmeticsWiki was created by Nicki Zevola and Sean Colombo, who saw a need that could be filled by a wiki. The site is seeking advertising and has referrals to locations where you can buy the products mentioned. The CosmeticsWiki revenue model is to earn a percentage on sales of the cosmetics and skincare items that people buy from links on the pages. Much of the site is empty, waiting to be filled. Such wikis with commercial aspirations are a relatively new phenomenon, and it remains to be seen whether thriving communities will form around them.

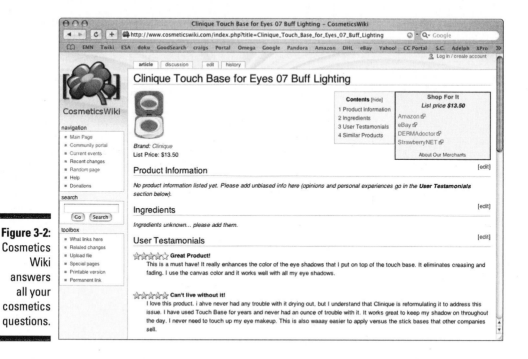

Figure 3-2:
Cosmetics
Wiki
answers
all your
cosmetics
questions.

Sharpening skills with hobbyist wikis

No matter how mainstream or obscure your area of interest or hobby, there's likely a wiki to help you learn more or enhance your experiences. The beauty of hobbyist wikis is that the truly passionate enthusiasts are the ones creating, updating, and adding to the sites, helping ensure that information is up to date and thorough. And, the interactivity of wikis means that you can join in the online community of like-minded hobbyists if you have something to add. The wikis described in the following sections show how wikis can enhance a variety of hobby experiences.

PokerWiki

```
http://poker.wikia.com
```

While away from the table, poker aficionados can read about poker strategy, rules, philosophy, tournaments, game selection, bankroll management, and casino reviews in nearly 600 articles on PokerWiki.

PokerWiki defines a specific purpose for itself that is complementary to other well-established sources of information about poker.

CookbookWiki

www.cookbookwiki.com

Whether you're craving a dish from Bosnia or Brazil, CookbookWiki aims to please all palates. The site's mission is to "document every culinary tradition of the world." As of early 2007, CookbookWiki contained more than 37,000 recipes. It also features forums for readers seeking recipes or tips on different types of cooking and baking, or ingredients. The wiki — as shown in Figure 3-3 — aims to act as a central repository for recipes that until now were scattered over countless countertop cookbooks — some of which might be out of print or too splattered with sauce to be useful for future generations.

CookbookWiki has an engaging and inspiring mission statement that explains why the site was created and what it hopes to accomplish.

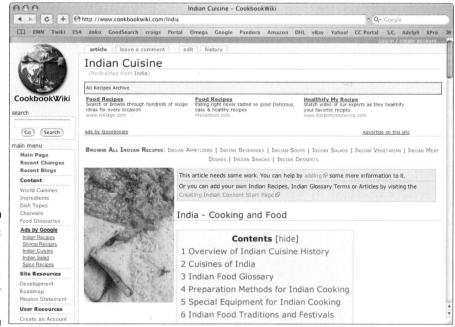

Figure 3-3: Cookbook-Wiki can help with almost any kind of food.

The Encyclopedia Gamia

```
http://egamia.com
```

Gamers — primarily those permanently attached at the thumb to a video console — will find articles on PC games, trading cards, board games, and written games at The Encyclopedia Gamia, shown in Figure 3-4. Offshoots include pages on TV shows about games and actors who voice video games, as well as tech issues related to gaming.

The Encyclopedia Gamia offers those who create pages a rich selection of templates that allow other material on the wiki to be referenced. For example, if you create a page about Donkey Kong, you can include the Donkey Kong template that provides links to all other elements related to Donkey Kong on the wiki.

Going around the world with travel wikis

One of the toughest things about travel planning is the difficulty of finding centralized, current information. By the nature of the publishing cycle and the reality of restaurant turnover, printed guidebooks can soon be out of date.

Figure 3-4: The Encyclopedia Gamia is the wiki-est resource for avid gamers.

Travel wikis — often updated by people who have just returned from a far-away locale — are easy to maneuver (even if the streets of your intended destination are not), and the information is likely to be current. A travel wiki might not fit into your back pocket as well as some guide books, but it's an avenue worth investigating.

One good example of a travel wiki is Wikitravel, located at `http://wikitravel.org`. Whether you're wondering where you can get the best plate of fried bluefish in the Pitcairn Islands (see Figure 3-5) or what kind of electrical adapter you'll need in Bahrain, Wikitravel is the place to go online before you go in person. The worldwide travel guide has nearly 13,000 destination guides and articles on locations near and far. Travelers can pick up tips on how to get to destinations, what to see and eat there, and the best places to stay — all kept up to date by users of the site. The home page has such features as Destination of the Month and Off the Beaten Path as well as travel news and fun facts about different destinations. (Did you know? "Noodles in Hanoi are often flavored with a few aromatic drops of crushed belostomatid, a giant water bug.")

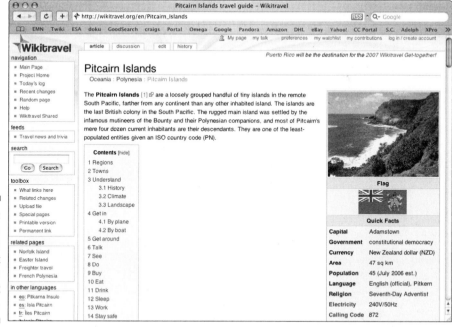

Figure 3-5:
The Pitcairn Islands and other great destinations await at Wikitravel.

Travel wikis represent a true hybrid of content- and process-focused wikis. Although much of the content is clearly reference material about places, the material is also about the process of taking a trip. ***Remember:*** More often than not, a wiki has properties that fit in more than one of the categories we discuss here.

Finding technical documentation wikis

One of the most popular applications of wikis in the world of engineering is to create a central spot for technical documentation. The ultimate purpose of documentation wikis is to provide reference material, but documentation wikis also benefit from being easy to use, which allows a large group of authors to contribute to and improve the content.

SAP Enterprise Services wiki

```
https://wiki.sdn.sap.com/wiki/x/LQ0
```

The SAP Enterprise Services wiki documents the Web services that SAP provides to allow developers to create new solutions. The wiki (see Figure 3-6) contains a general description of why the services were created, how they work, and how to use them. Scenarios for applying the services are suggested, and room exists for those who have used the services to comment on tips and tricks.

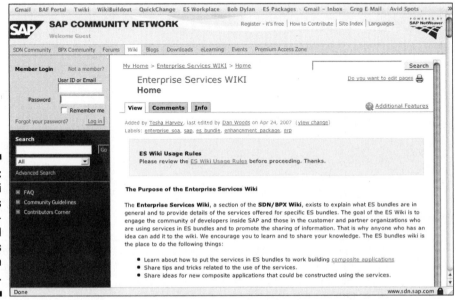

Figure 3-6: This wiki provides documentation and promotes information sharing.

Claroline Development wiki

```
www.claroline.net/wiki
```

The Claroline Development wiki is a complete set of technical documentation based on the Wikimedia wiki engine that covers everything going on with regard to the development of *Claroline,* which is an open source platform for creating e-learning courses. The site is a comprehensive source for all aspects of Claroline's development, including plans for new features, discussions of how the program is being restructured, and links to other forms of documentation.

SugarCRM Support and Development wikis

```
www.sugarcrm.com/wiki
```

The wikis of SugarCRM focus on asking and answering questions related to the use of SugarCRM. The Sugar Support wiki provides education and reference material about SugarCRM. The Sugar Development wiki covers new functionality and feature extension for SugarCRM. Both wikis provide detailed and complete information. The emphasis of these wikis is the information in them, not the formation of a community. The content seems to be in a wiki format more for ease of use in creating the content rather than to attract contributions from outside of Sugar. This is probably because the thriving user community at `www.sugarforge.org` makes other forms of community unnecessary.

Process-Focused Wikis: A Shared Space for a Shared Mission

Process-focused wikis are all about helping people collaborate and work together to get something done. Although process-focused wikis are awash in content, the goal of these wikis is not to create that content but to support a process: some other activity outside the wiki.

Wikis for project management are probably the largest category of process-focused wikis, but few of them are available on the Internet for inspection. After all, you can't have the whole world — or even just your competitors — looking at your top-secret projects! The key to getting these wikis going is providing a simple way to find the information you need to do your job and then to make sure that everyone gets the help they need to start changing wiki pages. These wikis thrive after they achieve critical mass and become the center of much of the activity in a company. Frequently, they grow organically throughout an organization as more and more people find out about them and want to use them.

Managing projects and productivity with wikis

The great thing about using a wiki for project management is that almost every aspect of a wiki works in your favor. The ease-of-use allows more people to start using the wiki right away without any training. The flexibility of the page structure is easily adapted to any need. Advanced features for structured wikis allow tables of information and simple database-like elements to be added to the wiki. After you use a wiki for project management, running a large project without one is hard to imagine.

The wiki used to write this book — hosted at Evolved Media Network — is typical of many project management wikis. The wiki has special pages devoted to tracking interviews and research documents. Each page has a form attached that allows lists of pages to be displayed in a table and sorted in various ways. In this way, the pages become sort of like database records. Other areas keep track of writer assignments, meeting notes from the project managers, schedules, and outlines for each chapter. Each page is easy to update and has a different form according to its special need.

Corporate or productivity wikis are typically password protected and are intended for smaller, private groups to collaboratively work on projects, or for large corporations to use internally. Large companies such as Google, Novell, SAP, Sun, and Motorola all use wikis to help run their internal operations, but access to people outside the company is prohibited.

Getting the job done with task-oriented wikis

Wikis are increasingly used by corporations, government organizations, and professional groups to share information, plan projects, and track developments related to their work. In such environments, research wikis are tremendous resources because accurate, timely information can easily be shared and updated by anyone in the organization.

eBay Wiki

    www.ebaywiki.com

eBay Wiki (www.ebaywiki.com), as shown in Figure 3-7, draws from the expertise of eBay users who contribute articles about buying and selling on eBay, eBay policies, seller tools, and more. Much of eBay Wiki is geared to more experienced eBay users, and you can also find a New User's Guide for surfers unfamiliar with how eBay works.

Figure 3-7:
eBay Wiki
is a
clearing-
house for
eBay
knowledge.

Intellipedia

http://en.wikipedia.org/wiki/Intellipedia

In 2006, John Negroponte, the U.S. intelligence czar, unveiled the government's own "spy wiki," called *Intellipedia* — a secure, online site available
only to intelligence analysts and officials with the proper clearance, and used
to share information among the country's 16 intelligence agencies. According
to news reports, the site had more than 28,000 pages and 3,600 registered
users as of late 2006. The creation of Intellipedia came after widespread criti-
cism following the terrorist attacks of September 11, 2001: namely, that government agencies were too closely protecting information (instead of sharing
it with each other) to prevent terrorist attacks and other events. Intellipedia
operates on the same software that runs Wikipedia, but its contents are not
available to the public.

Ganfyd

www.ganfyd.org

Ganfyd.org (see Figure 3-8) is the first free, collaborative medical reference
site and describes itself as an "evolving textbook of medicine." Begun by doctors and medical students in the United Kingdom, it now has more than 300

contributors from the U.K., Ireland, New Zealand, Canada, and Australia — all of whom are either medical doctors registered within the country they practice or invited guest experts. Only registered users can adapt content, but anyone is free to read the entries. Subjects include pages on medical and surgical specialties, primary care, public health, women's health, and a medical dictionary, among others.

Ganfyd.org is a clear example of how wiki culture can be adapted to the needs of a particular wiki. Because the quality of the information on Ganfyd.org is used in the practice of medicine, only medical doctors or experts are allowed to contribute content. The Ganyfyd.org wiki is also a hybrid between a reference wiki about medical information and a process wiki about diagnosis.

The name *Ganfyd* is derived from the usually pejorative slang phrase "Get a note from your doctor" — a case in which a patient needs a physicians' note to participate in or be excused from an activity, sometimes for legal reasons, for school or an employer.

Figure 3-8:
The Ganfyd wiki bills itself as an "evolving textbook of medicine."

TaxAlmanac

`www.taxalmanac.org`

Tax professionals come together on TaxAlmanac, a wiki developed by Intuit, which makes tax preparation products. TaxAlmanac — shown in Figure 3-9 — allows users to research tax law and peruse around 37,000 articles on the IRS, Tax Court decisions, Treasury regulations, and other topics useful in tax preparation.

WikiWikiWeb

`http://c2.com/cgi/wiki`

WikiWikiWeb is the first-ever wiki. WikiWikiWeb focuses on the "people, projects, and patterns" — or, the who, what, and how — in software development. Even if the topics and language on WikiWikiWeb seem impenetrable to anyone who's not a software engineer or computer programmer, the structure of the pages is what's ultimately important to general Web users. The idea of modifiable Web pages serves as the foundation upon which all other wikis (including Wikipedia) and wiki engines are built. The idea that anyone can modify or edit a page on a site to create a breathing, evolving document or community is taken directly from WikiWikiWeb.

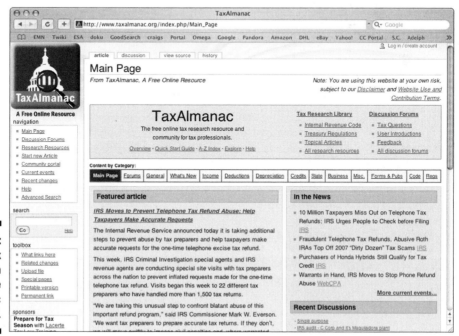

Figure 3-9:
Find tax information at the TaxAlmanac wiki.

WikiWiki means *quick* in Hawaiian. WikiWikiWeb — and wikis in general — were created by Ward Cunningham, a computer programmer who launched WikiWikiWeb on the site of his software consulting company, Cunningham & Cunningham, Inc. (c2.com) in 1995.

Wikinews

```
http:en.wikinews.org
```

Wannabe journalists can write to their heart's content at Wikinews, which bills itself as "The free news source you can write!" The site strives to maintain a neutral voice and cites all articles. The two most common types of articles on Wikinews are synthesis articles, which pull together numerous media reports drawn from traditional sources for a fuller view of the news, and original reporting, or firsthand reports from contributors who provide backup notes for their articles.

Making it happen with advocacy wikis

There are as many pet issues as there are people — global warming, recycling, renewable energy, clean water, and the ever-popular world peace. Communities are coming together online and using wikis to spread the word and sway folks to their side, share information about upcoming events related to their issues, update readers on legal or ethical developments, and track articles related to the causes.

Project Backpack

```
www.projectbackpack.org
```

Project Backpack was an effort to send backpacks and holiday letters to the children affected by hurricane Katrina. The simple wiki provided instructions about how to help and what to do. In the end, more than 50,000 backpacks were sent.

The About Us page has a message that captures the spirit of most advocacy wikis:

> You are Us. Join Us!

> Just get it done.
> Run with it. Take Ownership.

> No formal organization. No org chart.
> No money. No office. No phone. No fax.
> No email address of xxxx@projectbackpack.org

> No one is in charge. **Everyone is in charge.**

EvoWiki

`http://wiki.cotch.net`

Delve into Darwin on EvoWiki, created and edited by readers who want to promote evolution education, talk about biology, and offer scientific knowledge that counters the arguments of creationists. Topics include theories of evolution, common descent, creationism, intelligent design, political controversies, scientists, and lists of other evolutionist blogs.

SourceWatch

`www.sourcewatch.org`

Run by the Center for Media and Democracy, SourceWatch (see Figure 3-10) sees itself as an anti-spin site. Its self-professed goal is to "produce a directory of the people, organizations and issues shaping the public agenda," with an eye on tracking public relations, propaganda, and the manipulation of public perception. It also serves as a directory of think tanks, industry organizations, and experts who may speak on behalf of corporations, government, and special interest groups.

Figure 3-10: Untangle spin at the Source-Watch wiki.

CAISI (Client Access to Integrated Service and Information)

```
www.caisi.ca/wiki
```

The CAISI wiki is the site of a Canadian nonprofit group that uses open source development to create software used for a group of homeless shelters and other agencies that help the Toronto homeless population. The software allows a greater integration of care and real-time information for employees and volunteers at agencies and centers that help the homeless, with a goal of reducing chronic homelessness.

Wikocracy

```
http://wikocracy.com
```

On Wikocracy, anyone with a computer can play legislator. Everything from the U.S. Constitution to local zoning ordinances — as well as hot-button issues like the Patriot Act and the Defense of Marriage Act — are up for edits and rowdy, written jousting between collaborators with opposing viewpoints. Obviously, none of the revisions are legally binding, but it's nice to take a stab at creating your own Utopia online.

Finding educational wikis for students and teachers

Teachers and students are turning to wikis to collaborate on classroom projects, turn in and grade papers, share curriculum, plan studies, and link to information that can be helpful in lessons. These are being used on a small scale by single classrooms or on a large scale to disseminate curriculum that might not otherwise be broadly (or cheaply) available. In fact, *wikispaces.com,* a hosted wiki that allows you to quickly create a wiki on their servers, is sponsoring a program to distribute 100,000 wiki pages at no charge to educators to help them broaden and enrich their students' experiences. Some educational wikis include

- ✔ **Curriki (www.curriki.org):** Derived from the words *curriculum* and *wiki,* Curriki (see Figure 3-11) is the wiki of the Global Education and Learning Community, a project started by Sun Microsystems to develop and freely distribute curriculum materials worldwide. Content is created collaboratively by educators and other experts online. The project currently focuses on materials for kindergarten through 12th grade and the subjects of math, sciences, technology, reading, and languages.

- ✔ **Westwood Schools (http://westwood.wikispaces.com):** Vicki Davis' wiki for Westwood schools covers many topics and classes at the school, making excellent use of wikis as both a community building tool and as a storehouse of reference information.

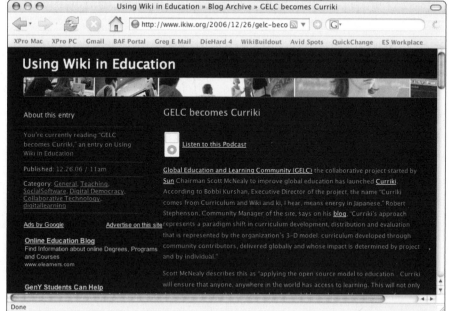

Figure 3-11:
Find
educational
curriculum
materials at
Curriki.

- **Mr. Lindsay's Room 15 Wiki (`http://mrlindsay.pbwiki.com`):** This is a beautiful wiki that shows what a wiki can do for a classroom. Features include demos of students' work, book reviews, poems, stories, and tons of other resources. It's a wiki run "by the students, for the students."

- **CAS 100B Course at Penn State (`http://cas100b.pbwiki.com`):** The CAS100B wiki supports the class covering effective speech at Penn State University. The wiki contains a syllabus, assignments, schedules, class notes, and different sections for different classes.

Community Wikis: Exploring Common Bonds

To find out the answer to the eternal question, "How will it play in Peoria?," you might want to check out the Peoria wiki. (Yes, there is one.) Community wikis can give new and old residents of towns, universities, or big cities all the latest information on where to live, places to go, where to eat, things to do — and what to avoid.

If your community doesn't already have a wiki, you might want to start one yourself. Check out these great community wikis for inspiration:

- ✔ **JhuWiki (`http://wiki.jhu.edu`):** This wiki (as shown in Figure 3-12), maintained and composed by students and others at Johns Hopkins University, says its mission is to "increase the quality of student life." To that end, JhuWiki contains articles on everything from where to get your eyebrows waxed at a salon that feels "rich and snooty" to buying used textbooks. On- and off-campus housing guides are included, along with lists of sororities and fraternities for those interested in the Greek life.

- ✔ **ArborWiki (`http://arborwiki.org/city/Main_Page`):** This wiki (as shown in Figure 3-13) is a collection of information about Ann Arbor, Ypsilanti, and other places in Washtenaw County, Michigan. ArborWiki encompasses information on politics, entertainment, local issues, and education. It incorporates a section dedicated to the University of Michigan with information for students, faculty, and staff. The site is committed to maintaining a free and public wiki for the collection of facts, figures, memories, and visions about anything pertaining to the area.

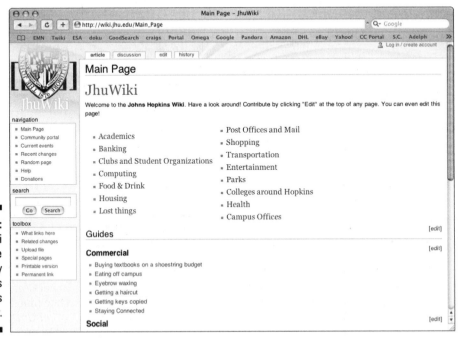

Figure 3-12:
The JhuWiki serves the community at Johns Hopkins University.

Figure 3-13:
ArborWiki is
dedicated to
serving the
Ann Arbor
area.

Community wikis don't have to be just for people who live near each other. Wikis can also serve people in fan communities, clubs, or other groups with shared interests. The following sections describe some nongeographical community wikis.

Goofing off with entertainment wikis

Star Wars nuts make up one of the most frequently updated and popular wikis on the Web: Wookiepedia. In a world where fan sites exist for nearly every show, book, or other pop-culture offering you can think of, and deal in all the minutae that true fans seek out, check out these well-designed examples before starting your own fan or entertainment wiki:

✔ **Marvel Database Project (www.marveldatabase.com):** Launched in 2005 and edited by both Marvel employees and Marvel Comics fans, the Marvel Database Project has expanded from reference materials about Marvel Comics like *The Official Handbook of the Marvel Universe* to include original content, profiles on Marvel contracted employees, cover art, and other images and comics listings and synopses.

✔ **Star Trek wiki (`http://memory-alpha.org`):** This wiki includes the most mind-blowing details about *Star Trek,* including facts, ships, weapons, timelines, and more.

✔ **Wookiepedia (`http://starwars.wikia.com`):** Sci-fi fans can get the 411 on the six popular George Lucas films that make up the *Star Wars* saga on *Wookiepedia,* a wiki devoted to all aspects of *Star Wars.* With more than 40,000 articles, the encyclopedic English-language version of Wookiepedia was the largest Wikia-hosted wiki on the Web, as of late 2006, according to article count. Many articles on the site read more like a fictional history book than a fan site. Contributors describe in great depth the battles, governments, creatures, and characters of the *Star Wars* films. The site also includes articles about the real-life culture of *Star Wars* fans and creators.

✔ **LyricWiki (`www.lyricwiki.org`):** Useful for brushing up on linguistic stylings ahead of a turn at the karaoke mike, or seeking sentiment from the lyrics of a favorite love song, LyricWiki has what song lovers are looking for. With more than 240,000 content pages, it is among the largest MediaWiki on the Web and is searchable by song, artist, album, genre, hometown, label, and language. Most notably it has a no-banner, no-popup ad policy, a relief to music lovers dogged by such annoyances on similar sites. iTunes addicts will find handy quick links to iTunes top songs running along the front page.

✔ **Lostpedia (`www.lostpedia.com`):** If the numbers 4-8-15-16-23-42 keep flashing through your mind, visit Lostpedia to help unravel the mysteries — or at least bat around theories — about the engaging but often-confusing TV program *Lost,* which revels in hidden messages and cryptic storylines that both intrigue and frustrate loyal fans. The wiki also summarizes episodes, delves into character biographies, and posts recent news related to *Lost* and the actors on the show.

✔ **Uncyclopedia (`http://uncyclopedia.org`):** Uncyclopedia is to Wikipedia what *The Onion* is to *The New York Times.* Uncyclopedia describes itself as "an encyclopedia full of misinformation and utter lies." You might say that it puts the *psych!* in en-*cyc*-lopedia. Heavy on sarcasm and inside jokes, the satirical wiki (a parody of Wikipedia) calls itself "content-free." However, content does actually exist in the form of humorous pieces such as misquotes, made-up news, and "helpful" how-to articles such as "How to smell like a fish."

Hanging around at clubhouse wikis

One of the most popular uses of wikis is to create a space to keep track of happenings in a club. If you go to any of the hosted wiki sites mentioned in Chapter 5 and search for the world *club,* you will find hundreds of listings of wikis dedicated to clubs and other similar organizations. You can find cycling clubs, yacht clubs, eating clubs, and on and on. The club sites have information about the clubs, schedules of events, and all the other information you would expect.

Getting nerdy with technology wikis

Given the popularity of wikis with engineers, it's no surprise that technology communities are frequently supported by wikis. Almost every significant form of technology has a wiki associated with it. Just go to a search engine, type in any technology brand or product name, and add *wiki* as the second search term to find at least one wiki (and sometimes many) devoted to the topic such as the following examples:

- **SuperHappyDevHouse (http://superhappydevhouse.org):** *SuperHappyDevHouse* is a wiki dedicated to organizing hackathon events in the San Francisco Bay Area in the spirit of the famous Homebrew Computer Club that played a key role in the development of the personal computer. *Hackathons* are extended gatherings of people who get together to work on their projects and share ideas. The PBwiki-hosted wiki gained a huge boost at a SuperHappyDevHouse event.

- **E398 Essentials (http://e398essentials.wikispaces.com):** The *E398 Essentials* wiki has a huge trove of information about the Motorola E398 cellphone: basic information about the phone along with many tips and tricks for hacking it in all sorts of ways. This sort of wiki is typical of many technology wikis that have a huge amount of information about a very narrow topic.

- **The Greater IBM Connection wiki (http://greateribm.wikia.com/wiki/Main_Page):** The Greater IBM Connection wiki exists to allow alumni of IBM (so-called Greater IBM'ers) a place to collaborate on issues of common interest.

Ease-of-Use Wikis: Web Site Creation Made Easy

Most of the attention paid to wikis focuses on how the simple mechanisms of wikis create new ways of collaboration. But the ease-of-use of wikis all by themselves have democratized the web. In about five minutes, anyone can now create a Web site. The configuration and customization mechanisms of hosted wikis allow you to make Web sites look almost any way you need or want. Ease-of-use wikis aren't focused on how a group works together but rather how quickly individuals can create wikis to get their content on the Web.

Creating small business brochure wikis

Whether the local florist, a small chain of dry cleaners, or a restaurant in the neighborhood, more and more small businesses are using wikis to create their standard brochureware Web sites. EditMe.com, a hosted wiki described in Chapter 5, makes changing the layout as easy as possible. *Warning:* It ain't that easy. After you get the hang of it, though, you can really make a site shine without having to work with (or pay) specialized programmers. www.tortoisetours.com is a fine example of a wiki that just looks like a great Web site.

Making connections with personal and family wikis

Personal wikis are great places to store information and keep notes, to-do lists, appointment books, thoughts, diaries, password lists (in the case of password-protected wikis), pictures, blogs, and anything else you might like. The beauty of a personal wiki is that all your information is available to you anywhere you have an Internet connection. If you leave your appointment book at home but you track your schedule on your wiki, you can basically "take it with you" as long as you're online.

Many people keep personal wikis private or share them only with small groups via password sign-in, but some examples are public. Here are a few to get a feel for what a personal wiki can do:

- http://raymondyee.net/wiki/RaymondYee
- www.memoryarchive.org/en/MemoryArchive
- http://guykawasaki.pbwiki.com/Book-Ideas

Similar to personal wikis are family wikis. These are used to track genealogy, post family histories and pictures, provide reunion records, post personal blogs, coordinate event calendars, or host online "brag books" of trips, vacations, or new relatives. Some good examples of family wikis include

    ✔ http://ringfamily.wikispaces.com

    ✔ www.brooksby.org

    ✔ www.sternfeldt.com

Hunting for More Wikis

Searching for wikis, unfortunately, isn't as easy as your typical Google search. Many wikis exist only for small groups of users and are private or password protected, meaning that they don't turn up in Web searches.

However, if you're searching for a wiki on a popular topic that you suspect might have a publicly accessible page, the easiest thing to do is to start with the granddaddy of all wikis, Wikipedia. Just type a search term in the Wikipedia Search box and see what pops up. (See Chapter 4 for more on using Wikipedia.) The following Web sites might also be helpful:

✔ **http://en.wikipedia.org/wiki/List_of_wikis:** Wikipedia maintains this "wiki of wikis," which also lists the Web's largest wikis.

✔ **http://meta.wikimedia.org/wiki/List_of_largest_wikis:** This is another list of the largest wikis.

✔ **http://wikiindex.org:** WikiIndex is dedicated to cataloging wikis.

Alternatively, a Web search on Google, Yahoo!, or any other popular search engine can turn up a wiki of interest by typing in your subject matter (for example, *gardening* or *classic cars*) plus the word *wiki*.

Often, smaller wikis or corporate wikis are kept private so that they can be edited or read only by small groups of people. If you want to know what kinds of companies use wikis in their businesses, some wiki providers offer client lists like the one found at http://en.wikipedia.org/wiki/Corporate_wiki.

Finally, hosted wikis (or wiki farms) of the sort described in Chapter 5 sometimes provide directories of wikis that are publicly available on their site if you feel like browsing. Check out lists of hosted wikis like the one at http://pbwiki.com/public.php. Hosted wikis, such as WikiSpaces.com (www.wikispaces.com/site/top), also have lists of the most active wikis on their sites.

Chapter 4

Using and Improving the 800-pound Gorilla of Wikis: Wikipedia

*O*nce upon a time, encyclopedia dealers came to your door to sell you their multivolume wares so that you and your offspring could truly live among the educated. These tomes, which publishers have groomed and updated over the course of decades (in some cases, centuries) were long ago digitized and put online. Even then, the information maintained the musty, authoritative air of a high school reference bookshelf. Just like book sales, stock trading, and paper mail, the encyclopedia system appeared to be working just fine, thank you.

Then, in 2001, something Wikipedia this way came.

The reasons for the success of Wikipedia — now the largest reference Web site on the Internet — are a direct result of its wiki-ness. In fact, Wikipedia grew directly from an attempt to create a free online encyclopedia (originally called *Nupedia*) that was peer reviewed. Nupedia was a nonstarter until one of the founders was introduced to Ward Cunningham's WikiWikiWeb.

Then, pow! The idea for a collaborative, informal, rapidly changing reference Web site blossomed.

Because Wikipedia is the largest publicly accessible wiki available, it's an excellent resource for learning more about wikis in general. This chapter shows you how to use Wikipedia as a research tool as well as how to become part of the community that supports the project through article editing and updating.

At this point, you might conclude that if any old clunkhead can update Wikipedia, it can't be too accurate. To be sure, the accuracy of the information on Wikipedia has come under scrutiny. And before this chapter concludes, we scrutinize that even more.

Understanding How Wikipedia Works

Finding entries on Wikipedia couldn't be easier. To begin exploring Wikipedia, visit www.wikipedia.org and then click the link for your preferred language. The home page for your language appears, as shown in Figure 4-1. From the home page, you have three ways to drill down to a desired entry:

- ✔ Click one of the subject areas listed in the upper-right corner of the page (such as Arts, Biography, or Geography).
- ✔ Click the Categories link just below the subject listings.
- ✔ Enter text into the Search field on the left margin of the page and then click the Go or the Search button.

Wikipedia is so vast that you might never return from this adventure. Along the way, though, you might also find an entry that's incomplete, incorrect, or in need of some TLC. That means its time for you to go native: Join the Wikipedians and become an editor.

Before you begin editing an entry, understand what separates Wikipedia from any other encyclopedia. Table 4-1 compares the Encyclopaedia Britannica Online with Wikipedia to highlight the differences.

Figure 4-1:
The Wikipedia home page gives you many browsing options.

Table 4-1   Encyclopaedia Britannica Online versus Wikipedia

Encyclopaedia Britannica Online	Wikipedia
Founded in Scotland in the 18th century.	Founded in England in the 21st century.
Contributors are experts in their field.	Contributors are volunteers.
Includes hyperlinks to other articles both within and outside the reference material.	Includes hyperlinks to other articles both within and outside the reference material.
Articles are peer reviewed.	Articles are reviewed by readers but not necessarily experts.
Entries are largely free of bias.	Entries can be biased, especially when first posted.
Changes are rare.	Changes are constant.
Updates annually.	Updates constantly.
Removed information vanishes.	Removed information is always available for review.
Over 12,000 articles.	Over 1 million articles.

(continued)

Table 4-1 *(continued)*

Encyclopaedia Britannica Online	Wikipedia
Sometimes lacks entries on subjects you would like to learn about.	Often includes entries on outlandish or arcane subjects.
Available in four languages.	Available in 14 languages (and parts have been translated into some 100 languages).

Run by volunteers

The phenomenal growth of Wikipedia is a direct result of its collaborative nature. There are over 1 million registered users of the English version, and that doesn't account for the millions of unregistered users. (You don't even need to register to edit the pages.) If the entries were subjected to the same stringent processes used by formal encyclopedias, it would contain far fewer articles.

Wikipedia itself is the best source of information on just how quickly it is growing. Figure 4-2 shows a chart that is part of the entry titled *Size of Wikipedia.* As you can see, Wikipedia started slow but quickly entered a growing spurt as more and more volunteers climbed aboard.

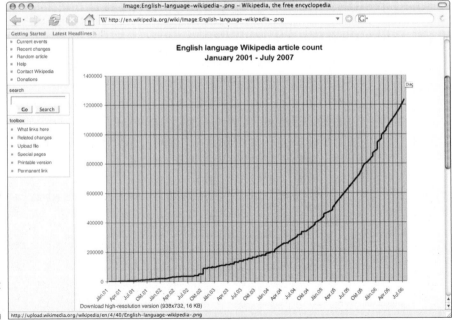

Figure 4-2: Wikipedia experienced sharp growth in recent years.

Here is the logic to the rapid growth in the number of articles on the Web site. Simply put, more entries lead to more traffic, which leads to more people who edit and create pages, which in turn, generates more entries. This cycle is potentially never ending.

Editing Wikipedia entries

Editing Wikipedia falls into two categories:

- ✔ Creating new entries
- ✔ Updating or changing existing entries

Most Wikipedia entries can be edited freely by anyone; you don't need an account or log-in. However, if you edit an article without logging in, your IP address will be logged. If you plan to participate in Wikipedia, we recommend that you click the Create Account link in the upper-right corner of most Wikipedia pages and create your own account.

Many of the examples used in this book are based on TWiki and wikispaces.com. Wikipedia, however, uses a different wiki engine called MediaWiki. The information in this chapter pertains to MediaWiki only and might not be applicable to TWiki, wikispaces.com, or any other wiki you're using.

The easiest way to start editing Wikipedia is to update an existing entry. First, find a suitable page or entry to edit. For this example, we use the Wikipedia:Sandbox, which is an area where you can experiment without permanently changing any of the real content. To add new information to the Sandbox page, follow these steps:

1. **Type** Wikipedia:Sandbox **into the Wikipedia Search field and then click Go.**

2. **Click the Edit This Page tab at the top of the Sandbox page.**

   A new page opens with a big, white editing space in the center. This is where you type your own text to make changes.

3. **In the editing area, enter the words:** This is a test of the Wikipedia broadcast system. It is only a test.

4. **Click the Save Page button that's underneath the white box.**

   Congratulations! You just edited your first Wikipedia entry!

Dressing up your Wikipedia entries

After editing the Wikipedia sandbox (as described in the preceding section), see how the text you entered looks a little, well, plain. Not to worry! Wikipedia lets you dress up the appearance of your text. To change the appearance of text, click the Edit This Page tab again and take a look at some of the more advanced formatting features of this page. Just atop the white box, where you enter text, is a line of square icons, as shown in Figure 4-3. These are your basic formatting options. From left to right, they are

- **Bold:** Styles the text in boldface

- **Italic:** Styles the text in italics

- **Internal Link:** Allows you to insert an internal link to another Wikipedia article

- **External Link:** Allows you to insert an external link to a Web address

- **Level 2 Headline:** Makes the text a level 2 headline, used for major headings within an article

- **Embedded Image:** Embeds a picture in the article

- **Media File Link:** Creates a link to a media file

- **Mathematical Formula:** Formats text as a mathematical formula

- **Ignore Wiki Formatting:** Used if your text could be inadvertently parsed as Wikipedia formatting code

- **Your Signature (With Timestamp):** Adds your signature and editing timestamp to the article

- **Horizontal Line:** Inserts a horizontal line across the page

- **Redirect:** Causes the article to redirect to a different location

- **Strike:** Draws a line through the text (strikethrough)

- **Line Break:** Inserts a line break

- **Superscript:** Formats the characters as superscript, like a footnote number or exponent

- **Subscript:** Formats the characters as subscript, like the 2 in H_2O

- **Small:** Makes the characters smaller than the surrounding text

- **Hidden Comment:** Inserts a comment that won't be displayed when you view the page

- **Picture Gallery:** Inserts formatting for two images with captions

- **Block Quote:** Inserts formatting for an indented block quote

- **Table:** Inserts formatting for a table with two rows and three columns

Figure 4-3: Control text appearance and function with the formatting buttons.

Adding any of these options to your text is a cinch. For example, to add bold-face to one of the words you just added to the page, do the following:

1. **Open the Sandbox page for editing as described earlier in this chapter.**

2. **Highlight the word *test*.**

   If the word *test* isn't on the page anymore, that's okay. Just select any word that you want to make bold.

3. **Click the B (for Bold) icon.**

   The word *test* now has three apostrophe marks on either end. This is the *markup,* or code, that tells Wikipedia to turn on boldface.

   To delete the boldface that you just added, simply backspace and erase those apostrophe marks from around the word.

Previewing and saving your changes

As you edit a sandbox page at Wikipedia (as described in the preceding sections), look at the options underneath the big, white edit window. The most important element here is the rectangular Edit Summary box. This space is used for making a few quick notes about what changes, if any, have been made to the page. Underneath that are three buttons:

✔ **Save Page:** Click this to save and publish your edits to a Wikipedia page.

✔ **Show Preview:** Click this for a sneak peek at the edits you made to a page.

✔ **Show Changes:** Click this to look at every version of the page leading up to the current version.

These two links round out the options:

✔ **Cancel:** Click here to exit the page without saving any of your changes.

✔ **Editing Help:** Click here to open a new window showing instructions on how to edit the page.

Finally, you'll see a big box full of characters and symbols with the word *Insert* in the upper-left corner. Should you require a special (perhaps non-English) character in your text — such as Ü or Ω — you can add it by clicking one of the characters in this box.

Linking pages and Web sites in Wikipedia

In the course of editing a Wikipedia entry, you will undoubtedly arrive at a moment when you want to create a hyperlink or link from a page you're work-ing on to another area where the reader can find more or related information about that page's content. The types of links that you can create on Wikipedia fall into three broad categories:

✔ Linking to another Wikipedia entry

✔ Linking to a specific section of another Wikipedia entry

✔ Linking to an external Web site

Creating a link to another entry within Wikipedia is the simplest of all three. Start by editing a page:

1. **In the white, edit window, type** Wiki For Dummies is part of the For Dummies series of books.

2. **Add two sets of square brackets around the words *For Dummies*, like this:** [[For Dummies]].

3. **Click the Save Page button.**

   When you look at the page, the words *For Dummies* should now appear in blue. This signifies a link. Click this link, and you are taken to the Wikipedia entry on the *For Dummies* series of books.

This method of linking can be used for any entry. Just determine the name of the Wikipedia page, put double square brackets on either end, and Wikipedia does the rest. The title of each entry appears at the very top of its page.

You will sometimes find that you want to link to another part of the page you're already editing. Wikipedia entries can be long and have many parts. Consider the entry on James Bond; it has a section devoted to the original Ian Fleming novels, and one about the filmed adaptations. Here's how you would link specifically to the section of the entry that is about the films or the books:

1. **In the white edit box, type:** James Bond is the star of James Bond Films and James Bond Novels.

2. **Add double square brackets around the words *James Bond Films* and *James Bond Novels*.**

   The text should look like this: `[[James Bond Films]]` and `[[James Bond Novels]]`.

   Make sure to capitalize *Films* and *Novels*. More on that in a bit.

3. **Insert a number sign (#) between *James Bond* and *Films*, and another number sign between *James Bond* and *Novels*.**

   The result looks like this: `[[James Bond#Films]]` and `[[James Bond#Novels]]`. The number sign tells Wikipedia to link to the James Bond article, and to the Films and Novels sections, respectively.

4. **Click the Save Page button.**

   The links should work. But they don't look too elegant, do they? You can fix that.

5. **Edit the page again, scrolling down to find the James Bond links.**

6. **Adjust the text to look like this:** `[[James Bond#Films|James Bond films]]` and `[[James Bond#Novels|James Bond novels]]`.

   You're adding a pipe character (usually found on the key above the Enter key on your keyboard).

7. **Save the page.**

   The links should be a bit more appealing — not to mention correctly capitalized and punctuated!

Wikipedia links are case sensitive. For example, the link `[[James Bond#films]]` takes you to the James Bond entry but not the Films section. In order to go directly to the Films section, you need to enter the link with a capital F: `[[James Bond#Films]]`.

It's hard to imagine that you would need to link outside Wikipedia for something because Wikipedia has entries on most everything. But references, which are one aspect of making good Wikipedia entries, require outside links. You might want to link directly to a company's home page or a newspaper article, for instance.

The best way to link to sources outside of Wikipedia is through a *named link*. Creating a named link is quite simple. Here's how it works:

1. **Copy an external Web address and paste it into the white, Wikipedia edit box.**

2. **Place a single square bracket at the front of the Web address.**

3. **At the end of the link, add one space and then type the name of the link, followed by another square bracket.**

   The link should look something like this:

   ```
   [http://www.wiley.com John Wiley & Sons]
   ```

4. **Save the page.**

What Wikipedia Can Do For You

Sure, Wikipedia is handy to have around in case you are the friend who gets phoned on *Who Wants to Be a Millionaire?* And it's certainly a reliable way to settle bets of all sorts, but there must be a more serious way to use this vast trove of information. The following sections show you how to best use Wikipedia as a research tool, evaluate the reliability of Wikipedia entries, and contribute to Wikipedia in a valuable way.

Using Wikipedia as a research tool

The reasons for choosing Wikipedia as a research tool over more traditional forms of reference material might include that

✔ **Wikipedia is extremely up to date.** Events that would otherwise take months or years to enter the record books can show up as entries on Wikipedia in a matter of days.

✔ **Wikipedia contributors come from all across the globe.** This means that the entries can represent a wide range of opinions and expertise from all over the world.

✔ **Wikipedia has an enormous number of visitors.** This often leads to errors that are caught and corrected quickly.

If you do use Wikipedia as a source — and you should probably first check whether the person or publisher you're writing for accepts Wikipedia as a source — cite it in a way that acknowledges its unique form. For one thing, the entries that you cite are written collectively, so obviously no single author can be attributed. The entries are always changing as well, and you have no reason to believe that the person who follows up on your citation will see the same information you saw unless you supply detailed information such as a permanent link to the page along with the exact time, date, and version of the article.

Open a History tab — found at the top of each Wikipedia entry — to determine the time, date, and version of the page you're referencing.

The exact citation style that you use varies depending on your preferred (or required) citation format. Most styles require you to include the date on which you accessed the entry along with the direct Web address leading to the page. For examples of how to cite Wikipedia in research papers, visit the Wikipedia entry titled "Citing Wikipedia."

Is Wikipedia reliable?

The creators of Wikipedia are the first to admit that not every entry is accurate and that it might not be the best source of material for research papers. Here are some points to consider:

- ✔ **Look for a slant.** Some articles are fair and balanced, but others look more like the Leaning Tower of Pisa. If an article has only one source, beware.

- ✔ **Consider the source.** Even if an article cites external sources, check out those sources to see whether they are being cited fairly and accurately — and do, in fact, reinforce the article's points.

- ✔ **Look who's talking.** If you research the contributors themselves and find that they are experts in their fields, you can be more confident in the entry.

- ✔ **Start here, but keep going.** Wikipedia should be a starting point for research but not your primary source for research material.

In December 2005, the scientific journal *Nature* published the results of a study comparing the accuracy of Wikipedia and the printed Encyclopaedia Britannica. The researchers found that the number of "factual errors, omissions or misleading statements" in each reference work was not so different — Wikipedia contained 162, and Britannica had 123. The makers of Britannica have since called on *Nature* to retract the study, which it claims is "completely without merit."

When visiting controversial entries, look out for *edit wars*. Edit wars occur when two contributors (or groups of contributors) repeatedly edit one another's work based on a particular bias. In early 2004, Wikipedia's founders organized an Arbitration Committee to settle such disputes.

Wikipedia does have some weaknesses that more traditional encyclopedias do not. For example

✔ There is no guarantee that important subjects are included or given the treatment that they deserve.

✔ Entries can be incomplete or in the middle of being updated at any given time.

✔ The writers of entries often fail to cite their original sources, thus making it hard to determine the credibility of the material.

These issues should not deter you from using Wikipedia. Just weigh the limitations of Wikipedia — and, for that matter, reference works in general.

Sharing your knowledge on Wikipedia

Here is a very simple way to make Wikipedia more reliable: by editing, improving, or creating an entry based on your own expertise.

The best way to find entries that are ripe for updating is to look for stubs. *Stubs* are entries in Wikipedia that don't contain enough information to be considered complete articles. Wikipedia keeps an ongoing list of the stubs most in need of attention; just enter **Most Wanted Stubs** in the Search field to find them.

Before writing anything on Wikipedia, here are three rules that any contributor must abide by:

✔ **Your entry must be original.** If you cut and paste text from another Web site; or copy directly from a newspaper, magazine, book, song, film, television show, or comic; you commit a copyright violation. Any such material will be removed from Wikipedia as soon as it is discovered — and the history files for the entry will tell Wikipedians exactly who is responsible for the copy job.

✔ **Write with a neutral point of view.** Wikipedia should not be used as a soapbox. The goal is to create a reference work that achieves a common good for all people. If you want to spread a message, then think about starting your own Editorialpedia.

✔ **Use references.** As we state earlier, one of Wikipedia's greatest failings is that its entries often do not include citations that would help the reader of the entry find second and third sources to support the article's claims.

Wikipedia has several sister projects, including Wiktionary, Wikiquote, and Wikispecies. They are all run by volunteers like you. If your article idea would fit more neatly into one of these projects, consider adding the information there instead of just at Wikipedia.

Wikipedia is founded on collective action. And in that spirit, you should not feel the need to act alone when you find a stub worth updating — and you don't need to. Wikipedia's Community Portal (just enter **Community portal** into the Search field) is an excellent way to find collaborators and to-do lists as well as learn about the latest projects getting underway.

Part II
Making Your Own Wiki

The 5th Wave
By Rich Tennant

"I started a wiki about making successful marriages, but my ex-wife keeps editing it with corrective posts."

In this part . . .

This part takes you from the general idea of wikis straight into the details of setting up a wiki, creating wiki pages, and making sure that the design looks great. Chapter 5 tells you how to find the right hosted wiki for your wiki — and also explains just what the heck a hosted wiki is.

After you get your wiki set up, Chapter 6 shows you how to make the words on a wiki page dance and sing and look just how you want them to. In Chapter 7, you can see how to link pages and add links to images and movies and the like. Part II comes to a close with Chapter 8, which provides advice about how to design your wiki to keep the information well organized and easy to find.

Chapter 5

Finding a Hosted Home for Your Wiki

. . . .

In This Chapter

▶ Sampling the hosted wiki tasting menu

▶ Comparing hosted wiki features

▶ Choosing the right hosted wiki for you

. . . .

For the first seven or so years of the history of wikis (1995–2002), the only people who could use wikis were those who could set up their own server, install the software, and get a wiki engine running. This barrier to wiki adoption goes a long way to explain why during this period, wikis were mostly used in engineering departments and other organizations that were highly technical. Starting in 2002 and accelerating in 2005, this situation changed to bring wikis to the rest of us. Many different groups of people with various motivations got together to create *hosted wikis* — wiki engines that are installed and hosted on public servers, removing the administration burden associated with running your own. Hosted wikis also provide design templates, so that you can literally have a wiki up and running within an hour. Hosted wikis, also known as *wiki farms,* opened the floodgates of wiki usage and are speeding the way forward for wikis to become part of the mainstream. Now you can choose from scores of hosted wikis. A wiki in every pot!

No Wiki Academy exists that dictates just how wikis should work or even what a Web site must do to be classified as a wiki. Every hosted wiki has a different idea of what it should be and how it should work. Wikis are like styles of cooking, and each hosted wiki is a different meal of many courses. Using a wiki is the best way to really understand whether it's right for you, but the number of wikis is quite large, and each wiki offers a different set of features. Most of us have the time to try a few hosted wikis, but nobody has the time to try a few dozen. That's where this chapter comes in: It's a hosted wiki menu guide to help you narrow down the list.

Choosing a hosted wiki is like looking at a vast list of multicourse meals, each with a different set of dishes. When you start out, it's not easy to figure out whether you want two appetizers or one, or whether you should order a salad or a cheese course. If you ask for spicy, will it be too spicy? To compare hosted wikis, we present the equivalent of a tasting menu that introduces the different aspects of hosted wikis. The first part of this chapter reviews many different hosted wikis and provides advice to help you find the one that's right for you. Then we get you started using WikiSpaces, which is one of the most popular and simplest hosted wikis.

Because the wiki landscape changes rapidly, the menu we present here is by no means complete. WikiMatrix is a Web site (www.wikimatrix.org) with an extensive menu of hosted wikis as well as wiki software packages. Another of its great features is the WikiMatrix Choice Wizard that can help you find the wikis that match your personal needs. (We discuss this wizard further in Chapter 10.)

Choosing the Right Hosted Wiki

Most hosted wikis share many of the same features. In the "Creating a Hosted Wiki with WikiSpaces" section, we describe some of that hosted wiki's specific features. For now, though, you can get down to the business of figuring out which hosted wiki you should use, or at least narrow the list of the hosted wikis you want to play with. The criteria to consider when choosing the right hosted wiki include

- **Ease of setup:** Some wikis are just needed for a few weeks to manage a ski trip or a quick project. (You can read about a real-life ski trip planning example in the upcoming section, "Creating a Hosted Wiki with WikiSpaces.") Ease of setup may always be important for you, but it's especially important for those ephemeral wikis that you need for only a month or two.

- **User invitations and limits:** If you anticipate hundreds of users, make sure that inviting people is easy and that they can manage their own accounts. Also, a large number of the free hosted wikis are free only if you have about five users.

- **Storage space:** Some hosted wikis charge if you use more than a fixed amount of storage space.

- **Open to all comers or just for friends:** Some hosted wikis allow private wikis only for paying customers.

✔ **Page protection:** Some wikis allow individual pages to be protected, and others can protect only all pages in a wiki or none. *Protection* means that only authorized users can change the page in question.

✔ **Cost:** As we allude, many hosted wikis are free — that is, if they have a stripped-down set of features. Others carry advertising on your wiki pages unless you pay for a subscription.

✔ **Customization capabilities:** Some customizations are free, and others cost money.

✔ **Number of wikis:** Will there be more wikis like yours, and will they need to link to each other? If you need a hosted wiki of your own, you might want to use a private label option (see "Adding premium services and advertising," later in this chapter) or consider running your own wiki engine, as described in Part III.

✔ **Data export capabilities:** If you plan to start with a hosted wiki and move it internally later, you need to be able to export the data from the hosted wiki.

Now comes the hard part for us as authors. How can we give useful general advice about which hosted wiki will work best for your specific situation? Well, the truth is we cannot tell you for sure which wiki is precisely right for you. We can offer some help, though. Throughout the rest of this section, we list the wiki categories that we outline in Chapter 3 and suggest an appropriate hosted wiki for each. Keep in mind that some hosted wikis are great for creating ease-of-use wikis, and others have features that make them just right for content-focused wikis, and so on.

Using a hosted wiki is the fastest and easiest way to get a wiki up and running. These benefits are sometimes not the most important factors, though. Hosted wikis might be the wrong choice for wikis used inside a company, especially if the wiki contains sensitive information. Or if you plan on building advanced structured wikis, hosted wikis probably won't give you the control you need. Hosted wikis also might not merge seamlessly into an existing computing environment, such as a corporate portal or directory services. The latter means that your users need to remember yet another login and password combination. In these situations, you might need to get your own server and install a wiki engine on it to meet your needs. Chapters 10 and 11 cover how to do that.

Exploring hosted wikis

The number of hosted wikis has exploded in the past few years. Every few months or so, it seems that several new worthy offerings hit the Internet. We can't identify and include a description of every hosted wiki. So instead, we provide the following selection of hosted wikis, chosen based on our wanderings and good taste. If a hosted wiki that you run across isn't on this list, don't read too much into it: It might turn out to be the best hosted wiki out there. Likewise, just because a hosted wiki is on this list doesn't mean that it's perfect. We found that each hosted wiki is special in its own way.

First, we describe the hosted wikis included in this chapter. Then we recommend wikis for various uses. (If you want to participate in a continuing conversation about what's going on with hosted wikis, please visit `www.evolvedtechnologist.com`, where Dan will be monitoring new developments and reporting on new hosted wikis as they arrive.)

- ✔ **BrainKeeper** (`www.brainkeeper.com`): BrainKeeper calls itself an *enterprise wiki*. Its focus is knowledge management and corporate communication, offering features such as workflow for approvals of content. A subscription for nine users is $35 per month or $385 per year, increasing based on the number of users. This is a wiki for business.

- ✔ **Central Desktop** (`www.centraldesktop.com`): Central Desktop's motto is "organize, share, collaborate," and this site adds anything and everything needed to collaborate in the workplace to the idea of a wiki. In fact, the wikiness of Central Desktop is sort of obscured, but many people include it in lists of wikis. Features for project management, shared calendars, and discussions are all free for up to five users and two workspaces. Pricing for up to ten users starts at $25 per month.

- ✔ **cospire** (`www.cospire.com`): cospire is a site for creating communities that uses blogs and wikis along with a system of categorizing and searching content. You must register to start or join cospire communities, but the site is free. The mission of the company that created cospire is "To make knowledge sharing practical and addictive."

- ✔ **EditMe** (`www.editme.com`): EditMe is a wiki focused on making building Web sites as easy as possible based on a wiki model. Following the desires of its user base, EditMe has advanced features for access control, support for blogs, and an easy to use WYSIWYG (What You See Is What You Get) editor. EditMe costs $4.95 per month for its most basic offering and goes higher from there.

- ✔ **JotSpot** (`www.jot.com`): JotSpot, which calls itself the first application wiki company, was purchased by Google in October of 2006. JotSpot focused on extending wiki functionality in all directions so you could have a shareable, easy-to-edit environment in any application, such as documents, spreadsheets, calendars, or photo galleries. JotSpot is currently being integrated with Google products, and a launch date of the combined offering has not been announced as of the writing of this book.

✔ **Nexdo** (www.nexdo.com): Nexdo is a straightforward, simple wiki offering that has a free version for up to five users and a paid version for six users that starts at 44 euros per month and increases in price as more users are added.

✔ **PBwiki** (www.pbwiki.com): PBwiki aims to make creating a wiki as easy as making a peanut butter sandwich. PBwiki is one of the simplest and easiest to use wikis. It offers a free version and several levels of paid versions, starting at $9.95 per month, that include more storage and extra features.

✔ **seedwiki** (www.seedwiki.com): seedwiki is a streamlined, bare-bones wiki that is perhaps the most similar of all hosted wikis to the original wiki created by Ward Cunningham. seedwiki offers a free version as well as a paid version that adds features such as access control and notifications, starting at $10 per month.

✔ **Socialtext** (www.socialtext.com): Socialtext describes itself as the leading enterprise wiki that is most trusted by Global 2000 corporations. (Ross Mayfield, Socialtext's CEO and founder, is one of the most cited sources on wikis.) Socialtext has advanced features for e-mail integration, searching, weblog publishing, and file management. You must call SocialText to obtain pricing information.

✔ **StikiPad** (www.stikipad.com): Stikipad is a full-featured wiki solution that offers the ability to create and edit wiki pages along with advanced abilities for e-mail integration, control over the design of the pages, mobile access, spam management, and page locking. StikiPad has a free version and also paid versions, starting at $4.95 per month that offer advanced administration and technical support.

✔ **wetpaint** (www.wetpaint.com): wetpaint is a simple and very easy-to-use wiki that has one of the best WYSIWYG editors. wetpaint offers the ability to comment on each page as well as a wide gallery of styles.

✔ **Wikia** (www.wikia.com): Wikia, which was created by Jimmy Wales (the founder of Wikipedia), offers hosted wikis that use the MediaWiki engine (the engine used at Wikipedia). Wikia is not for personal wikis but is intended to host wikis that will attract large communities of editors.

✔ **Wikidot.com** (www.wikidot.com): Wikidot offers free hosting for wikis; unlike most hosted wikis, Wikidot has no advertising or premium service of any kind.

✔ **WikiSpaces** (www.wikispaces.com): WikiSpaces is an extremely easy-to-use and reliable wiki that is great for beginners; it has a large number of educational users. WikiSpaces has premium levels of subscription, starting at $5 per month, which offer more storage.

Ease-of-use wikis

Ease-of-use wikis are those that allow you to do it yourself. Without training or expertise, people can exploit the simplicity of wikis to create Web sites of various kinds. The sites that fall into this category simply ignore many of the aspects of wikis that have made the idea of wikis so important, such as shared authorship and free-form collaboration.

For example, a woman with a small business could use a wiki to quickly create a site to explain her business. The simplicity of wikis would make it easy to create the site. She wouldn't have to spend a lot of time working with Web designers or programmers. Then, as she gains confidence, she could use more and more of the features of the wiki to customize the look and feel of the site. Here are some of the features most important to a small business wiki and other ease-of-use wikis:

- ✔ **Step-by-step simplicity:** You should be helped through each task of the wiki with wizards and step-by-step instructions.

- ✔ **Protected pages:** You should be able to stop others from editing certain pages. A description of a small business is not a collaborative subject.

- ✔ **Customizable layout, graphics, and fonts:** You might not want your ease-of-use wiki to look like a wiki at all. You do want it to look sharp and polished.

Of course, the idea of an ease-of-use wiki applies to any simple Web site that you want to create. Web sites for individuals, families, and volunteer groups are all fine examples of ease-of-use wikis. Creating a simple wiki in one of these categories is a perfect way to get started with wikis.

Any of these hosted wiki are a good choice for ease-of-use wikis:

- ✔ **EditMe:** www.editme.com
- ✔ **WikiSpaces:** www.wikispaces.com
- ✔ **PBwiki:** www.pbwiki.com
- ✔ **wetpaint:** www.wetpaint.com
- ✔ **StikiPad**: www.stikipad.com
- ✔ **Wikidot.com:** www.wikidot.com

Community wikis

Community wikis are centered around some shared interest, whether it's a place, a topic, a technology, or a club of some sort. With this sort of wiki, simplicity and ease of use is important. To make many of these wikis thrive, though, collaboration is important so that everyone in the community can add their two cents. Communicating through e-mail is important, as are facilities for inviting users, managing accounts, and promoting the wiki.

Any of these hosted wikis are a good choice for community wikis:

- ✔ **WikiSpaces:** www.wikispaces.com
- ✔ **PBwiki:** www.pbwiki.com
- ✔ **wetpaint:** www.wetpaint.com
- ✔ **JotSpot:** www.jot.com

Process-focused wikis

Process-focused wikis are all about getting work done. Process-focused wikis capture all the information about some process and help track its execution. Project management wikis are probably the most common form of process-focused wiki. Unlike ease-of-use or community wikis, process-focused wikis often must manage tabular information and use wiki pages like database entries. Spreadsheet-like functions are quite helpful, as is the ability to notify people via e-mail when certain pages change. Because process-focused wikis are frequently used by corporations or large organizations, the ability to tightly integrate with e-mail, word processors, calendars, and other productivity tools is crucial.

Any of these hosted wikis are a good choice for process-focused wikis:

- ✔ **JotSpot:** www.jot.com
- ✔ **Socialtext:** www.socialtext.com
- ✔ **BrainKeeper:** www.brainkeeper.com
- ✔ **Central Desktop:** www.centraldesktop.com
- ✔ **Nexdo:** www.nexdo.com
- ✔ **seedwiki:** www.seedwiki.com

Content-focused wikis

Content-focused wikis are aimed at creating large communities focused around creating and maintaining a large body of content. Content-focused wikis need to be able to present templates for pages to be created and provide instructions to those who would join the community of contributors who create and maintain the content. Content-focused wikis also need to have facilities for adding images to pages as well as other features, such as special pages for discussions or facilities for managing changes to pages or rolling back changes if pages are vandalized.

Any of these hosted wikis are a good choice for content-focused wikis:

- **Wikia:** www.wikia.com
- **cospire:** www.cospire.com
- **WikiSpaces:** www.wikispaces.com
- **PBwiki:** www.pbwiki.com

Creating a Hosted Wiki with WikiSpaces

WikiSpaces — created by Dominick Bellizzi, James Byers, and Adam Frey in 2005 — is a great example of a hosted wiki as a user-friendly consumer product. The reason for this lies in the story of its creation: James Byers was planning a ski trip with a group of friends. The e-mail thread regarding plans grew ridiculously long, and he found existing wiki options lacking — so he created his own. The focus on simplicity, ease of use, and premium offerings abound in this hosted wiki, all of which might be useful to you while your wiki grows.

James Byers says that he views managing a wiki like tending a garden — and, fittingly, the site's logo is a bonsai tree. "In the garden, the influx of content will happen a lot early on — that's the filling in of the flower beds that were left early," says Byers. "Then there's weeds that have to be plucked constantly — adding a little content here, changing a spelling mistake here. In a healthy wiki, that's going to happen constantly. Then later, more weeding, more trimming, more pruning."

WikiSpaces is a safe first choice for anyone getting started using wikis, and that's why we focus on it here. To set up a wiki on WikiSpaces, just follow these steps:

1. **Go to www.wikispaces.com.**

   The WikiSpaces home page (shown in Figure 5-1) is what you first see.

2. **In the Join Now - Free! area, enter a username, a password, and an e-mail address.**

   Hold off on entering a space name at this point. You can do that in a minute.

3. **Click the Join button.**

   You see a screen that looks like Figure 5-2.

Figure 5-1:
WikiSpaces
makes it
easy to
create
your own
hosted wiki.

Figure 5-2:
Choose the
type of wiki
you want to
create.

4. **In the Make a New Space Now area, enter a name, decide what kind of wiki you want, and then click Create.**

You have three choices:

- *Public:* Absolutely anyone can edit a public wiki. This type of wiki is free.

- *Protected:* A *protected wiki* can be viewed by everyone but can be edited only by those invited to the space. This type of wiki is also free.

- *Private:* A *private wiki* can be viewed and edited only by those invited to the space. On WikiSpaces, this kind of wiki is free for 30 days but then costs $5 per month.

For the purposes of these steps, we're choosing a protected wiki because it fits the greatest variety of uses. After you click Create, your wiki comes to life, as shown in Figure 5-3. You now have your own wiki.

Create a new page by clicking this button.

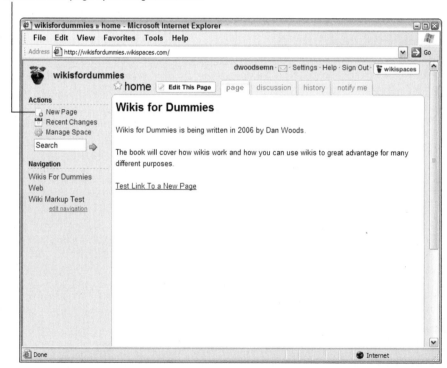

Figure 5-3:
The new home page of your wiki looks like this.

5. Click the Edit This Page button and rock on with your bad wiki self.

Put up a fan site for Eldridge Cleaver or Whittaker Chambers or something. Use your power wisely. Invite others to work with you. Manage a project. Write a new book on wikis.

The experience you just went through is pretty much the same for most hosted wikis. The differences can start to appear most profoundly when you start creating pages and working with others. The rest of this section deals with the tasks involved in wiki creation: creating individual pages, editing and linking pages, and so on.

Creating pages

One of the most useful features of wikis is how they are friendly to unfinished or partially completed content. In the first generation of wikis, pages were only created by editing a page, inserting links to pages you wanted to create, and then saving that page. Then the links to unfinished pages would appear in some special way that would allow you to click them and create them.

Although this form of page creation was popular with engineers who were accustomed to writing HTML or other programming languages, it wasn't the easiest way for your average bear to create a page.

Most wikis still support this method, but many others use the page creation method that WikiSpaces employs. A New Page button appears at the top left of each page (refer to Figure 5-3). When you click the New Page button, a form appears, as shown in Figure 5-4. Enter a name and then click Create to create the new page. After it's created, you can start entering content.

Figure 5-4:
Enter a name for your new page and click Create.

Editing pages

The method for editing pages differs among hosted wikis. Here are the two ways how pages are edited:

- **Through a WYSIWYG editor, which is similar to a word processor:** Figure 5-5 shows a WYSIWYG (What You See Is What You Get, or *visual*) editor.

- **Through wiki markup:** Figure 5-6 shows a wiki markup editor. (See Chapter 6 for more on wiki markup.)

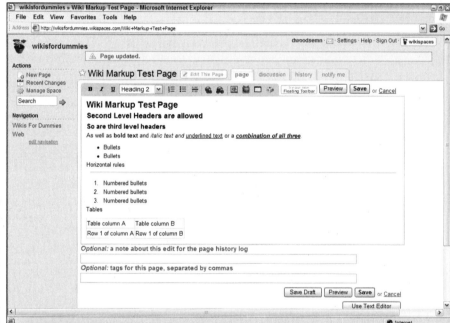

Figure 5-5: The WikiSpaces. com WYSIWYG editor is easy to use.

If the wiki markup in the text editor looks odd at first, it becomes second nature after a while. For more about creating pages and content, check out Chapter 6.

Figure 5-6:
You can also edit pages using wiki markup.

We all want WYSIWYG editors on wikis to work well. However, the unfortunate truth is that they are a long way from the quality, ease of use, and reliability of the word processors on our desktops. Most people who add content to wikis on a daily basis end up learning enough markup to do what they need to do using the wiki markup editor instead of a WYSIWYG editor.

Linking pages

Linking pages is the same story. To create links, wikis started out with a nerdy, efficient, and hard-to-understand technique, but modern hosted wikis have come up with a much easier method.

The easy hosted wiki way to create a link is to use forms and simple drop-down menus to help you add a link. When you're in a WYSIWYG editor, click the Link button on the toolbar. A form pops up (as shown in Figure 5-7), which asks you for all the information needed in the link.

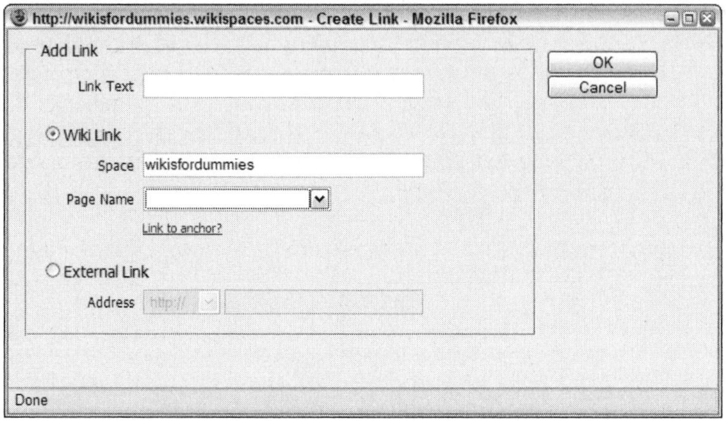

Figure 5-7:
A WYSIWYG
editor
makes it
easy to add
a link.

If you prefer to use the text editor and wiki markup, links are added by using markup that looks like this:

```
[[Wiki Markup Test Page|Test Link To a New Page]]
```

If you save the page on which you entered this text and then click the link, you're taken to a page named Wiki Markup Test Page. Note that WikiSpaces puts some default information on empty pages that makes it hard to understand that the page is new. However, if you look at the top of the page, you can see that the page is named Wiki Markup Test Page — and if you click the Edit button, you will start with a blank page. You can read more details about linking pages in Chapter 7.

Protecting pages and wikis

One way to use wikis is to let anyone edit any page. This is how Wikipedia works. Many other wikis work this way as well — when the people using and editing the wikis are well intentioned and well behaved. Sometimes, though, when wikis are public or have controversial content, all kinds of commotion breaks loose in the wiki. Spammers have also discovered wikis, sometimes entering spam messages in them. In many cases, restricting who may edit your wiki makes sense.

The first wikis had no ability to protect pages. It was considered decidedly un-wiki to restrict access. Later, though, many of the early versions of wiki engines added features for controlling access to pages in various ways. WikiSpaces and a number of other hosted wikis have continued this development trend: One of the most important ways that hosted wikis vary is how they restrict access to wiki pages.

WikiSpaces has a direct and simple approach to restricting access to editing pages. If you are the organizer of a wiki, you have access to the Manage Space menu choice in the column on the left side of the page. (If you don't have this button, you are not an organizer and can't change settings that control the wiki.) After you click the Manage Space button, you see a page with many options. Under Space Settings, click the Members and Permissions link to open the page shown in Figure 5-8.

The Space Permissions grid at the top of the Manage Space page offers three choices:

- ✔ **Public:** This allows pages to be viewed and edited by anyone.

- ✔ **Protected:** Pages can be viewed by anyone but edited only by space members.

- ✔ **Private:** Pages can be viewed and edited only by space members. This is a premium option only, available for a monthly fee.

These three choices meet the needs of most people. You can have a totally public wiki, you can restrict editing of pages but still have them be available for viewing, or you can keep the whole wiki behind closed doors.

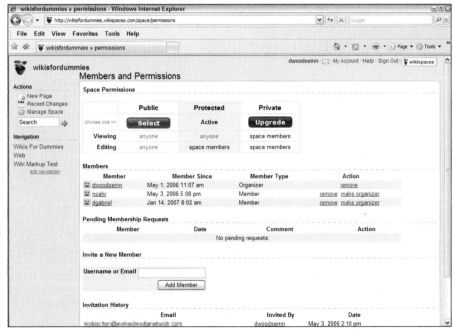

Figure 5-8:
Control member permissions here.

Other hosted wikis go further than this and allow you to control what can happen to individual pages. Some pages can be read only, some can be edited by everyone, and some can be completely private. Some hosted wikis offer private wikis as the only option for protecting a wiki. If you need to know more about protecting your wiki, Chapter 13 goes much more deeply into this topic.

Inviting others to your wiki

After you have enough content in your wiki, get others involved. If you have a public wiki, this can be as simple as sending around the Web address of the wiki. The WikiSpaces wiki created for this book is located at `http://wikisfordummies.wikispaces.com`. Most hosted wikis create a special Web address for your wiki when you create it.

If you have a wiki that restricts editing to members of the wiki or is completely private, people who want to edit pages or see the wiki must create accounts (which usually involves creating a username and password and supplying an e-mail address) at the hosted wiki where your wiki lives.

Most hosted wikis make inviting users quite easy. If you look at the bottom of the Manage Space page in Figure 5-9, you can see four sections:

- ✔ **Members:** Shows the members of the wiki

- ✔ **Pending Membership Requests:** Shows requests that have been sent but not yet accepted

- ✔ **Invite a New Member:** Allows you to start the process of inviting a new member

- ✔ **Invitation History:** Shows all the invitations that have been sent out

All you have to do to invite a new member is enter an e-mail address or an existing WikiSpaces username in the Invite a New Member section and then click the Add Member button. You can enter a list of e-mail addresses or usernames if you like. When you click Add Member, a prefilled form like the one in Figure 5-9 appears. This form allows you to adjust the invitation message before sending it.

Other hosted wikis offer similar mechanisms for inviting users. After users are invited, you have to worry about getting people to participate in the wiki — a topic that we cover in Chapter 11.

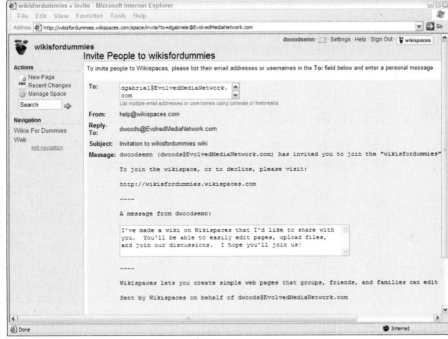

Figure 5-9:
Use this
form for
sending
invitations
on
WikiSpaces.
com.

Changing the look, feel, and design of a wiki

Hosted wikis have many different approaches to changing how a wiki looks.
The sort of things you can change are

- The logo that appears on the wiki
- Header and footer text
- Fonts used on each page
- Menu items
- Colors used on the pages
- The layout of the pages

There are usually two broad categories of devices to change the appearance of a wiki: ones that are easy to use and those that require much more advanced technical knowledge. WikiSpaces offers both ways to change how your wiki looks. To change the overall appearance of your wiki, do the following:

1. **Sign in to your WikiSpaces wiki.**

   You must be signed in to make changes.

2. **Click the Manage Spaces link for your WikiSpaces wiki.**

3. **Under the Space Settings section, click the Look and Feel link.**

4. **Click a link to change one of the following aspects of your wiki:**

   - *Theme:* This option is the easiest way to change your wiki. Click the Change or Make New Theme link to change the theme of your pages. The *theme* is a collection of settings for how the pages look grouped together in a bundle, the colors on the pages, the style sheet used on the pages, and the logo on the pages. Free wikis have fewer choices for themes.

   - *Colors:* This option is almost as easy. Enter a six-letter *(hexadecimal)* HTML color code to change the background, menu, text, and link colors. Or, click Pick Color to open a graphical color chooser.

   - *Wiki Stylesheet:* Here you can customize the Cascading Style Sheet (CSS) used for your wiki. This feature is available only with paid WikiSpaces services and requires some CSS knowledge. In other words, this is the hard way.

   - *Logo:* Click Browse to select and upload your own custom logo for the wiki. (Another easy and free feature.)

You can also create templates for pages so that new pages start out looking a certain way. This can be useful if some pages have information that should be on every page or certain sections that should be filled in. Templates are also used to control the navigation that appears on the left-hand side of the page with links to important pages. Click the Manage Templates link on the Manage Space page, and then edit the `space.menu` template to add links to the navigation bar on the left side of all pages in your wiki.

Templates and style sheets really let you go in many different directions, but you have to know what you are doing. We cover this topic in much more designing detail in Chapter 8.

Adding images, video, and other widgets to a wiki

The typical wiki page allows you to have headings; text in bold and italic, and underlined; bullet points to various levels; horizontal rules; tables; and links to other pages inside or outside the wiki. Most wikis also allow you to upload and display images. Web pages these days include

- YouTube videos
- Links to RSS (really simple syndication) feeds
- MP3 files
- JavaScript programs to get information from other sites
- Ease-of-use features, such as drop-down menus

And the list goes on. You also have the option of adding some or many widgets to your wiki pages that

- Provide special navigation
- Simplify adding content
- Notify you via e-mail about changes to pages
- Enable you to add information in tables or forms so that pages can become like database records or spreadsheets

Enhancing pages in this way creates what are known as *structured wikis,* which we describe in detail in Chapter 14.

It is a challenge for anyone to construct a page with all these elements because they all work so differently. Hosted wikis have many different approaches. WikiSpaces offers wizards that guide you through the most common ways of adding special content such as links, images, and tables. An Embed Media link helps manage the insertion of the sort of HTML needed to link to video, audio, or other elements so they can be accessed from a wiki page. We cover how to link to this sort of content in Chapter 7.

Adding premium services and advertising

Hosted wikis are businesses. To keep operating, they must collect money to pay their expenses and reward their founders. Hosted wikis have two revenue streams:

✔ Subscription fees charged for premium services

✔ Revenue from placing advertising on pages

Most hosted wikis allow wikis to be hosted without charge if they are public, and charge only if the wikis are made private. Some hosted wikis, such as WikiSpaces, add advertising to wiki pages. Subscription charges might also be required to gain access to premium services.

The WikiSpaces.com premium offering is pretty typical of hosted wikis. For a charge of $5 per month or $50 per year, you get the following:

✔ Advertising no longer appears on your pages.

✔ The wiki can be made completely private.

✔ You can create custom themes.

✔ You can create custom style sheets.

✔ You can use encryption when you communicate with your wiki.

Some hosted wikis charge for how much space your wiki pages use or for how much bandwidth is used by people who download pages.

WikiSpaces also offers another plan to organizations who want to set up their own space of multiple wikis. This option — Private Label — allows a whole space of wikis to be created, one for each department of a company or one for each class in a school, that all live under the same administrative environment. For more information about these services, click the Upgrade link at the bottom of any WikiSpaces page.

Chapter 6

Creating Content for Your Wiki

In This Chapter

▶ Putting on wiki makeup with wiki markup

▶ Reviewing the basics of wiki markup

▶ Applying HTML to your wiki pages

▶ Sorting out the different modes for wiki pages

The "secret sauce" of wikis is that they are simple and easy. When it comes to making content look pleasing and readable, though, don't get fooled into thinking that there is nothing much to wikis. The various ways how you can control the appearance of content on wiki pages might not give you the unlimited power of a program like Adobe Photoshop, but one look at Wikipedia or another advanced wiki shows that the pages can look attractive and nicely designed.

This chapter shows you how to make your wiki pages shine with clarity. The early sections build on the quick start provided in Chapter 2, showing you the tools that wikis provide for organizing content with headings, bullets, and tables. We show you how to add images to pages and also compare how to edit pages with wiki markup and WYSIWYG (What You See Is What You Get) editors. And don't miss the tricks for using HTML (HyperText Markup Language) tables to give your wiki pages more complicated layouts.

How most wiki pages are designed and organized falls into one of three patterns, or *modes:*

✔ **Document mode:** Pages might look like word processing documents.

✔ **Thread mode:** Pages can have comments added one after another in a conversational thread.

✔ **Structured mode:** Pages might have more advanced structures.

The characteristics of each of these styles is described and compared in the latter part of the chapter.

Applying Markup as Content Makeup

If content is the star of the show on a wiki, formatting content is like applying makeup. When formatting content, you attempt to highlight the best features of a page so that when someone takes a look at it, he knows at a glance what the page is about. Good formatting helps someone scan a page and quickly get an idea what it is about, making it easier to dive into the most interesting parts.

In the examples in this chapter, we use the Sandbox area of TWiki.org, which we describe more fully in Chapter 2. If you decide to use any of the other hosted wikis mentioned in Chapter 5, you should be able to follow along easily. The TWiki.org sandbox is located at

```
http://twiki.org/cgi-bin/view/Sandbox/WebHome
```

Scroll down and pick a Sandbox page in which to practice. The first time you try to edit a page in the TWiki.org Sandbox web, you are asked for a user name and password. Use *TWikiGuest* as the username and *guest* as the password to be allowed to edit the page.

Editing Pages with Wiki Markup

Here are the two ways to apply formatting to a wiki page:

- ✔ Use wiki markup.
- ✔ Use a WYSIWYG editor (explained later in this chapter).

Wiki markup is a set of simple character patterns that makes your content appear differently. For example, if you put asterisks around a word like this:

```
*blockhead*
```

That word appears in bold when the page is displayed:

blockhead

In many ways, wiki markup is a throwback to the early days of word processing programs, which worked the same way. To apply wiki markup to a page, click the Edit button on the page. You see the page in a simple text box that shows the wiki markup for the page, as shown in Figure 6-1. The page shown in Figure 6-1 is the same sample page that was created in Chapter 2. If your Sandbox page has been changed by someone else, delete the text in the Sandbox page and re-enter the text and markup exactly as shown in Figure 6-1.

After entering the text, scroll down to the bottom of the page and click the Save button. You see the page shown in Figure 6-2.

Figure 6-1:
Wiki markup
gives you
control
over text
appearance.

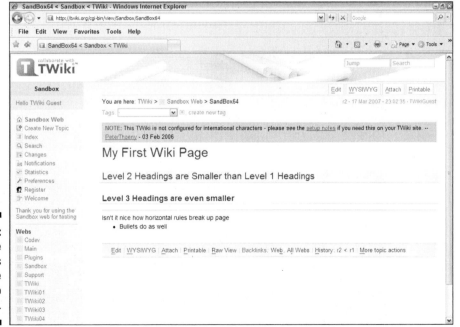

Figure 6-2:
When the
page is
saved, the
wiki markup
is applied.

Wiki markup dialects

No global wiki markup standards exist. Each wiki engine handles markup a bit differently although you'll find some common patterns. For example, here are some different ways to indicate a level 1 (main) heading:

✔ **TWiki.org:** Use ---+ at the beginning of a line.

✔ **MediaWiki** (used by Wikipedia): Use two equal signs on each side of the text: ==Text for Level 1 Heading==.

✔ **wikispaces.com:** Use one equal sign on each side of the text.

Each element of wiki markup has its variations. The markup for bullets is usually pretty much the same for most wiki engines, but markup for tables can be wildly different. Fortunately, wiki markup is not a complicated affair. When you start using a wiki, you can easily learn the rules. Most wiki engines have links to Help pages. If you click the Show Help link on the Twiki.org Edit page, for example, the information in the figure is shown. Wikipedia has a comprehensive cheat sheet for its markup at http://en.wikipedia.org/wiki/wikipedia:cheatsheet.

SandBox64 (edit)

⊡ Hide help

Formatting help:

- **bold** put word/phrase in asterisks: *your phrase*
- **bullet list** 3 spaces, asterisk, 1 space: * your text
- **headings** 3 dashes, 1 to 6 pluses, 1 space: ---++ Your Heading
- **italic** put word/phrase in underscores: _your words_
- **links** use topic name or URL: WebHome, http://yahoo.com, or [[http://yahoo.com/][link to Yahoo]]
- **monospaced** put word/phrase in equal signs: =your words=
- **paragraphs** separate with blank line
- More formatting help and hints on good style

```
---+My First Wiki Page
---++Level 2 Headings are Smaller than Level 1 Headings
---+++Level 3 Headings are even smaller
----
Isn't it nice how horizontal rules break up page
  * Bullets do as well
```

The point of wiki markup is to control the way the text appears by following some simple rules. The following sections tour the various forms of wiki markup.

Creating hierarchy with headings

The most commonly used markup is for headings. Headings introduce a wiki page and its various subsections, thereby providing structure and hierarchy on your pages. The TWiki method for doing this uses three dashes to indicate that a line is a heading followed by one, two, three, four, or more plus signs to indicate the level of the heading. One plus sign equals Heading 1, two equal Heading 2, and so on, as shown in Figure 6-3.

Figure 6-3:
The TWiki
method to
denote
headings
uses a
series of
dashes and
plus signs.

```
---+Heading 1 —
```
Heading 1
```
---++Heading 2 —
```
Heading 2
```
---+++Heading 3 —
```
Heading 3
```
----Horizontal Rule — _____
```

The exact font and size for headings is controlled by the user's Web browser and is usually specified in a style sheet or a skin of the sort that we discuss in Chapter 8.

Inserting bullets

Bulleted text is probably the second most popular type of wiki markup after headings. Bullets are particularly useful in lists because they aid readability. (We use bulleted lists throughout this book.) The formula for TWiki bullets is simple:

```
* [Three Spaces]* = First level bullet
* [Six Spaces]* = Sub-bullet
* [Nine Spaces]* = Sub-sub-bullet
```

There is no limit to how many levels of bulleted text you can present. To get to a deeper level, just add three more spaces.

To create numbered bullets, replace the asterisks with numbers, such as 1. Any number is okay because the wiki engine will number the bullets properly for you. For example, write

```
1 bullet
1 next
1 one more
```

to get

```
1. bullet

2. next

3. one more
```

You need three spaces in front of the number for TWiki; use one for MediaWiki.

Bulleted text goes only to the end of a line of text. This means you cannot have text under a bullet that contains any *carriage returns* (what you create when you press Enter while entering text). Nevertheless, you can add line breaks with the %BR% variable: BR stands for *break*.

Building tables

Anyone who has used a spreadsheet can attest to the value of tables. Virtually all wikis support tables in some form. Although creating a basic table in TWiki is a cinch, how tables work in other wikis is one of the biggest areas of variation.

TWiki creates tables by using vertical bar characters *(pipes)*. To define a table, simply enter text separated by vertical bars like this:

```
| *Column One Heading* | *Column Two Heading* | *Column Three Heading* |
| Row one info for Column 1 | Row one / column 2 | Row one / column 3 |
| Row two info for Column 1 | Row two / column 2 | Row two / column 3 |
| Row three info for Column 1 | Row three / column 2 | Row three / column 3 |
```

You get a page like the one shown in Figure 6-4. This is the basic way to create a table. TWiki.org table markup is quite powerful. Table 6-1 lists some TWiki table formatting markup.

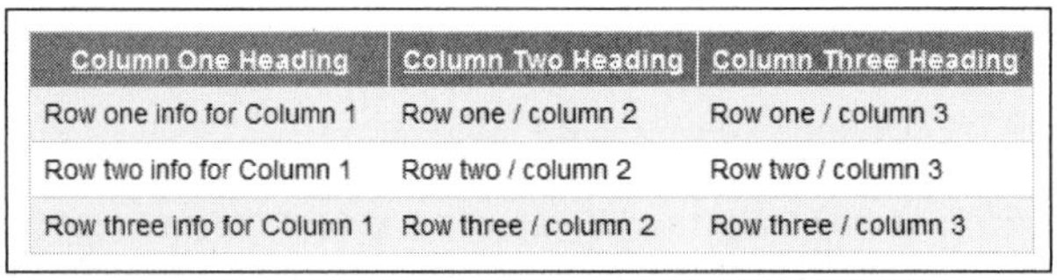

Figure 6-4:
Use wiki markup to easily create tables.

Column One Heading	Column Two Heading	Column Three Heading
Row one info for Column 1	Row one / column 2	Row one / column 3
Row two info for Column 1	Row two / column 2	Row two / column 3
Row three info for Column 1	Row three / column 2	Row three / column 3

Table 6-1	TWiki.org Table Markup
Markup	*Description*
`| *bold* |`	Header cell with text in asterisks
`| center-aligned |`	Cell with at least two spaces on either side (must be an equal number)
`| right-aligned |`	Cell with more spaces on the left

Markup	Description
`| 2 colspan ||`	Multiple | characters next to each other allow the cell to span multiple columns
`|^|`	Follow-up row of multispan rows
`\`	At the end of each line, splits rows over multiple lines

The text in table cells can be formatted just like any other text, and image links can also be included in tables. (Text formatting is described in the next section; image links are described in Chapter 7.) After you get the hang of basic table creation, you can start thinking outside the cell, so to speak.

Formatting text

Text formatting isn't uniform across wikis although all wikis use formatting methods that are simpler than HTML. Table 6-2 lists wiki markup rules for popular text styles in TWiki.

Table 6-2	Wiki Markup for Text Formatting		
To Get This	**Do This**	**Example**	**Looks Like This**
Bold text	Enclose words in asterisks.	`*Bold*`	**Bold**
Italic	Enclose words in underscores.	`_Italic_`	*Italic*
Bold italic text	Enclose words in double underscores.	`__Bold italic__`	***Bold italic***
Fixed font	Enclose words in equal signs.	`=Fixed font=`	`Fixed font`
Bold fixed font	Enclose words in double equal signs.	`==Bold fixed==`	**`Bold fixed`**

Plain text	Enter plain text that is already formatted with spaces, tabs, and line breaks.	`<verbatim>`
		`Text that is`
		`  Indented or`
		`uses tabs`
		`</verbatim>`
			Text that is indented or uses tabs

The promise and tragedy of WYSIWYG

Wiki markup can easily be compared with HTML or other formatting methods, but it isn't easy to compare with a word processing program like Microsoft Word. Early word processors used basic markup for text formatting, but modern word processors have abandoned markup in favor of a one-step process. You simply click toolbar buttons to make text bold, format headings, or create tables. This sort of editing was an innovation in word processing: What You See Is What You Get, or *WYSIWYG* for short.

Most modern wiki engines have WYSIWYG editors. On each page displayed by the TWiki.org engine, the WYSIWYG button allows the page to be edited by using the Kupu editor, as shown in the figure here.

The Kupu editor works like most word processors. You select text and then click a toolbar button to format text. In theory, WYSIWYG is yet another wiki feature that removes barriers to Web publishing because you don't even have to learn wiki markup.

Applying WYSIWYG editing to wikis has one major challenge: the browser. The text edit box that is used to edit wiki markup is simple and works the same way in almost every browser. However, WYSIWYG requires browser plug-ins that don't always work reliably. WYSIWYG plug-ins are highly sensitive to browser versions; the more complex your formatting, the less likely that the WYSIWYG editor will work.

Some WYSIWYG editing plug-ins work better than others. JotSpot, the wiki purchased by Google, has been one of the leaders in making WYSIWYG work. With all its engineering resources, perhaps Google will be the first to get it right. In the authors' opinion, if you want to use wikis, you're better off using wiki markup in a text box rather than WYSIWYG.

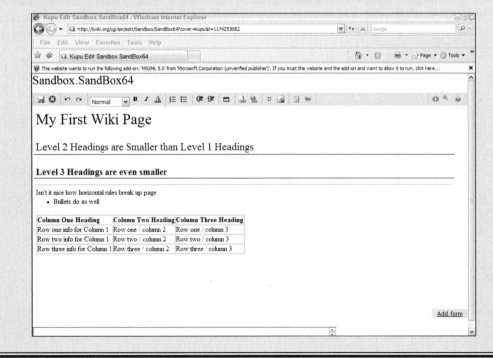

Wiki markup is important, but don't get carried away with it. Keep in mind that the key purpose of a wiki is to share content. Focus first on making content available, and improve the appearance of the content later.

Controlling Layout and Formatting with HTML

HTML is another way to format wiki content and give pages a bit more structure than plain wiki markup allows. In some wiki engines, such as TWiki.org, you can use HTML; in others, you can't. HTML is harder to read and maintain, so use it sparingly. Having said that, if the wiki markup syntax doesn't offer the formatting you need and you're familiar with HTML, it's usually an option. For example, many forms of wiki markup have no equivalent for strikethrough text. In HTML, though, you can enter `<strike>deleted text</strike>` to get ~~deleted text~~.

HTML is also useful for controlling page layout. For example, the home page for the wiki web that we used to write this book was designed by Peter Thoeny, the creator of TWiki.org, using HTML. Peter created the layout shown in Figure 6-5 by combining wiki markup with an HTML table.

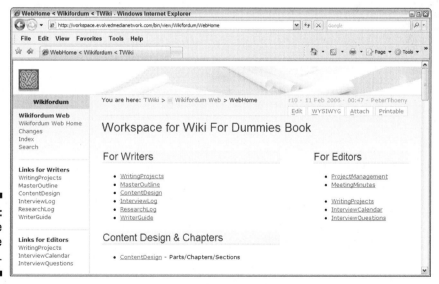

Figure 6-5:
A wiki page can use HTML.

The wiki and HTML markup for the page shown in Figure 6-5 looks like this:

```
<table width="100%"><tr><td valign="top">
---++ For Writers
   * WritingProjects
   * MasterOutline
   * ContentDesign
   * InterviewLog
   * ResearchLog
   * WriterGuide
---++ Content Design & Chapters
   * ContentDesign - Parts/Chapters/Sections

</td><td valign="top"> </td><td valign="top">
---++ For Editors
   * ProjectManagement
   * MeetingMinutes
   * WritingProjects
   * InterviewCalendar
   * InterviewQuestions

</td></tr></table>
```

This use of HTML allows screen space to be used more efficiently. A complete explanation of HTML is beyond the scope of this book, but if you already know HTML, you can probably use that knowledge as you build your wiki.

Choosing Wiki Page Modes

One of the magical aspects of wikis is that flexibility never goes away. When you put information in a database, you have to spend a lot of time designing how the information will be stored; later, changing that structure isn't easy. With wikis, though, the information can be captured and structured; how the information is organized can be easily changed. Wikis also easily accommodate many different forms of organization for the same information.

In Chapter 1, we show how wikis can imitate almost any kind of Web site. Wikis can emulate bulletin boards, forums, traditional Web pages, and more. The three fundamental patterns of wiki pages are

   ✔ **Document mode:** Pages using this mode are formatted with headings, bullets, tables, and images, like the pages of a book or a Web site. Ongoing collaboration is summarized at the top of the page and (in many cases) is summarized by an editor. Document mode pages are usually written in third person and unsigned. Although the page is still subject to editing by anyone using the wiki, it's an authoritative informational page.

   ✔ **Thread mode:** Thread mode pages are akin to e-mail conversations, similar to what you might see on a Web message board. One person writes some text, the next person responds, another person adds his two cents, and so on. The new entries might appear on top of the older ones, or you might have to scroll all the way to the bottom of the page for the latest comment. Threaded discussions are usually written in a conversational, first-person manner.

✔ **Structured mode:** These pages are like forms with boxes for each field, such as name, address, and ZIP code. Structured pages have locked-down structures with clear separations for each type of information.

Within each project, topic, or web, some pages might rely on document mode collaboration while others fit better for thread mode discussions. Which mode you use is a matter of who will use the page and how. Front pages are, by and large, written in document mode for the simple reason that they act as portals into the rest of the information in the web or topic. Threaded pages proliferate more frequently within webs or topics, though, because of the free form and open discussion they facilitate.

Sometimes combining document mode and thread mode in the same page makes sense. For example, you might need a design document (in document mode) at the top, followed by a feedback section (in thread mode). The MediaWiki engine used by Wikipedia has separate discussion pages (in thread mode) for each article page (in document mode). Table 6-3 lists pros and cons of each mode. Then throughout the rest of the chapter, we discuss each mode in more detail.

Table 6-3	Document Mode versus Thread Mode versus Structured Mode	
Mode	*Pros*	*Cons*
Document mode	Makes the subject easily accessible to newcomers. Leverages the knowledge of all participants to create an authoritative entry on a given subject. Combined with links, it facilitates the navigation of other areas within the wiki.	Does not promote open conversation. Requires editors and overseers. Can easily become outdated.
Thread mode	Fast and easy way to share ideas. Promotes open dialog and collaboration. Ensures that you own your own words. (No one can modify or delete your writing.) Supplies a historical record of ideas and who contributed them.	Conversations can become messy and hard to follow. Newcomers to the project will have difficulty getting up to speed. Can become bogged down in arguments rather than discussions.

(continued)

Table 6-3 *(continued)*

Mode	Pros	Cons
Structured mode	Presents information in a highly controlled format. Clearly labels different types of information. Allows structured information from databases to be displayed or captured by wiki pages. Provides a way to automate wiki pages.	Much more complicated to create and maintain than other forms of wiki pages. Difficult to change.

Using document mode

Organizing wiki pages in document mode is simple enough: That is, you present content in the format used by most documents. Wikipedia pages explaining various topics are great examples of document mode. By reading a document mode wiki page, someone who is new to the information can get up to speed by simply reading from top to bottom.

Comparatively, the general structure of document mode pages (except fiction) is an inverted triangle. Go ahead and draw a triangle in the margin of this page with the tip pointing down and the base at the top. This inverted triangle represents the information on a document mode page. The top of the page (the long, flat end of the triangle) contains general information or a broad summary of the subject matter. As you work down the page, the writing becomes more specific until you reach the last and most detailed data on the subject matter at the tip of the triangle. Each level of detail in the triangle is identified by the size of the heading. Larger headings identify more general information, and smaller headings point to more specific sections.

Avoid putting too much detail on a single page. Your trip to the tip of the document triangle presents natural places for links to other parts of the wiki that offer expanded information.

A page that uses document mode still has multiple contributors. Comments can pile up, especially toward the bottom of the page where the information gets more detailed. Document pages periodically need to be edited to remove some comments. Refactoring pages is one of the tasks performed by wiki managers, as we describe in Chapter 12. Refactoring is acceptable, but here are guidelines to follow to respect the original commenter and the participatory nature of wikis:

 ✔ The text that replaces the comment should accurately reflect the original.

 ✔ Always give credit where due.

 ✔ Maintain a complete list of contributors.

Attaching relevant documents to the bottom of a document mode page (covered in Chapter 2) is another excellent way to enhance content. Avoid attaching materials that would be a better fit for another page within the same topic. The documents, spreadsheets, and presentations included on a page should offer general overviews of the topic, thus serving the goal of the document mode structure.

Implementing thread mode pages

It's tempting to think that wiki pages organized in thread mode require zero upkeep. Although this is often the case, you have ways to enhance these pages as well. Figure 6-6 shows a typical page in thread mode, with one comment after another.

> ### Answer
>
> △ If you answer a question - or have a question you asked answered by someone - please remember to edit the page and set the status to answered. The status is in a drop-down list below the edit box.
>
> I'm getting the same error message. on Red Hat Linux ES 4.
>
> edit: removed unrelated Perl errors
>
> -- MackHooper - 25 Jan 2007
>
> OK. managed to fix this on my system. The problem stemmed from not following the install directions *exactly*. In particular, the bin/LocalLib.cfg file *MUST* have been created and edited to reflect the correct path prior to running bin/configure.
>
> -- MackHooper - 25 Jan 2007
>
> YES! MackHooper is right. When I removed everything, unzipped again, and corrected bin/LocalLib.cfg as the first thing, everything works fine.
>
> Thanks. MackHooper
>
> -- TonyAlbers - 26 Jan 2007
>
> See also Perl5ErrorsTemplateProblem.
>
> -- PeterThoeny - 18 Mar 2007
>
> [   ] [Add comment]
>
> Change status to: [AnsweredQuestions ▾]

Figure 6-6:
A typical thread mode page looks like this.

In addition to the comments, a thread mode page should include the following types of information:

✔ A brief summary of the discussion topic at the top of the page

✔ A set of ground rules for the discussion (for example, "No sticks and stones, but name calling is okay")

✔ A list of the discussion owners or leaders, along with contact information or links to their personal pages

In general, the more participants writing entries on a thread mode page the better. That said, a thread mode page can grow so large that it becomes difficult for even the participants to navigate. One excellent way to avoid the never-ending scroll to the bottom of a thread mode page is to offer alternative ways to view the discussion. By using various structured wiki techniques, you can parse threaded discussions by author, subject, or date, for example. This requires advanced wiki skills but can be well worth the time investment after a thread mode page grows into a robust, thriving discussion with multiple participants.

One sign of a successful and constructive threaded discussion is that it eventually yearns to be transformed into a document mode page. Sometimes the document mode page replaces the threaded page.

Using structured mode

Structured mode pages offer a third way to create wiki pages. Pages organized in structured mode follow a predefined template that makes it clear how and where comments are to be added. The templates for structured mode pages are created by whoever designs the wiki. Chapter 14 explains how to create structured wikis and wiki pages. Figure 6-7 shows a structured mode page for capturing information about an interview.

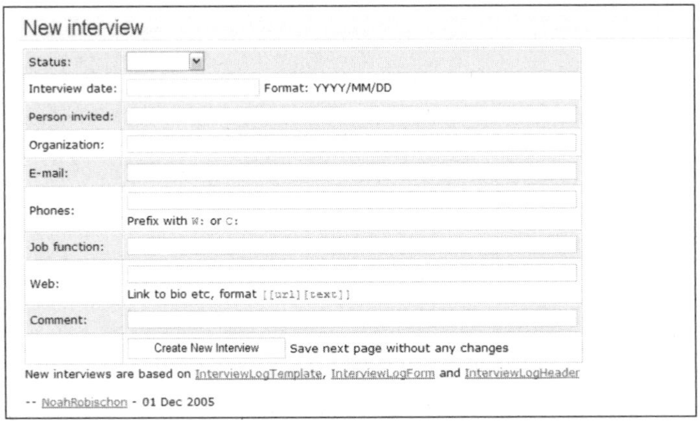

Figure 6-7:
Structured
mode pages
often
include form
fields.

New interview

Status:	
Interview date:	Format: YYYY/MM/DD
Person invited:	
Organization:	
E-mail:	
Phones:	Prefix with W: or C:
Job function:	
Web:	Link to bio etc, format [[url][text]]
Comment:	

Create New Interview   Save next page without any changes

New interviews are based on InterviewLogTemplate, InterviewLogForm and InterviewLogHeader

-- NoahRobischon - 01 Dec 2005

Data fields describe various aspects of the interview, including

✔ The name of the person being interviewed

✔ The date of the interview

✔ The e-mail address of the person being interviewed

There are usually rules governing how and when to edit or contribute to a structured mode page. Sometimes these rules are self evident (as in the interview page shown in Figure 6-7). Other times, you might need to spell out the rules at the top of the page.

Chapter 7

Linking, Categorizing, and Tagging Wiki Pages

*E*ven without links, wikis are an easy way to create and share content. With links, though, each page has depth because each link is an invitation to read more, explore, and jump to another topic. Because links are easier to create in wikis than in any other sort of Web technology, you have no excuse not to use them. The readers of your wiki will thank you for helping them find the information they need.

Of course, linking in wikis has its own strange history. As we describe in Chapter 2, wikis use camel case links. *Camel case* was created as a quick and easy linking scheme by Ward Cunningham, the inventor of wikis. As the wiki concept has grown, other needs arose, and camel case is no longer the only way to create a link. For example, *free linking* provides more flexibility and has become quite popular, especially because Wikipedia adopted it in lieu of using camel case. This chapter tells you about both types of linking, including the ways that wiki links go beyond the sort of links you see in plain old HTML Web pages.

Two other kinds of links used in wikis are adding images and linking to YouTube videos. Including pages — that is, inserting an entire Web page into your wiki page — can be considered a form of linking as well, albeit an extreme one. Using categories and tags also creates links to pages, so we cover them here, also.

Linking Wiki Pages

When most people think of links in wikis, they usually compare wiki links with links on Web pages, but this is a big mistake. Links in wikis are much more than just a way to move from one page to the next. The following sections show you the true power and capabilities of wiki links. This method and other linking methods are explained in this chapter.

In order for links to work, pages need unique names. Wikis use *namespaces* to ensure unique page names. The web is then the namespace, and each page name is a combination of the page name and the web name. You could think of the page name as a first name and the web name as a last name. There might be a lot of Dans, but only so many Dan Woods (and even fewer Peter Thoenys). This also makes it easier to have a common structure in all your webs. A wiki might have 50 webs representing 50 different clubs, but each club could have its own MeetingMinutes page without fear that the Bridge club and the mud wrestling club would get their meeting minutes mixed up.

Some wiki engines allow one namespace covering the entire wiki engine (this would not be the right wiki engine for the 50-club wiki). Other wiki engines, such as TWiki.org, use webs as namespaces.

Linking WikiWords automatically

In Chapter 2, we explain the basics of automatic linking using camel case links. Camel case links are formed by using words with a special character pattern that uses capital letters inside the words. The following examples show what is and is not camel case:

- ✔ ThisIsCamelCase
- ✔ Thisisnot
- ✔ thisisnoT
- ✔ thisIsNot
- ✔ THisisnot
- ✔ ThisIs
- ✔ SoisthiS

Camel case describes a string of letters that meets three rules:

- ✔ The string begins with an uppercase letter.
- ✔ The string doesn't contain any blanks.
- ✔ The string has at least two uppercase letters separated by at least one lowercase character.

Camel case words used for wiki links are *WikiWords.* To create a link in a wiki page, simply put in a camel case word and then save the page. If the page named by your WikiWord exists, the word shows up as a link to the appropriate page. If the page doesn't exist, the link shows up in the page but it doesn't lead anywhere — yet. When you click the link, you create the page as described later in this chapter. (See the section, "Creating pages using links.")

The good thing about WikiWords is that you can create links lickety-split. For example, you're writing furiously when you think of a topic like rhubarb pie, which is important to the page that you're writing. All you have to do is type **RhubarbPie**, and there you have it — the link is created. What could be easier?

Most wiki engines are trending away from WikiWord linking in favor of free linking, which we describe later in this chapter. Many engines turn off WikiWord linking by default. Check the settings for your engine for whether WikiWord linking is enabled for your wiki.

Preventing false WikiWord links

WikiWord linking does present some problems. First of all, some words don't really lend themselves to camel case linking. For example, if you want to link to *rhubarb* instead of *rhubarb pie,* what do you do? One trick is to write RhubarB or RhuBarb, both of which would result in a link. The problem is that both of these words look like typing mistakes.

Another problem is the growing trend of using camel case-style syntax in brand names. For example, NetWeaver (the SAP business technology platform) looks like a WikiWord, as do some surnames (such as McCullough). Without intervention, these words would be seen as links in most wiki engines.

The remedy to false WikiWords used by TWiki.org and some other wikis is to have a special character that stops camel case linking from happening. In TWiki.org, any of the following methods stop automatic WikiWord linking:

- ✔ `<nop>McCullough`

- ✔ `!McCullough`

- ✔ `<noautolink>`

  No text here would be automatically linked, not even
  `McCullough</noautolink>`.

TWiki.org can also stop automatic WikiWord linking for specific words in
every wiki by using a plug-in. See Chapter 14 for more on using wiki plug-ins.

Free linking

Free linking provides more flexibility than WikiWord linking, but you do have
to type some extra characters. Suppose you're writing a Wikipedia page, and
you want to add a link to a page about rhubarb pie. With free linking, you
would type

```
[[rhubarb pie]]
```

When you save the page, a link is created to the page named *Rhubarb pie.* (Note
how MediaWiki capitalizes the first letter when it creates the new page, even
though the link was lowercase. Maybe the developers decided that otherwise
the pages would look like they were all written by ee cummings or k.d. lang.)

When MediaWiki (the wiki engine that runs Wikipedia) encounters words in
double square brackets, like the ones shown in Figure 7-1, it turns them into
links when you save the page. The resulting links, shown in Figure 7-2, appear
without the brackets and in a different color so that users know they can
click those words and be taken elsewhere. Red means the link doesn't exist;
blue means it does.

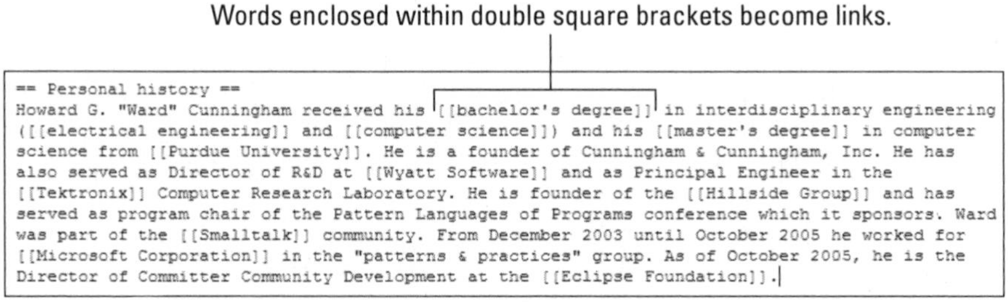

Words enclosed within double square brackets become links.

Figure 7-1:
Perform free
linking by
typing
double
square
brackets
around
words.

```
== Personal history ==
Howard G. "Ward" Cunningham received his [[bachelor's degree]] in interdisciplinary engineering
([[electrical engineering]] and [[computer science]]) and his [[master's degree]] in computer
science from [[Purdue University]]. He is a founder of Cunningham & Cunningham, Inc. He has
also served as Director of R&D at [[Wyatt Software]] and as Principal Engineer in the
[[Tektronix]] Computer Research Laboratory. He is founder of the [[Hillside Group]] and has
served as program chair of the Pattern Languages of Programs conference which it sponsors. Ward
was part of the [[Smalltalk]] community. From December 2003 until October 2005 he worked for
[[Microsoft Corporation]] in the "patterns & practices" group. As of October 2005, he is the
Director of Committer Community Development at the [[Eclipse Foundation]].
```

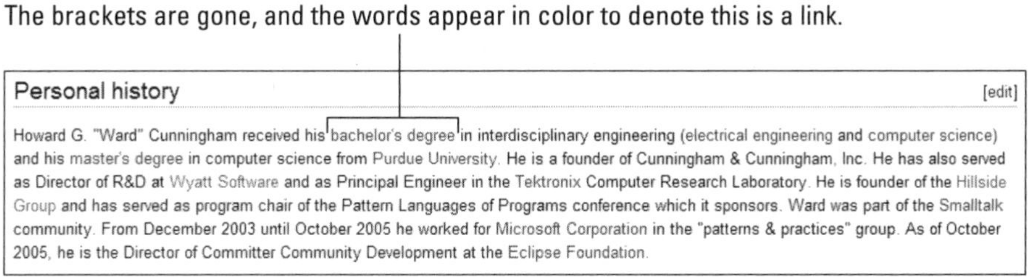

The brackets are gone, and the words appear in color to denote this is a link.

Figure 7-2:
When the
page is
displayed,
free links
appear as
links.

> **Personal history**   [edit]
>
> Howard G. "Ward" Cunningham received his bachelor's degree in interdisciplinary engineering (electrical engineering and computer science) and his master's degree in computer science from Purdue University. He is a founder of Cunningham & Cunningham, Inc. He has also served as Director of R&D at Wyatt Software and as Principal Engineer in the Tektronix Computer Research Laboratory. He is founder of the Hillside Group and has served as program chair of the Pattern Languages of Programs conference which it sponsors. Ward was part of the Smalltalk community. From December 2003 until October 2005 he worked for Microsoft Corporation in the "patterns & practices" group. As of October 2005, he is the Director of Committer Community Development at the Eclipse Foundation.

The MediaWiki engine has some other tricks as well. Table 7-1 lists some of the link methods available in MediaWiki and many other engines.

Table 7-1	Free Linking
Link Syntax	*Result*
`[[rhubarb pie]]`	The link shows up as `rhubarb pie` onscreen and links to the *Rhubarb pie* page.
`[[rhubarb pie]]s`	The link shows up as `rhubarb pies` onscreen but links to the *Rhubarb pie* page. This is *blended linking*.
`[[rhubarb pie|my favorite pie]]`	The link shows up as `my favorite pie` onscreen but links to the *Rhubarb pie* page.

For more linking tips and tricks, visit

`http://en.wikipedia.org/wiki/Wikipedia:How_to_edit_a_page#Links_and_URLs`

Creating pages using links

Perhaps the most important difference between wiki links and Web links is that wiki links can be used to create new pages. When writing a wiki page, a common practice is to create links to a topic that you'll come back to later, or perhaps to a topic that you think someone else should come back to later.

When you save a page on which you inserted a link, one of two things happens:

✔ The page to which you link already exists, in which case clicking the link goes to that page.

✔ The page to which you link does *not* exist. If you click this type of link, a new page is automatically created, ready for you to add content.

Most wikis indicate when a link leads to a page that doesn't yet exist. For example, TWiki puts a question mark after the link, as shown in Figure 7-3. On wikispaces.com and Wikipedia, links to pages that don't exist are shown in red. If you click these indicators — a TWiki question mark, or a Wikipedia red link — a new page is automatically created.

Figure 7-3:
Question
marks
suggest
that these
are links to
pages that
don't yet
exist.

Giving life to stubs

Creating links to pages that don't yet exist has some important implications for how you edit and use wikis. Someone creating a link to a page that he thinks should exist and then that same person going back to fill it in is a pretty straightforward process. It is sort of like saying, "Note to self: Remember to add this page later."

However, when someone creates a link to a page that he thinks someone else should fill in, that's a different matter altogether. It is a request to the community: "Hey community! Does someone else know enough to create this page?" If you think of such links as requests or votes, you have a way to see what types of pages the wiki community wants to see created. Chances are that the pages with the most requests or votes are the ones that the community wants most.

Many wikis keep lists of pages that don't exist or have just a small amount of information in them. These pages are *stubs* or *short pages*. Figure 7-4 shows the stubs page for BibleWiki. If you're looking for a good way to contribute to your favorite wiki, peruse that wiki's stubs page to see what needs to be done.

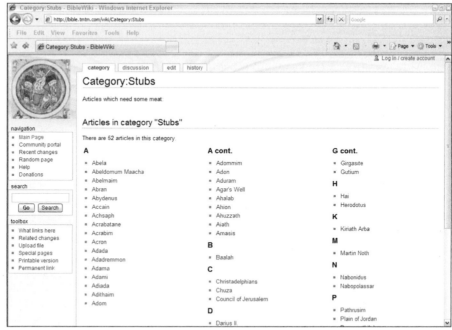

Figure 7-4:
This page at
BibleWiki
lists page
stubs.

Viewing all links to a page

Unlike HTML-based Web sites, wiki engines are aware of every link. This leads to some very powerful capabilities, including the ability to quickly see all the links that point to a given page. This can be useful both for wiki maintenance as well as for finding related information. To see how link listing works, follow these steps:

1. **Visit Wikipedia and view the article on Ward Cunningham, the inventor of wikis.**

   Chapter 4 shows how to find specific pages at Wikipedia.

2. **On the left side of the Ward Cunningham page, locate the link labeled Toolbox.**

3. **At the top of the Toolbox list, click the What Links Here link.**

   A list of all pages that link to the Ward Cunningham article appears, as shown in Figure 7-5.

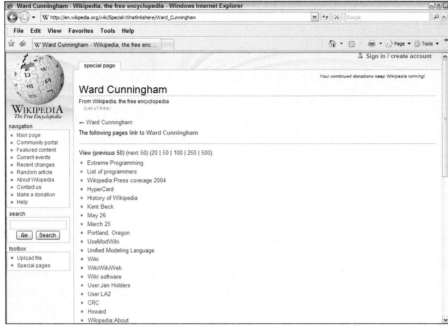

Figure 7-5:
Wiki engines
can easily
list all links
to a given
page.

Lonely pages that have no links leading to them are *orphans*. How do you get to an orphan page? The only way is to jump directly to the page if you know its name; or you can navigate to the page displaying a list of all the pages on the wiki. (In TWiki, you click Index to display such a list.) Removing orphan pages is one of the tasks performed during wiki management, which we describe in Chapter 12.

Renaming all links in a web

Another extremely useful wiki feature is the ability to simultaneously rename a page and all the links leading to that page. TWiki probably has the best implementation of this feature. There, you can rename a page and all the links to that page in one command. TWiki.org not only searches the web in which the page resides but all webs run by the wiki engine. To rename a page in TWiki, follow these steps:

1. **Scroll to the bottom of the page in question and click More Topic Actions.**

   TWiki displays a More Actions on Topic page. This page lists a variety of actions you can take, including deleting and renaming pages.

2. **Click the Rename/Move Topic link that specifies that it looks for references in all public webs.**

   TWiki displays a page where you can rename the page.

3. **In the Topic Name field, enter the new name for the page and click the Rename/Move button.**

   TWiki changes all the links as well as renames the page.

On some other wikis, the process is a bit more complex. If you rename or move a page on MediaWiki or WikiSpaces, for example, links to the old page are redirected to the new page. You must manually change each link to skip the redirection step. Confluence, a commercial wiki, behaves like TWiki and changes links automatically (and the process is also a little easier; you rename right from the editing page).

Linking Outside Your Wiki

The creators of wikis try to provide all the information a reader needs, but there are always good reasons to link to information outside your own wiki. In the following sections, we introduce you to many different ways to create external links.

Linking URLs

The surefire way to link to a Web site outside your wiki is to use a *URL,* which is the common Web site address that usually looks something like this:

```
http://anywebsite.com/anydirectory/anypage.html
```

Most wikis recognize URLs as links. In some wikis (such as MediaWiki), you need to type single square brackets around URLs like this:

```
[http://anywebsite.com/anydirectory/anypage.html]
```

When a page containing a URL is displayed, it automatically links to the URL's destination. In many wikis, URL-generated links are followed by special icons, as shown in Figure 7-6. These icons tell you that if you click the link, you will be taken to a location outside the current wiki.

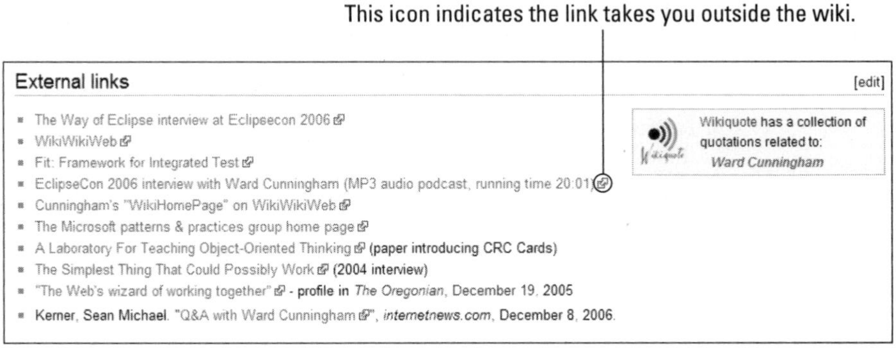

This icon indicates the link takes you outside the wiki.

Figure 7-6:
Arrow icons
indicate
external
links on
most wikis.

External links   [edit]

- The Way of Eclipse interview at Eclipsecon 2006
- WikiWikiWeb
- Fit: Framework for Integrated Test
- EclipseCon 2006 interview with Ward Cunningham (MP3 audio podcast, running time 20:01)
- Cunningham's "WikiHomePage" on WikiWikiWeb
- The Microsoft patterns & practices group home page
- A Laboratory For Teaching Object-Oriented Thinking (paper introducing CRC Cards)
- The Simplest Thing That Could Possibly Work (2004 interview)
- "The Web's wizard of working together" - profile in *The Oregonian*, December 19, 2005
- Kerner, Sean Michael. "Q&A with Ward Cunningham", *internetnews.com*, December 8, 2006.

Wikiquote has a collection of
quotations related to:
Ward Cunningham

Linking between wikis using Interwiki names

Wikis often link to other wikis. In the early days of wikis, this was done by using long URLs, which worked like any other external link. This became a bit tedious because it meant entering long URLs every time you wanted to link to other wikis.

To solve this problem, Interwiki link prefixes were created. Prefixes identify the external wiki to which the link points. Interwiki prefixes are unique. The Interwiki name for BibleWiki, for example, is BibleWiki. The format of an Interwiki link is the same as a normal free link except that the Interwiki name is used as a prefix. So, instead of entering this URL to get to the Book of Deuteronomy page:

```
http://bible.tmtm.com/wiki/Book_of_Deuteronomy
```

you enter a wiki free link, prefixing the page name with the Interwiki name and a colon, like this:

```
[[BibleWiki:Book_of_Deuteronomy]]
```

Most wiki engines that use Interwiki prefix names put external link icons after the link (refer to Figure 7-6). You can find the list of Interwiki link prefixes at

```
http://meta.wikimedia.org/wiki/Interwiki_map
```

Linking to other webs and namespaces

Larger wikis are often organized into webs (sections or subsets of a wiki). The TWiki.org wiki that was used to write this book, for example, has more than 30 webs. Sometimes linking from one web to another is useful. TWiki.org handles cross-web links by using prefixes. To link to a page in a web called Otherweb, enter

```
[[Otherweb.PageName]]
```

This link takes you to the PageName page in the Otherweb web.

Some wikis have multiple namespaces, and the exact method for linking across namespaces varies with each wiki. In MediaWiki, for example, you prefix the page name with the namespace name, like this:

```
[[Help:Link]]
```

Linking to Files, Images, and Multimedia

One of the least standardized but most valuable wiki linking tools involves attaching files to pages, including images and multimedia. Like with many things about wikis, the general approach to attaching files or inserting images is pretty much the same for most wiki engines, but the details are vastly different. The basic similarities include

- ✔ **Most wiki engines allow file uploads.** Sometimes, the files are attached to individual pages (like at TWiki.org). Other times, they are put in a central area (like at MediaWiki, PBwiki, and WikiSpaces).

- ✔ **Images are uploaded as files and then can be linked to from wiki pages.**

- ✔ **Multimedia elements are included via URLs, JavaScript, or both.** These links bring videos or advanced functionality, such as calendars, into pages. Some wikis use wizards to help add such elements to pages.

In Chapter 1, we introduce you to PBwiki and the `Wikisfordummies.pbwiki.com` site that can be used as a sandbox. If you don't have your own wiki, use this wiki to practice adding files, images, and multimedia elements to wiki pages in the following sections. We point out some of the differences between various wikis along the way.

Uploading attachments

Attaching files to a wiki page is much like attaching files to an e-mail in that you usually just click an Attach Files button and then browse to the desired file. Wiki file attachments are particularly handy if you need to share PDFs or other file types with other wiki members. In PBwiki, the easiest way to attach files is to use the point-and-click editor. Follow these basic steps, which are similar in most wikis:

1. **Create or open a PBwiki page to which you want to attach a file.**

   If you open a page, click Edit Page to display the page in the editor.

2. **Make sure you are in the Point and Click editor, which displays icons, rather than the Classic Mode editor, which displays wiki markup.**

   The link in the upper-right corner should read Switch to Classic Mode. If it reads Point-and-Click Mode instead, click that link to go to Point-and-Click Mode.

   A page like the one shown in Figure 7-7 appears.

Click to insert an image

Click to attach a file

Click to insert a plugin

Figure 7-7:
Open your
PBwiki page
for editing.

The editing toolbar has three buttons that are of interest to you (as shown in Figure 7-7):

- *Attach File:* Click this button to attach a file, such as a PDF or a ZIP archive.

- *Insert Plugin:* If you have a plug-in to use with the wiki page (see Chapter 14 for more on plug-ins), click this button to attach it.

- *Insert Image:* Click this button to insert an image.

3. Click the appropriate button for the type of file (file, plug-in, or image) that you want to attach.

A screen like the one in Figure 7-8 appears.

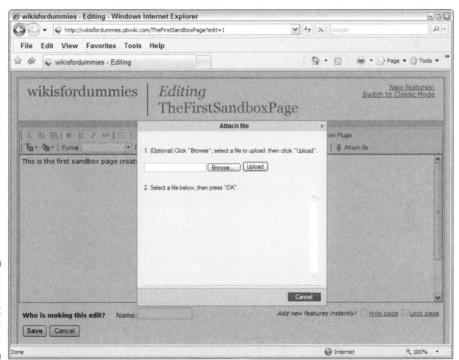

Figure 7-8:
Browse to the file that you want to attach.

4. Click the Browse button and then navigate to the file that you want to upload.

5. Choose the file and then click Upload.

When the file finishes uploading, it appears in the list of the page's attached files, as shown in Figure 7-9. In this example, we attached a JPEG file containing the logo of a legendary children's soccer team in New York.

This image is now attached.

Linking to file attachments

Attaching a file to a wiki page is usually just the first step in making use of uploaded files. After attaching the file, you might want to use it in a page somewhere. You can always see what files have been uploaded to a wiki by clicking the Files button at the top of every page.

To insert a link to an uploaded file, simply go to the Files page and hover your mouse over the file to which you want to link. Right-click the file and choose Copy Link from the menu that appears. Then paste the link into a wiki page. The syntax for a link in PBwiki looks like this:

```
<a href="/f/filename.ext">link text</a>
```

If you're familiar with HTML, the preceding syntax should look familiar. In PBwiki, all uploaded files go to the /f directory. The preceding link names this directory in the path to the filename.

In some wikis — such as those running the TWiki.org engine — uploaded files are attached to specific pages instead of the wiki as a whole. In this case, you use the special variable %ATTACHURL% to link to page-specific files. A link looks like this:

```
<a href="%ATTACHURL%/filename.ext">link text</a>
```

In Wikipedia, a separate namespace is used. Linking to a file looks like this:

```
[[Image:filename.ext]]
```

As you can see, you'll find variations in how different wikis handle file attachments. More advanced features — such as thumbnails, graphic sizing, and captions — are more complex and unique to each wiki engine. Whatever wiki engine you use, spend time discovering its file attachment specifics.

Inserting images

If you know the basics of uploading and linking to wiki file attachments, using images is quite easy. If you want to insert an image into your wiki page, first upload it as a file attachment, as we describe earlier in this chapter.

After the image file is uploaded, click the Insert Image button on the editing screen of the desired page. A window like the one shown in Figure 7-10 appears. Select the image that you want to insert and then click OK to produce a link tag that looks something like this:

```
<img src="/f/littlepebblesB&W.jpg" border="0" />
```

After you save your edits, the image appears in the page, as shown in Figure 7-11.

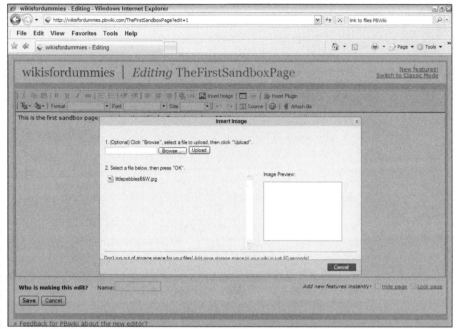

Figure 7-10:
Insert
images into
pages from
this window.

Figure 7-11:
An image
is inserted
into a
PBwiki
page.

Before clicking OK to close the Insert Image window and insert the image, right-click the image (Control-click, Mac) to access advanced options and properties, such as size and alignment.

Linking to multimedia

Links to multimedia files — such as MP3s, movies, or YouTube videos — work much like links to images. You either upload the files and then link to them, or link to the source from which the videos are streamed. Multimedia links are also frequently associated with inserting advanced features, such as calendars or tables with lots of fancy elements. In PBwiki, all these things are handled by the Insert Plugin button. Click this button while editing a page to open the window shown in Figure 7-12.

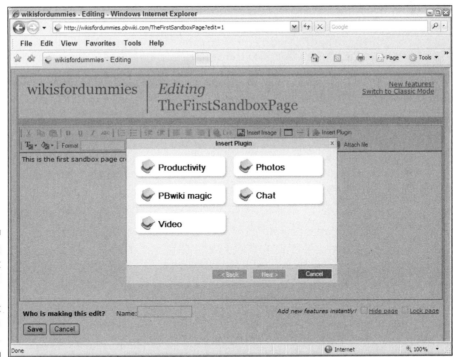

Figure 7-12: Insert advanced features via the Insert Plugin feature.

The Insert Plugin window has choices for all sorts of multimedia elements and structures, such as calendars, Google gadgets and maps, stock charts, Web site stats, links to photo sharing sites, YouTube videos, chat rooms, and more.

Categorizing and Tagging Pages

Most wiki engines use categories and tags to organize and link related pages. Both categories and tags have the same mission: to associate pages into groups so that people can easily find related content. Wikipedia uses categories extensively, and they are open to any site that uses the MediaWiki engine. Other wikis like TWiki.org have extensions that allow users to tag pages. The following sections show you how to use categories and tags in various kinds of wikis.

Using MediaWiki categories

Chapter 8 discusses categories from the perspective of a wiki designer. In wiki parlance, a *category* is a label applied to many pages so you can find all those pages that share the same label. Any given page can have more than one category. For example, the Wikipedia page about Ward Cunningham is assigned to the following categories: 1949 births | Living people | American computer programmers | Wiki | Extreme Programming | People from Portland, Oregon | American technology writers | Purdue University alumni. Here, our goal is to show how the MediaWiki engine can insert links that either put a given page in a category or display a list of all the pages in a category.

Including a page in a category is incredibly easy. If you create a page about this book *(Wikis For Dummies),* and you want to include it in a category called *Books about wikis,* just include the following link at the bottom of the page:

```
[[Category:Books about wikis]]
```

The MediaWiki engine creates that category if it didn't already exist, and then it includes the page in that category. So, if the category already existed, the page will be added. If the category didn't exist, a new category will be created, and the page will become the first member of the category.

In addition to including a page in a category, you might sometimes want to create links to the category pages themselves. You have to be careful here because if you include a category link of the sort shown earlier, the page on which the link is included becomes part of the named category, which is not what you want. You just want to link to that category. To avoid this problem, add an extra colon in front of the word Category, like this:

```
[[:Category:Books about wikis]]
```

Using categories is a complicated topic with lots of ins and outs. For all you ever want to know about categories and how to make them work, visit

```
http://en.wikipedia.org/wiki/Wikipedia:Categorization
```

Tagging content

Tags are similar to categories, but tags are intended to be a bit more inclusive. To use categories, you have to know how to use category links and manually edit them. Tags, though, can easily be entered by almost anyone. *Tags* describe topics or keywords in articles, and wiki search engines use these tags to rank search results. In other words, tags are pretty much the same as categories but they are assigned to pages differently, and you search for pages included in each tag differently, as well.

In TWiki.org, the Tag-me plug-in allows you to involve users in the tagging process. Figure 7-13 shows how the Tag-me plug-in adds tags to the tops of pages. (We don't go into the process of adding the Tag-me plug-in to a page. See Chapter 14 for more about plug-ins.) Anyone reading the page can click a tag to add a vote for it, or they can use the text box to add new tags. To add a tag to a page, follow these steps:

1. **Select a tag from the drop-down box.**

2. **Click the plus sign just to the right of the drop-down box to add the tag to the page.**

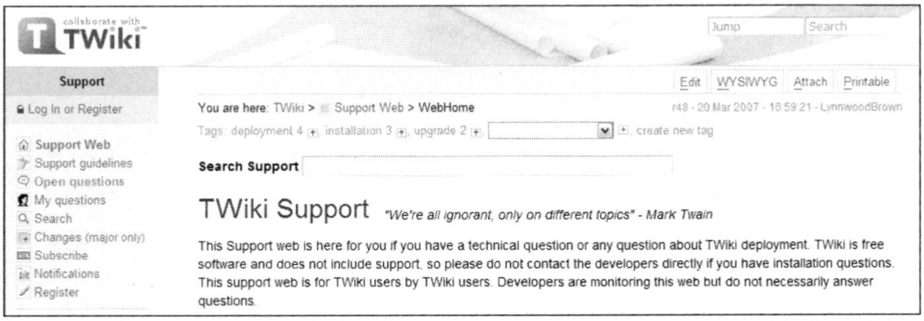

Figure 7-13: Tag-me adds tags to the top of TWiki.org pages.

Navigating by using tags is different from navigating through categories. The Tag Cloud plug-in displays tags, as shown in Figure 7-14. Tags with larger type have more pages associated with them. To use the Tag Cloud plug-in (which, like the Tag-me plug-in, must be installed), you just click a word in the tag cloud to see a list of pages associated with that tag.

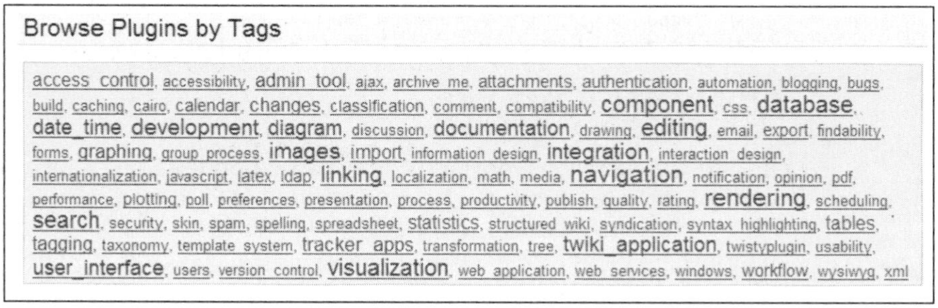

Figure 7-14:
Larger type
means more
pages.

Browse Plugins by Tags

access control, accessibility, admin tool, ajax, archive me, attachments, authentication, automation, blogging, bugs, build, caching, cairo, calendar, changes, classification, comment, compatibility, component, css, database, date_time, development, diagram, discussion, documentation, drawing, editing, email, export, findability, forms, graphing, group process, images, import, information design, integration, interaction design, internationalization, javascript, latex, ldap, linking, localization, math, media, navigation, notification, opinion, pdf, performance, plotting, poll, preferences, presentation, process, productivity, publish, quality, rating, rendering, scheduling, search, security, skin, spam, spelling, spreadsheet, statistics, structured wiki, syndication, syntax highlighting, tables, tagging, taxonomy, template system, tracker apps, transformation, tree, twiki_application, twistyplugin, usability, user_interface, users, version control, visualization, web application, web services, windows, workflow, wysiwyg, xml

Chapter 8

The Four Dimensions of Wiki Design

Designing a wiki means putting together all your wiki skills and knowledge to create a useful form for your wiki. The best wikis look a lot more like a Volkswagen Beetle — that is to say, utilitarian — than a sleek Ferrari, but they are beautiful all the same. Ideally, the design of your wiki should help people find what they want and join the content creation process if they feel so moved. To help you create such a design, throughout this chapter, we discuss the four dimensions of wiki design:

1: Find the right structure for your information. When designing your wiki, the key thing to remember is that the structure of the information being captured must be in charge. *Information architecture* — taxonomy — is a fancy name for organizing the content of your wiki. Whatever the name you give this process, finding the right structure for your information is the secret sauce to making a wiki sing.

2: Create a clear way to navigate a wiki. Everything you see when you encounter a wiki, from the front page to all pages deeper inside, must keep reminding you where you are, what sort information you're looking at, and how you can find your way around. Of course, the reason to navigate a wiki is to find just the right page that has the information you want.

3: Design the structure of the pages. Use the techniques shown in Chapters 6 and 7 (which cover content and linking, respectively), but also employ the benefits of the page template. Templates, by nature, ensure consistency in a user-friendly way.

4: Adjust colors and fonts, adding images where needed, to make your wiki pleasing to the eye. Use themes and colors to give visitors visual cues about organization and navigation. By adding logos and other graphical elements, you personalize the wiki as well as make it unique.

Designing a wiki is an ongoing process. Wikis were made to be changed. The design that you start with should be improved as experience and ideas from those using the wiki point to ways to make it better. This chapter gives you the conceptual foundation of a well-designed wiki so that you can quickly get your wiki up and running and then have the fun of redesigning it over and over again.

Architecting the Information in Your Wiki

In Chapter 1, we introduce the idea of index cards to explain wikis. (The gist is this: If you have a box of index cards, you can add cards to the box, remove them, search through them, change the information on them, and so forth. Likewise, you can do the same with information on a wiki.) *Information architecture* is all about how many types of cards you have, how they are related, and what to write on each card. But what good is a box of cards if you can't find the card you want? *Taxonomies,* effective patterns of linking, and clear page names (all covered in this section), are the foundation of a well-organized wiki. Having the information architecture show up on the front pages and section front pages of your wiki makes your wiki easy to navigate. We cover that in the following section.

Understanding wiki taxonomy

One way to begin organizing your wiki is to act like a biologist. Biologists love to classify things. They're not satisfied with calling people *humans;* instead, they call us *Homo sapiens.* Biologists systematically classify the animals and plants in our world by using *taxonomy.* Taxonomy is a way to classify things based on their relationships to one another and is a key part of any good information architecture for a wiki.

Taxonomy has nothing to do with that stuffed moose head hanging on the wall. (Still, those folks who attend the National Taxidermists Association probably know the difference between *Antilocapra americana* and *Antilocapra anteflexa,* which are taxonomic names for different families of pronghorn antelope.) Flashback to high school biology class: Each species belongs to a

Prof. Tufte's design advice

Edward Tufte, a professor emeritus at Yale University, taught courses in statistical evidence, information design, and interface design. Over his long and continuing career, he wrote many books on the design and display of graphical information. Prof. Tufte also periodically teaches a wonderful course that includes one piece of advice so valuable that it should be the foundation of your approach not only to designing wikis but designing pretty much everything else.

Prof. Tufte says that rather than seeing design as a problem of invention or a challenge to create something new, look at design as a research problem in which you find something that already works to copy. Boy, does this approach make design much easier, and it fits right into the open source, evolutionary ethos of wikis.

So, in reading this chapter and considering how to design your wiki, don't feel nervous and pressured that you have to come up with something new. Rather, think about the wikis you like most from Chapter 3 or other wikis, books, or content that you enjoyed. Take a look at Tufte's books. Copy what you like and then improve it as you gain experience.

genus; each genus belongs to a family; each freshman can't wait for summer vacation. (It is high school, after all.)

With wikis, the equivalent of species and genus are wikis, webs, and pages:

- **Wiki:** A *wiki* is usually defined as all the pages under the umbrella of one domain, such as `www.mywiki.com`.

- **Web:** A *web* is a self-contained group of pages inside a wiki, which are intended to be linked. Linking pages across a web usually requires some special notation.

- **Page:** A *page* is a unit that is edited and displayed. A page contains text, images, and any other content included in the wiki.

If a wiki followed the hierarchical organization of species used in biology, it would look something like this:

Wiki

Web

Page

Okay, that's easy enough for the average *Homo sapien* to grasp on a conceptual level. So how, exactly, does the concept get turned into reality? Simple! Just think of how the project you are involved with is organized already.

Inside a web, the pages can be grouped in many different taxonomies. In a project management wiki, for example, each project can have its own web; or, one web can have many projects, each with its own group of pages. (A *project* is anything you might undertake, from compiling a Girl Scout troop cookbook to coordinating a Harley-Davidson club road trip to writing a grant for the study of penguin mating patterns.) Or, for a wiki on The Beatles, each album might have its own web, and each web might have a group of pages dedicated to each song. Wikipedia uses a set of basic topics, as shown in Figure 8-1.

Figure 8-1:
Basic
topics for
Wikipedia.

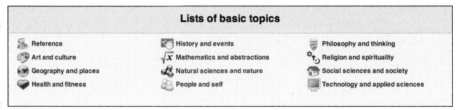

Each of these basic topics is a web within Wikipedia. Because of the sheer scale of Wikipedia, these webs also have sub-webs for subtopics, as shown in Figure 8-2.

Figure 8-2:
A Wikipedia
topic uses
subtopics.

Surveying common wiki taxonomies

One of the biggest favors that you can do for yourself is to use a taxonomy that everyone using the wiki already knows, clearly depicting the taxonomy on the front page of the wiki. You can see an example in Figure 8-3. Here are some popular taxonomies used to organize the pages inside wikis:

✔ **Whole, parts, and subparts:** Many things that wikis track have natural groupings to them. For example, albums have songs, books have chapters, software has different menu areas and screens, and cars have makes and models. Content-focused wikis of the sort described in Chapter 3 usually are organized around the natural groupings of the topic being discussed. For example, the front page of the Case Western Reserve University Wiki (`http://wiki.case.edu`) shows several categories (People, Academics, Organizations, Campus Life, Around Case, Other Categories), each with subcategories listed.

✔ **Organizational chart:** The boss is at the top, and every department that reports to her branches outward, like a big, happy family tree. This is an effective structure for smaller internal wikis that are being used primarily for project management or are otherwise process-focused.

✔ **Actions in a sequence:** Open an order, place a bid, add data — this type of taxonomy is useful for process-focused wikis. For the wiki used to write this book, we have a list of pages that mimic the steps taken to write a book: project management and planning, content design, research, interviews, and writing.

✔ **Alphabetical or other natural order for a list:** When in doubt, use A–Z. Topics, projects, webs, and registered users can all be organized this way and be quite effective in steering visitors to their destination. If a natural order to the content exists that would be easily recognized and understood, use it. For example, BibleWiki, (`http://bible.tmtm.com`) has a list of the parts of the Bible and a list of the books in each part.

✔ **Timeline:** Whether you're engaged in a project on the history of the species or one that has distinct phases and a strict deadline, organizing the pages in time order can help keep everyone on track and on time. For project management applications, this can mean having a list of all the steps taken on the front page. For a research project, the timeline could show the events of the topic being discussed it chronological order. WikiTimeScale (`www.wikitimescale.org`) is a good example.

✔ **Order of importance:** An old-fashioned to-do list is a good way of drawing the user's attention to the most important topics or projects on a wiki. This is a great structure for a punch list of items to be completed at the end of a project.

✔ **Geography:** When the information you're organizing is associated with regions, states, countries, or other geographical boundaries, use that to your advantage. For example, Wikitravel (`www.wikitravel.com`) divides its contents by continents.

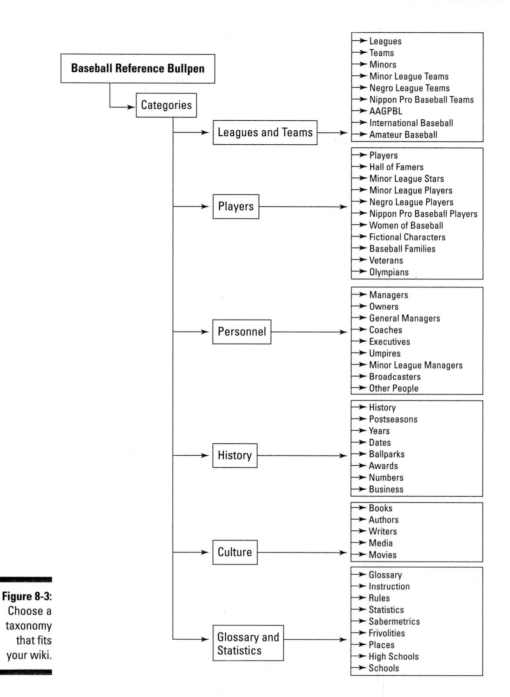

Figure 8-3:
Choose a
taxonomy
that fits
your wiki.

These taxonomies cover most cases. Your wiki might end up following one of these taxonomies, a combination of several styles, or even another taxonomy of your own design.

Don't over-think your taxonomy. It should be a natural fit for the information that you're organizing. The goal is that when users of your wiki arrive at the front page, they should know exactly where to go to find what they need. The easiest way to do this is to build on a structure they already know. Put yourself in the mindset of a user and make a mental picture of what the front page should look like. Also, remember that wikis are inherently organic. Start simple, study the patterns of usage, and add structure in iterations as needed.

Linking in patterns

Think about the different ways in which people will want to access information on your wiki.

For example, suppose you're creating a wiki on The Beatles. Depending on the depth of the content, you probably need page albums that have all the descriptive information for each respective album, and another type of page that has information for each song. Such a structure allows all sorts of flexibility:

- ✔ Create separate pages for two versions of the same album and then link to the individual song pages for songs shared by each album.

- ✔ Create playlist pages that have lists of links to song pages. As many playlist pages can be created as you like without duplicating the song pages.

- ✔ Link to an individual song page when you discuss that song in other locations on the site. Using such links draws people into finding more content on the wiki.

- ✔ Create pages that summarize or compile certain kinds of content. For example, a wiki covering The Beatles can include a page listing all songs written by Ringo Starr. This short but useful list could then link to the individual song pages.

All this linking is possible if the information on a page is properly designed. By *properly,* we mean that the information that goes together naturally is grouped on a certain type of page. Understanding what goes together naturally might be easy to figure out — such as with the example of albums and songs — or it might be harder to determine. The great thing about wikis is that if you get it wrong, you can always change it later.

Teach your users that adding many links in wiki pages is a good thing. This makes it easy to find related content. Make frequent use of WikiWords, which are linked automatically to pages of that name. (See Chapter 7 for more on using WikiWords.)

What's in a page name?

A successful wiki will quickly grow many content pages. Correctly naming content pages allows you to create links easily, makes pages easier to find, and lays the foundation for certain types of automation discussed in Chapter 14.

Suppose that you're creating a project management wiki. On the one side, having consistency on your wiki is a good thing. Say that Project A has a schedule yet Project B features a calendar: Both pages do the same thing — that is, track important dates — but things can get confusing for the user. When you have multiple pages on a wiki with similar, interchangeable names, it can inadvertently sow the seeds of mass confusion. To understand why, just think of what happens when you enter the word *schedule* into your wiki's search engine. It spits back a list of pages titled *Schedule,* but you have no clue to which project each schedule relates.

Hence the need for good naming. Remember those biologists and their taxonomies? They use Latin because it's descriptive — you know that *Antilocapra americana* and *Antilocapra anteflexa* are related just by reading the name. The pages on your wiki should work that way, too. Okay, you don't have to name your pages in Latin, but the name of the page should hold the key to decoding the page's specific contents. Table 8-1 identifies several common patterns that appear in wiki page names.

Table 8-1	Common Patterns for Page Names
Page Name Pattern	*When Used*
WidgetSchedule WidgetCalendar WidgetJournal	The Widget prefix defines several types of documents related to the Widget project.
ProposalNewcorp20070228	The date suffix identifies a version.
ContactsExternal ContactsInternal	The Contacts prefix identifies the type of information, and the suffix divides it into a group.

You can always hide the page's true name through linking. For example, if you name a page *ProjectASchedule20060928,* but all you want the user to see is the word *Schedule,* link it like this:

```
[[ProjectASchedule20060928][Schedule]]
```

See Chapter 7 for more on creating and formatting links in wikis.

Webs can also be a source of naming ambiguity. If you find that multiple webs have the same name, the problem is likely that the web names aren't general enough. In other words, the webs are being named as if they were topics. Consider the word *Schedule* again. Even if the web is a collection of important company-wide dates, it is better to name it descriptively, such as Holiday Schedule or Human Resources Schedule.

Plotting Navigational Paths through Your Wiki

When designing wikis or Web sites, *navigation* is the term used to describe how information architecture is presented to users. The navigation for your wiki includes the links that appear on the three sorts of pages in every wiki: the front pages (including the section and category pages), the content pages, and the supporting pages. Front pages and section front pages summarize the information in various groups of pages and tell you how to find what you need. Supporting pages describe the process of creating content. Graphics and colors make everything look pretty and clear. Navigation also includes headers, footers, and the left-hand side of content pages. By following Prof. Tufte's advice and using proven navigation models, you can find the right structure for your home page in no time. (See the sidebar, "Prof. Tufte's design advice.")

Designing the front page

The *front page* of your wiki is the first thing that people see when they arrive, so it better tell them right away what the wiki is all about and how to find what they're looking for. To design an effective front page, start by asking yourself some basic questions:

> ✔ **Is your wiki content- or process-focused?** Or do you have a community wiki or some sort of brochureware? (See Chapter 3 for more on wiki categories.) Depending on the type of wiki you're designing, the content, process, community, or product should be the star of the show on the front page.

- ✔ **Will people who arrive at the wiki know how the wiki fits into their lives?** If this is a project management wiki inside a company, everyone using the wiki might know what it is before they arrive. If it's a content wiki on the web, you might have to explain the wiki's purpose.

- ✔ **Will people arrive at the wiki knowing their own role?** If you want people to contribute, you must ask them to do so on the front page. If they're just looking for information. you must tell them how to find it.

- ✔ **How nerdy are the users of the wiki?** Do they know all about wikis and how to use Web sites, or are they newbies? Skilled Web surfers are more familiar with the conventions of interactive design. For example, they intuitively understand how to browse a long list of links as a result of, say, shopping at Amazon.com.

The answers to these questions will illuminate the proper design of your front page.

Fundamentally, your front page must tell visitors how to use your wiki. The front page is your billboard that people see as they drive by. It shouldn't be subtle. It should grab the reader's attention and yell out the wiki's purpose. Some examples of what should be on the front pages of wikis include the following:

- ✔ **A content-focused wiki seeking input from new users:** This should say clearly what content is being created on the wiki and how the content is organized, providing interesting examples to inspire people. If the content-focused wiki is just getting started, the front page should spend more time recruiting new contributors and provide links to instructions on how to contribute content. If the wiki is well established, perhaps appeals for donations are more appropriate. The BibleWiki home page shown in Figure 8-4 touches all these bases.

- ✔ **A process-focused wiki used for project management:** This should start with a clear list of all the projects on the wiki. If the population using the wiki is really nerdy, not much needs to be explained. If this wiki introduces project management to a bunch of newbies, the front page should include a huge link to a page explaining what the wiki is all about and how to use it.

- ✔ **A process-focused wiki used for capturing tips on how to perform a task:** This should clearly show the steps involved in the task.

Figure 8-4:
The
BibleWiki
home page
explains
the wiki's
mission and
how to get
involved.

✔ **A community wiki:** This should have a front page that reflects the interests of the community. If the community is all about events, a listing of events should be right up front. If it is about educating people on a topic or issue, that topic or issue should be most prominent.

✔ **A brochureware wiki:** This need not explain that it is a wiki at all. Small businesses that use wikis to publish Web sites just need to display their products and services and provide contact information.

There is no single right or wrong way to design your front page. The goal is to start with something simple and then let the design emerge organically as the wiki is used. In some cases, the organic design of a wiki might not become obvious until after it's being used regularly and you hear complaints or ideas from the user community. Changing the front page is a cinch — just click Edit and redesign it to fit your needs. Three days or three months later, it might be time to change the front page again based on new feedback from the users. This is part of the natural evolution of a wiki.

Designing section pages

As your wiki grows, the number of categories of information that it tracks will likely expand quickly. One project becomes many, and you can branch out into whole new areas.

Section pages are the home pages for each category in a particular web of your wiki. Section pages provide more detail about specific topics.

Section pages can be used in all sorts of ways:

✔ **For a content-focused wiki,** you might have one section for each basic topic. Figure 8-5 shows a section page for branches of technology at Wikipedia. This section page serves as a portal to various technology topics.

Branches of technology		[edit]
Types	**Major fields of technology**	
Applied science	Artificial intelligence | Ceramic engineering | Computing technology | Electronics | Energy | Energy storage | Engineering physics | Environmental technology | Materials science | Materials engineering | Microtechnology | Nanotechnology | Nuclear technology | Optical engineering	
Athletics and recreation	Camping equipment | Playground | Sports | Sports equipment	
Information and communication	Communication | Graphics | Music technology | Speech recognition | Visual technology	
Industry	Construction | Financial engineering | Manufacturing | Machinery | Mining	
Military science	Bombs | Guns and ammunition | Military technology and equipment | Naval engineering	
Domestic / residential	Domestic appliances | Domestic technology | Educational technology | Food products and production	
Engineering	Aerospace engineering | Agricultural engineering | Bioengineering | Biochemical engineering | Biomedical technology | Chemical engineering | Civil engineering | Computer engineering | Electrical engineering | Electronics engineering | Environmental engineering | Industrial engineering | Materials engineering | Mechanical engineering | Metallurgical engineering | Nuclear engineering | Petroleum engineering | Software engineering | Structural engineering | Tissue engineering	
Health and safety	Biomedical engineering | Bioinformatics | Biotechnology | Cheminformatics | Fire protection technology | Health technologies | Pharmaceuticals | Safety engineering	
Transport	Aerospace | Aerospace engineering | Marine engineering | Motor vehicles | Space technology | Transport	

Figure 8-5: Use section pages for portals to topics.

✔ **For a brochureware wiki,** you might have a section page for each type of product or service that your company offers.

✔ **For a content-focused wiki,** you might have a section page that shows how to contribute content, such as the TaxAlmanac page shown in Figure 8-6.

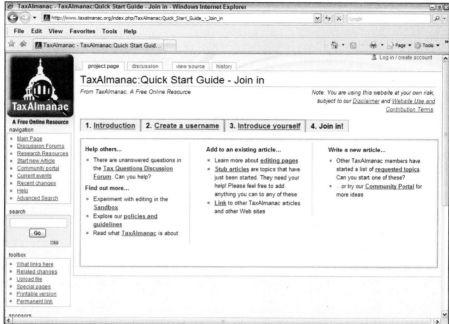

Figure 8-6:
The TaxAlmanac wiki shows the steps for joining and adding content.

> ✔ **For a process-focused wiki,** you might have a section page explaining the stages that a project goes through or the roles involved in managing each project.

Categorizing pages

The repeated tragedy of wiki design is that often just when you get the basic structure of front and section pages exactly right, a new idea occurs to you for another way to organize the content. *Categories* are the remedy for this problem because they allow many different groupings of content.

Categories are an alternate taxonomy to the one used in your information architecture. Categories create the equivalent of section pages that link to all the articles in a given category. Figure 8-7 shows the Wikipedia index of categories.

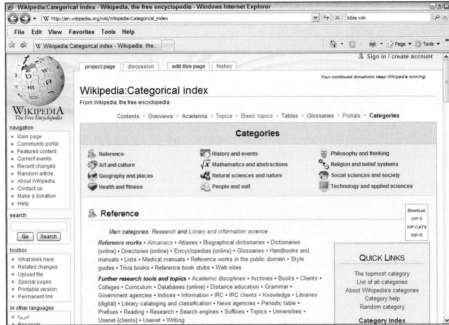

Figure 8-7:
The
Wikipedia
Categories
page has
hundreds of
categories.

Each category is a keyword tag indicating that an article is related to that category. For example, a Wikipedia article on Agile CMMI (a kind of software development) has the category tags shown in Figure 8-8. As you can see, a content page can be part of many different categories. Click a category name to link to its category page as shown in Figure 8-9.

Figure 8-8:
A content
page can fit
into several
categories.

Categories: Software engineering | Software development process | Standards | Quality

Pages in category "Software engineering"

There are 186 pages in this section of this category.

- Software engineering
- List of basic software engineering topics
- *
- List of software engineering topics
- List of software engineering topics (alphabetical)

A

- ATLAS Transformation Language
- Acette
- Actor modeling
- Agile CMMI
- AgileCMMI
- Analysis Effort method
- Application Development Facility
- Application and Data Integration
- Application software
- Architecture Tradeoff Analysis Method
- Artificial intelligence systems integration
- Aspect (computer science)
- Auditability
- Australian Software Engineering Conference
- Automated code review
- Autonomous agent
- Avionics software

B

C cont.

- Continuous integration
- Critical mass (software)
- Cross-cutting concern

D

- DO-178B
- De Novo Software
- Debates within software engineering
- Decomposition (computer science)
- Defensive programming
- Deprecation
- Derived Object
- Design-driven development
- Software development process
- Bug bash
- Distributed revision control
- Domain expert
- Domain-Specific Modeling
- Duplicate code
- Dynamic testing

E

- Electrical CAD
- Emios
- Encapsulated Process Object
- Encrypted function

K cont.

- Kernel streaming
- Knowledge engineering
- Knowledge engineers

L

- Larry Constantine
- Lean CMMI
- LeanCMMI
- Life-critical system
- Linguistic Method
- Literate programming
- Locality of reference

M

- Macro-Perimeterisation
- Management review
- Message queue
- Meta-Object Facility
- Meta-Process Modeling
- Meta-modeling technique
- MetaCard
- MetaEdit+
- Metamodeling
- Method stub
- Methodology (software engineering)
- Model Transformation Language

Figure 8-9:
Category pages list content pages in the category.

Most hosted wikis and installable wiki engines have support for categories. Categories are sometimes called *tags* or *tag clouds,* depending on the wiki farm or engine. For more on categories and tags, see Chapter 7.

Planning headers, footers, and left-hand navigation

With front and section pages, you can guide the user to certain parts of your wiki. But how do users get around after they arrive at content pages? As you've probably already seen, most wiki pages have links all over the place. As users click link after link, they can easily get lost, so the wiki needs some parts of the information architecture available on each and every page. Headers and footers provide this architecture on every page of the wiki. *Left-hand navigation* — the column of links often found on the left side of the screen — can do the same thing, or it can also provide links that are related to the current page.

Manually generate headers and footers for every page on your wiki is silly. Most wiki engines help you template or automate headers and footers. For now, consider how you want your headers and footers to look as well as how they can enhance your wiki. We discuss templates later in this chapter. (See "Using Templates to Design Content Pages.")

Now you can see how Prof. Tufte's advice can help you. (Read the sidebar on his work, elsewhere in this chapter.) Go to the wikis that you like. Look at what links and other explanatory information are in the headers, footers, and left-hand navigation. Make a list of the links you think would work for your site. Whenever you face another design issue, rinse and repeat.

The following sections show a few of the many well-oiled ways to use headers, footers, and left-hand navigation. The TWiki.org site — which is used as an example here — has been created over a period of eight years and has been honed to be as useful as possible. If you are going to follow Prof. Tufte's advice to follow proven examples, TWiki.org is a great example to copy. Plenty of other header designs could better fit your topic or web. Browse the wikis and Web sites that you admire, examine their navigation, and copy what works for you.

Using left-hand navigation

Wikis tend to follow the design conventions used by Web sites all over the Internet. Take a look at the TWiki.org page shown in Figure 8-10. Note that most of the links shown in Figure 8-10 are common to many wikis. The left-hand navigation links serve general housekeeping functions and include

- **Support Web:** These are links to the home page of the support web, allowing users to return to a known page from any location.

- **Support Guidelines:** This page explains general support practices.

- **Open Questions** and **My Questions:** These list support questions from the individual user and from other users.

- **Search:** These give quick access to the search page.

- **Changes:** These show recent changes to the wiki.

- **Subscribe:** These allow users to sign up for the wiki's RSS (really simple syndication) feed.

- **Notifications:** These allow users to sign up for e-mail notifications about changes to the wiki.

- **Register:** This sends users to the registration pages so they can create an account.

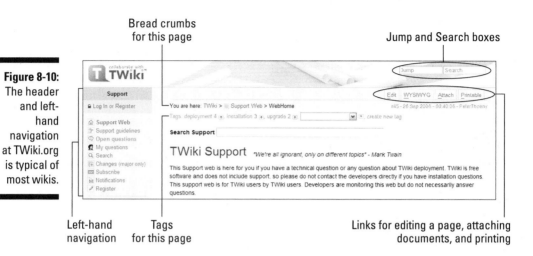

Bread crumbs for this page

Jump and Search boxes

Figure 8-10:
The header and left-hand navigation at TWiki.org is typical of most wikis.

Left-hand navigation

Tags for this page

Links for editing a page, attaching documents, and printing

On some hosted wikis, such as WikiSpaces and PBwiki, the left-hand navigation is simply a special page, and customizing that page to include your own left-hand navigation links is very easy. You might want to add links to all the webs within your wiki as well as links to the sections within the current web for easy navigation.

Creating effective headers

Like left-hand navigation, headers are a Web-wide standard, and most share some common elements. The header on the TWiki.org support web (refer to Figure 8-10) has several useful features:

- The header is a great place to play Hansel and Gretel — that is, to leave bread crumbs. *Bread crumbs* — the part of the page that begins with You are here in Figure 8-10 — show people where they are and how to get back to where they came from.

- Below the bread crumbs in the header are tags for the current page. This is another way that categories, mentioned earlier in this chapter, are implemented.

- In the top-right corner of most wiki headers are the Jump and Search boxes. Enter a page name in the Jump box and press Enter to quickly jump to that page. The search box allows you to search the entire wiki.

- Underneath the Jump and Search boxes are links that allow you to edit the page it text mode, edit the page in WYSIWYG (What You See Is What You Get) mode, attach files to the page, or display a printable version of the page. For more on using these features, see Chapters 2, 6, and 7.

The key to getting your headers correct — or any part of your wiki navigation, for that matter — is understanding how people use the wiki. Can everybody find what they need? That's great; maybe you don't need to update your headers or other parts of the navigation. If people can't find things they need, though, perhaps links to those materials should go in the header or other parts of the navigation. One way to listen to user input is to make sure that a link that provides feedback is prominent on all pages of your wiki.

Planning footers

The footer of each page is another functional space. Because the user is at the bottom of the page, he is likely to want a different set of functions than what he had at the top of the page although some navigational elements like bread crumbs should show up in both headers and footers. Figure 8-11 shows what the footers look like at TWiki.org. This footer contains the most common elements of a wiki footer, including these:

- ✔ **Edit, WYSIWYG, Attach,** and **Printable** links are repeated from the header. These are the most commonly used links, so having them in the footer adds convenience because people don't have to scroll back to the top of the page to find them.

- ✔ **Raw View** offers a way to view the underlying source code of the page. It is similar to the Edit button except that you can't save any changes. Raw View is useful if you want to copy and paste a bit of code or wiki formatting onto another page.

- ✔ **Backlinks** are links that search the web or the entire wiki for links to the page you are currently viewing.

- ✔ **History** provides links to recent versions and the changes made from version to version. For example, version numbers appear as r38 <r37 <r36, with older versions linked so that you can view them.

- ✔ **More Topic Actions** is a shortcut to a page showing more advanced changes that can be made to the page you are on, such as delete, rename, and move.

Figure 8-11:
A wiki footer includes basic navigational tools.

Edit | WYSIWYG | Attach | Printable | Raw View | Backlinks: Web, All Webs | History: r38 < r37 < r36 < r35 < r34 | More topic actions

Adding supporting pages to your wiki

Supporting pages add information to the wiki to meet special needs that are infrequent but necessary. Pages in the supporting cast can include any of the following:

- **Explanatory pages** that tell the rules of the wiki and describe community practices
- **Pages** that describe the processes for adding content
- **Site Map** (an overview of all the webs on the wiki)
- **Users** (a list of people who use the wiki)
- **Groups** (a list of the project groups or business divisions using the wiki)
- **Templates** that show how contributed pages should look
- **About Us pages** that explain who created the wiki
- **Frequently Asked Question (FAQ) pages**
- **Copyright and content licensing pages**

Although these pages aren't always the most exciting to create, they are a great investment most of the time because they help expand the range of your wiki to include newbies. Keeping up such pages is an important task in managing a wiki, which we discuss in Chapter 12.

Supporting pages are one place where Prof. Tufte's design advice ("copy what works") applies quite well. (See the sidebar, "Prof. Tufte's design advice.") Supporting pages are copied from one wiki to the next all the time. Sites running the MediaWiki engine (see Chapter 10) start off with an excellent structure for supporting pages, including pages that solicit donations and explain what is happening with the community.

Using Templates to Design Content Pages

The content pages are the heart and soul of every wiki. Chapter 6 covers all the ways that content can be added to a page using bullets, tables, images, and other formatting ideas. Chapter 7 walks through the various techniques for linking pages. Ideally, after a wiki gets going, the community of people using the wiki keeps busy adding and adjusting pages.

Wikis should be flexible, not trapping content into a rigid structure. However, the potential flexibility of wikis doesn't mean that structure is always a bad thing or that contributors to a wiki don't want or need help creating pages. When you look at a wiki like the Baseball Reference Wiki (www.baseball-reference.com) or Encyclopedia Gamia (http://egamia.com), you see pages and page elements that look just like one another. If your wiki has pages that look the same or share common elements, it makes sense to give wiki contributors a leg up on creating those pages. Page templates do exactly that.

The simplest sort of page template appears on hosted wikis like WikiSpaces, PBwiki, and others that focus on making wikis easy to use. Page templates on these sites offer a page that has headings for various sections, along with sample lists of bullets or table entries. Figure 8-12 shows the screen at PBwiki that allows you to choose from a variety of templates.

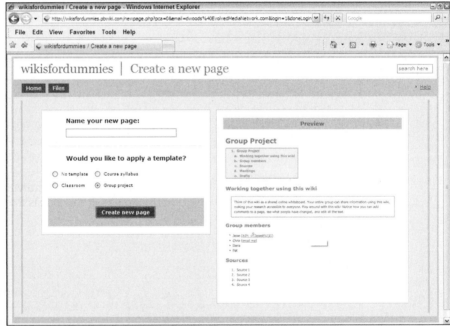

Figure 8-12:
Templates make creating a new page easy.

When a page is created from a template, some generic placeholder content is inserted in the new page, as shown in Figure 8-13. You can then fill in your own content for the new page. Most hosted wikis allow you to use predefined templates, and some allow you to create your own templates either in the free version or after an upgrade.

Figure 8-13:
Replace the template's placeholder content with your own.

The idea of templates applies to parts of pages as well as entire pages. Content-focused wikis, such as www.Baseball-Reference.com, feature hundreds of parts of pages than can be included in other pages to provide links to useful information. For example, the Baseball Reference Wiki includes pages discussing Major League Baseball ballparks. The page for each individual park includes a box with links to all the other ballparks. If this box is a template, it can easily be inserted on each page by entering the following text:

```
{{MLB ballparks}}
```

The box shown in Figure 8-14 appears as a result of this wiki markup.

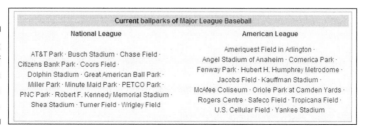

Figure 8-14:
This box of links is created with a template.

Creating templates for portions of pages is a process that varies widely depending on the wiki engine you're using. To get a general idea about how templates can be created and used, see the Wikipedia article on templates at en.wikipedia.org/wiki/Wikipedia:Template_namespace. Chapter 12 describes how to manage templates.

Another method for populating pages automatically is to use forms and variables. Forms are often filled in with variables that contain useful information, such as the name of the page or the name of the wiki. Forms and variables are discussed in Chapter 14.

Adding Visual Panache to Your Wiki

Black text on a white (or off-white) background has been used by newspapers for centuries as the standard way of presenting useful information. It works for wikis, too. The information age is not bound by the physical world of ink and paper, though. The color and images on a wiki can convey just as much information as the content of the webs, topics, and pages.

Take another gander at the Wikipedia home page. This time, go online (http://en.wikipedia.org/wiki/Main_Page) to see it in color. The Wikipedia front page has a blue section and a green section, and below those is a purple section. You know just by looking at the page, consciously or not, that those colors signify different sections. The page also has logos, icons, and photographs that make up the page's graphic design.

Graphic design is a subtle and tricky art. People spend entire careers perfecting the balance of type, color, and imagery that appear on a page. Wikis provide you with the basic knobs and dials to control the graphic look of pages. While doing it yourself, it is always a good idea to follow Prof. Tufte's advice and copy attractive designs. If your site really becomes popular, consider turning to a trained graphic designer to at least give your wiki a visual once-over.

Most hosted wikis and all the installed wiki engines allow a large degree of control over how pages look. Some of these changes — such as colors and graphics — are simple. Others — such as the ability to display your wiki on a cellphone or PDA screen — require advanced knowledge of things like Cascading Style Sheets (CSS), XSL Transformations (XSLT), and other ways of controlling the layout of pages.

Using themes and skins

Most hosted wikis offer a variety of visual themes to choose from. A *theme,* also sometimes called a *skin,* is a collection of all the advanced settings — color, fonts, backgrounds, text size, and more — combined to create a certain look. Sometimes themes and skins just change the colors and graphics. Other times they change the entire layout of a page. To change a theme on WikiSpaces (www.WikiSpaces.com), follow these steps:

1. **Click the Manage Space link in the left-hand navigation area.**

2. **In the Space Settings section, about halfway down the page, click the Look and Feel link.**

3. **Click the link under Themes to display the page shown in Figure 8-15.**

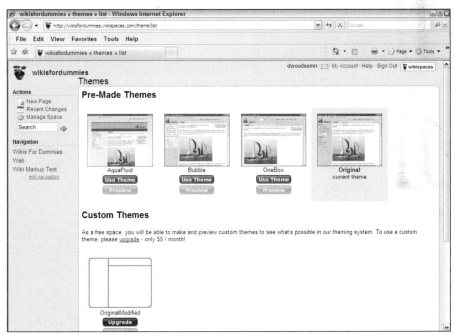

Figure 8-15:
You can choose one of several predefined themes on WikiSpaces.

4. **Select a theme and then select the appearance of all the pages on your wikis changes.**

By choosing a theme, you get a different combination of fonts, colors, graphics, and layout to give your wiki a new personality. You can create your own themes on WikiSpaces and other hosted wikis, but frequently, this involves an upgrade to a premium version of the site for a fee. Be aware that building new themes and skins usually requires some knowledge of CSS or XSLT.

Choosing color

One of the most effective uses of color on a wiki is to assign each web its own color. This does not mean that *all* the text, background, and other elements of the web should be shades of, say, orange. However, giving each web a small colored box next to its name, and then automatically having that color be used in key places throughout that web, can enhance a user's sense of place and make your wiki look professional.

For example, suppose that you have a wiki that's primarily used for collaboration, but a blog also resides on the wiki where users can post links to news articles. One way to differentiate the blog portion of the wiki from the collaborative sections is to give the blog web a different background color. That way, anyone visiting the blog will understand that this page has a different purpose than other parts of the wiki.

Note: Using color in page backgrounds should be handled with caution. It is all too easy to have background color overwhelm both the text and the rest of the page. That said, much like the use of colors to signify different webs, background colors on a page can be an excellent way to differentiate the type of information being presented.

One way to use colors is to explicitly enter the colors you wish for table backgrounds or fonts, as described in Chapter 6. Hosted wikis, such as WikiSpaces, make color choice easier. In the Look and Feel section of the Manage Space area of WikiSpaces, the form shown in Figure 8-16 allows you to change colors used for the background, text, and links in the wiki's theme.

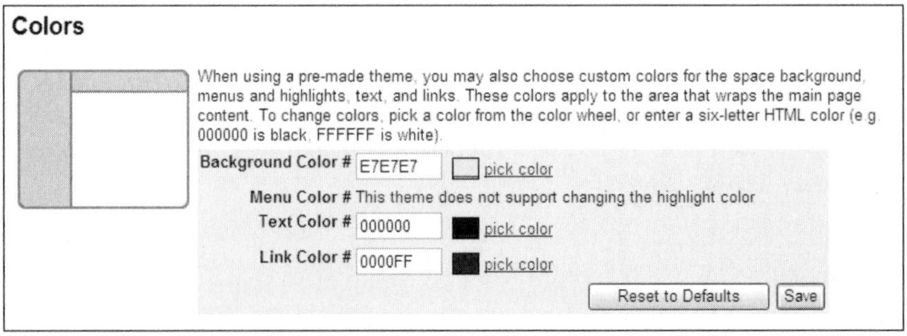

Figure 8-16:
Select
the colors
used in a
WikiSpaces
theme.

Colors

When using a pre-made theme, you may also choose custom colors for the space background, menus and highlights, text, and links. These colors apply to the area that wraps the main page content. To change colors, pick a color from the color wheel, or enter a six-letter HTML color (e.g. 000000 is black, FFFFFF is white).

Background Color # E7E7E7   pick color

Menu Color # This theme does not support changing the highlight color

Text Color # 000000   pick color

Link Color # 0000FF   pick color

Reset to Defaults   Save

Personalizing wikis with logos

If you don't already have a logo, you probably want one. Just a simple image can really set your wiki apart and make it more memorable. Logo design is an art unto itself, best handled by an artist or graphic designer. The question for wiki builders is not whether to use a logo but where?

The conventional use of logos, which has been evolving since the earliest days of Web sites, is to place the logo in (or near) the upper-left corner of the page. Visit Amazon.com, Motorola, or AOL — pretty much any well-known Web site — to see a logo in virtually the same place on every site. Of the many reasons for this placement, consider this: No matter how small you make your browser window, a logo in the upper-left corner will still be visible. Suffice it to say, it's a tried-and-true place to put your logo.

Putting your logo in the upper-left corner of every page is a simple exercise for most hosted wikis. In the Look and Feel section of the Manage Space area of WikiSpaces, for example, is a form that enables you to upload your logo.

If you want your logo to look good, make sure it is a size that will fit into the area allotted for it in the wiki theme. In the themes on WikiSpaces, logos are 150 x 150 pixels or smaller.

Another way to spruce up your wiki is with a *favicon*. Favicons are *favorite icons,* which are 16 x 16 pixels. Browsers display the small icons in the address bar, browser tabs, and bookmarks. Favicons help users find your wiki more easily. To add a favicon to your wiki, typically you upload an image file with the icon to the wiki and then refer to it using an HTML <IMG> tag. Some wikis, like TWiki, make this easier by creating variables that make inserting the favicons easier.

Part III

Promoting, Managing, and Improving Your Wiki

The 5th Wave   By Rich Tennant

"I got this through one of those mail order PC companies that let you design your own system."

In this part . . .

This part addresses the issues that you encounter when taking your wiki world-wide — or at least to the people whom you want to use your wiki. Chapter 9 presents the playbook for attracting users to your wiki. If you are in an organization that can't use a hosted wiki, we cover that here as well.

Chapters 10 and 11 explain choosing and installing the right wiki engine on your own servers. Chapter 12 explains how to manage a wiki, and Chapter 13 explains how to protect one.

Chapter 14, the most technically advanced chapter in the book, explains how to add special features to create a *structured wiki* — one that can automate tasks and treat wiki pages like records in a database.

Chapter 9

Attracting Users to Your Wiki

*A*s we show throughout this book, wikis are a great way to create and share information in an organization or group. You set up your wiki, open the doors, and — like an expectant shopkeeper — keep looking out the window for wiki customers. But where are they? And why aren't they wiki-ing?

Remember that new technologies take time to understand and (most importantly) accept. Imagine the early skeptical days of movable type, radio, telegraph, television, and microwave ovens. Now, those technologies are part of everyday life. A wiki is similar. It looks like something that everyone understands — a word processor document — but follows a strange set of new and odd rules. *Anyone can edit one? Anyone can erase anything in one? How can that be useful?*

This chapter shows you how to attract users. To attract users to your wiki, have your *elevator pitch* ready — a multisecond description of the project and its values. You can say something like, "With our wiki, we now have a great repository for all the Widget Sales Support information. I bet you want access." Those interested in both Widgets and Sales Support will probably jump at the chance. The folks in the Widget factory might not. But first, we talk about how *not* to attract users to your wiki.

Wiki Don'ts

Pitching a wiki to a busy executive, a community member, or an average Internet user is an uphill battle. With a number of competing stimuli — Web TV, mobile phone calls, e-mails pinging in the background — your wiki won't get the attention it deserves unless you're able to explain its value in a few simple words. To paraphrase that old mountain-climbing chestnut, you can't convince someone to use your wiki because "it's there" (or even because it's just plain cool). A wiki's value directly corresponds to how well your audience understands your goals and project.

Your primary decision is whether you want to publicize your wiki. If the wiki consists of private poetry on the life cycle of the naked mole rat, your audience is probably limited to a few biologists and fans of hairless mammals. If you're attempting to tackle a huge topic — The Beatles, skeet shooting, or training and breeding the common cockroach — you're ready to publicize.

Don't confuse your audience

State clearly what you wish to accomplish. Think about your first page. What does it include? MyCoolWiki is a horrible title because it tells the viewer nothing about your content. Comparatively, The Beatles Wiki is a great title. The Magical Mystery Tour Wiki is an even better title. Make it amazingly easy to understand what you're offering. Create a separate wiki for each project you work on — hey! they're free! — and don't try to do too much on one page.

Also, encourage the use of WYSIWYG (What You See Is What You Get) editors for new users, and allow users to attempt using markup languages when their skill level is up to snuff. (For more on WYSIWYG editing and wiki markup, see Chapter 2.) If they can't understand what you're asking them to do, it's almost impossible for them to do it.

Don't fire and forget

The worst thing that you can do is create a wiki and expect others to update it. The easiest part is obviously clicking a few links and starting up your wiki. (To see how easy it is to start a wiki, read Chapter 5, which shows how to get a wiki up on a hosted wiki in a matter of minutes.) The hardest part is convincing people to use it.

Don't just build your wiki and send an e-mail announcing it. Take and share ownership of this new project and be ready to educate those who don't understand what's going on. Whether you're working on a Midwest Regional Sales Office wiki or a Siamese Kitten wiki, you are the seed crystal around which everything else will coalesce. Nothing is sadder than seeing a lone wiki, sniffling in the rain, waiting for its owner to come back.

Don't spam

If people are interested in your wiki, they will stick with it after you show them what it is. You'll find no value in bombarding your audience with e-mails and reminders. Grab a few key members and teach them how to use a wiki; then ask them to bring others on board. If your wiki is public or part of a community, don't go to forums or message boards and trumpet your wiki's superiority. Don't visit Wikipedia and link to yourself. Wikis are made by networks of like-minded people, not by angry spam victims.

For a community wiki, talk to a few major blog and forum owners on your topic and ask them for help in fleshing out your project. If they see value, they'll quickly add to your initial progress. If they don't see value, they'll ignore it. Don't be pushy. In a corporate setting, grab a few close confidants and start your wiki. Make it a useful repository for information. Then, move on to other members of the team. Wikis are organic, accreting information and value over time.

Don't get the Field of Dreams syndrome

You watched the movie *Field of Dreams* and took to heart the mantra, "If you build it, they will come." You spent hours on your logo. You posted your first three paragraphs inviting the world to join you on a magical ride through the history of fine cheeses or the Form R-55515 in the XRZ 12-12 Advanced Motorized Mulch Extractor Manufacturing Directives. Yet no one has contributed to your wiki, and your hits have been dismal. It seems that only you and Mom want to read about brie, and even she stopped visiting last week.

Take control of your wiki and build it, but don't expect an instant audience. A wiki audience consists of people who trust your information and want to help it grow. If they happen upon your pet project and are interested, they will stay. Create a core group, seed your wiki, and let it grow. Don't force it.

The Wikitorial debacle

In 2006, the *Los Angeles Times* tried to create an open forum for readers to talk back and comment on editorials in the paper. Dubbed the *Wikitorial,* it heralded a new era in journalistic openness — or did it?

The result was a free-for-all of name-calling and nastiness that was taken down right away. The Internet sometimes reduces inhibitions and encourages our more base instincts to bare themselves. Therefore, use wikis where there is a chance that a cooperative community can form. Throwing a wiki at a controversy just means that you will end up with a nasty wiki.

Don't overdesign

The best wikis consist of a few blocks of text, an image or two, and a request for more updates. Of course, any text or images posted to the wiki should relate to the wiki's topic. Animated GIFs, pictures of your cat, and diagrams of the ancient pyramids, for example, don't belong on a wiki about fishing. File-download links and help pages should be easy to identify. Explain exactly what each page is about at the top. Your readers will thank you.

Don't overmanage

A wiki is like your little digital baby: It's hard to let it out into the world. You want to coddle it, take care of it, and make sure that no one defaces it. Well, relax, Mama or Papa! Wikis are designed to be constantly changing and fluid. If your audience wants to put up thoughts on advanced Needle-in-a-Haystack Finding Techniques on your procedural How to Mow the Grass wiki, let them go for it. You can always expand the wiki to encompass new information, or even start a new web or wiki. (For more on planning wikis and webs, see Chapter 8.) Be ready for surprises.

Don't go on wiki suicide missions

Wikis don't have magical powers. They cannot create camaraderie where none exists, nor can they streamline an out-of-control operation. They are not powerful information magnets, nor will they make your team better writers, more organized, or more intelligent. In short, without a strong guiding hand, wikis are useless.

Wikis cannot promise instant returns or unbelievable creativity. Wikis allow users to quickly and easily update and upload information. Wikis are no substitute for holding a meeting, contacting your team members, or doing hard work yourself.

Wiki Do's

In the preceding sections, we describe what not to do when implementing and promoting your wiki. Avoiding common mistakes will help prevent you from turning people away from the wiki. Instead, take positive actions to make your wiki better and more popular. The following sections show you some "wiki do's" that will help your wiki attract users and keep them coming back for more.

Seed your wiki

A useful wiki, from a user's point of view, is one that has a clear goal and some information already in place. Take Wikipedia, for example. When you visit a topic, you see a concise, hopefully coherent entry on a particular subject. If you find the information useful, it served its purpose, and you and Wikipedia can both go about your business. If you find the information lacking or incorrect, you can edit the entry and expand upon it. That's how wikis work.

But if that *seed* — some initial, useful information — isn't there, there is no impetus for others to create it. This is true with almost any page, from the lowliest procedural wiki to the most exalted managerial wiki. Whether you're creating a collaborative style sheet for a school newspaper or building an homage to *NSync, if you don't take the first step, we can guarantee that no one else will.

To begin, create an introductory page with links to the sub-pages you expect to create. Writing about The Beatles? Make pages for John, Paul, Ringo, George, and maybe even Pete Best. Index these pages on a main page and explain your goals. Create a page for their discography. Create a taxonomy (see Chapter 8 for more on taxonomies) that makes sense for you and your readers. Here's an example:

> *Welcome to Joe's Beatles Page. Our lofty goal is to create a compendium of knowledge on The Beatles and their many albums. It is a wiki, which means it consists of a set of linked pages that you can edit simply by clicking the edit button. Take note, however, that wikis have a set of commands and formatting tags that you will need to use when adding to or modifying this collection. Visit our Help page to learn how to edit this wiki.*

Your goal is to create something that

- A casual reader can understand and use immediately.
- Someone "in the know" can edit and update alongside your already pithy and useful work.

Remove barriers

Getting people to understand wikis is the first step in the long slog toward wiki Utopia. Productivity tools have come and gone. Anything that dilutes our attention (except, of course, videos of kittens wearing sun bonnets) is a potential drain on productivity rather than an improvement.

Your goal, then, is to make it abundantly clear that the wiki will help, not hinder, the average user. Here's how:

- **Educate:** Convincing your office mates to buy doughnuts on Friday is easy. Making them invest in a corporate or community wiki can be difficult. That's why you have to be the wiki evangelist. Reply to e-mails with a quick note — "Hey, this looks like some great content for the wiki. Check it out here. . . ." — and add their input in a logical place. Take a few hours and invite everyone into the conference room or club meeting place (*Hint:* bring doughnuts) and show them what a wiki is, how it works, and how easy it is to update. Wikis are like chess: They take a moment to learn and a lifetime to master. Who knows? There might even be some latent wiki savants in your group who take the project and turn it into something you never expected.

- **Instigate:** Create wikis from already existing documents. Send out, by e-mail, the URLs to specific wiki pages instead of including the content of the pages in the e-mail itself. Print out a wiki entry with the URL prominently displayed, and pass it out at your next meeting. Flatter your friends and tell them, "This is going into the wiki." Do it enough times, and they'll either stop calling you or ask what a wiki is. Your goal is to make your wiki as visible and useful as possible. Don't be afraid to use it.

- **Promote collaboration:** Trust networks between people can be strong or tenuous. If you have a good spirit of teamwork, take advantage of your existing trust relationships and work together on a local wiki. Then take it "national," as it were, by offering to make wikis for other departments and connecting them. With a little careful connectivity, you can create an organization-wide storehouse of knowledge.

Instilling a sense of ownership and involvement is doubly important for personal or public wikis. With these wikis, people are contributing during their (usually scarce) free time. Take advantage of your initial contacts with fans of your topic and offer to add their input to the group wiki. Then, reach out to other information sources and ask them for input or suggestions. People love giving advice: When they see their advice appear in a public wiki, they feel like they've contributed. Start local and work your way out to a wider network.

Encourage wiki-users to be bold

An old adage in computer training states, "There is nothing you can do to break the machine." No matter how many times you press the Enter key, move the mouse, or click the wrong thing, everything can be fixed with a flick of a switch. This is true of wikis — especially wikis with change control. Allow your wiki users to do whatever they want, whenever they want. Do they need to put up images of the internal workings of a jet engine? Help them compress the images to JPEGs and start posting. Do they need to create special web forms for user input? Show them how to build them. It's quite easy. (See Chapter 7 for more on using images in wikis; for more on web forms, see Chapter 14.)

This doesn't mean that your co-authors should populate the wiki with jokes, sound files, and pictures of puppies. Instead, it means you should tell your potential community members that there's nothing they can do to destroy the wiki. There is always a backup; no one will yell at them for posting something; and the more information on the wiki, the better it becomes.

Starting a Community Wiki

Say you're starting a wiki for a personal project, club, or obsession — a *community wiki*. The goal is simple: Catalog some interesting information on a particular topic. Whether it's a wiki on the life cycle of the common salamander or a bowling league players roster, a wiki is a great resource for research and information maintenance. The following sections provide tips on how to make your community wiki a powerful tool.

Focus the wiki

Don't fill the wiki with useless information. Create pages for each topic and keep the focus clear and uncluttered. Begin by creating a main page and then branch off from there, creating a tree hierarchy (as shown in Figure 9-1) that's easily managed and understood. Tell your co–wiki-ers to keep it simple as well. Decide what your wiki is about and stick with it.

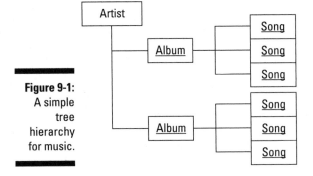

Figure 9-1:
A simple
tree
hierarchy
for music.

Advertise the wiki

No, you don't have to buy a billboard on Route 66 to advertise your wiki. All you have to do is explain your wiki and share your mission with the community. You can easily do this in a quick e-mail to friends or in a post on a community forum. Many potential users might not even know what a wiki is, let alone how it can help their cause or organize their obsessions. Explain the concept but don't harp on it. Discretion is the watchword — if people are interested, they will join you.

Assist the wiki

Become the group wiki expert. Be ready to answer questions and seed content that might come from other channels. Why not go through a group's forums and bring out definitions of terms or historical references? Grab some old discussions and create a FAQ list or glossary. Build a schedule or team roster, add some contact information, and show others where the information is located and how to edit it. Treat the wiki as an extension to your private Web site.

If you're creating a procedural wiki, ask for how-tos from your most active members. This will encourage more folks to stop by to read about your musings on model rocketry or interpretative dance. A wiki offers a more focused and condensed view of a procedure than a blog does. Blogs are organized by date and usually reflect opinions. Wikis are organized by topic. Wikis are like books, except that anyone can add a page at any time. Wikis are great for storing information. Be the person who shovels that information into the wiki, allowing everyone else to follow suit.

Promoting Wikis in the Office

Convincing your entire knitting circle to use a wiki might be hard, but what about convincing an entire office? As we discuss earlier in this chapter, attracting users can be a lonely row to hoe, but don't despair. Your goal is to begin the evangelization process and hope — or wait — for the rest of your office to fall into line. Some ideas that might help include the following:

- ✔ **Begin by focusing on private wikis.** Create pages for use in your own workspace and send those pages instead of Word documents when possible. Obviously, sending a web page when a formal report is due might not be a good idea, but creating a precedent for wiki usage is key.

  If the boss asks for a report that is traditionally sent in a Word document, do it in Word and then make a quick copy in the wiki. Send both to your boss, noting that you will update the report with any changes and update the wiki as well. This is a win-win situation because you followed the letter of office law while allowing the idea of wikis to intrude on your boss' psyche. Of course, this will work only if you get the go-ahead from the right person to use a wiki in the first place. Springing wikis on a group without consultation can succeed, but it can also blow up in your face.

- ✔ **Build templates for the office.** If you pass around meeting minutes, create a meeting minutes template that's easy to use and understand. If you need to store procedures, sit down with one of the team members who is well versed in a particular skill or system and ask him to help you create an example procedural page. Create a "best practices" page for your team, highlighting the best of the best in your particular department.

- ✔ **Determine where wikis will be most effective.** Help desks, programming teams, and other service-oriented departments are best suited to using wikis. Many expensive tools such as Lotus Notes and Microsoft Exchange have long promised wiki-like functionality, but only with wikis has the simplicity of adding and cataloging information allowed that promise to come to fruition.

✔ **Demonstrate wiki potential to the company.** When you first propose a wiki to people outside your direct sphere of influence, they'll probably look at you funny. You and your buddies in Accounting can finish each others' sentences, but the rest of the company might not be on the same page. Use your existing webs of trust to pitch and grow your wiki project. Don't expect the CEO to start posting if you can't get the mailroom folks to pitch in.

You can argue all you want — "This project will help us in the long run!" — but unless you create a small wiki biodome in your own department, no one will appreciate what you've done. By creating value in your own smaller environment and then — by using networks of trust — expanding it into other parts of the organization, you can at least be sure people will understand your mission and, tacitly, appreciate the effort.

✔ **Remember the hierarchy.** Just like you can't jump from department to department, you can't jump up the corporate ladder unless you have a key to the executive washroom. Pitch the wiki idea to the CEO's assistant. He or she can easily send the CEO some wiki links outlining procedures or executive decision trees and pique the higher-up's interest.

Living with Wiki Life Cycles

After your wiki is up and running, you can expect a wiki life cycle that will happen whether you're running a community or an office wiki. All wikis begin at the planning stage, and the following sections walk you through the normal life cycle of a wiki. Understanding this cycle will help you plan and implement your wiki as well as continue to be a key part of the wiki as it matures. The job of promoting wikis and encouraging their use doesn't end after they have successfully launched. You must keep spreading the word and helping in different ways as a wiki matures.

Deploying the wiki

After you have office or community buy-in for the wiki, the busywork begins. The initial deployment stage involves lots of fire-fighting and helping new users get up to speed. You'll also want to begin thinking about corporate branding and working with a design team to ensure that your new site matches the community or corporate identity.

Work out access controls and roll-back systems as well. This ensures that the people who are supposed to be using your wiki have access and also that interlopers can't mess up your hard work.

Growing your wiki

The growth phase involves getting everyone on the same page and expanding your wiki to other parts of the organization. At this point, you're ready to start repurposing old documents for use on the wiki and helping users create new ones using templates and other user-friendly tools.

The growth phase lasts as long as you let it, but this stage requires care and pruning so that the wiki doesn't become too overgrown.

Taming large wikis

A large wiki contains more than 50,000 pages. We know what you're thinking — who has time to read all that?! However, some wikis can become monsters — and the sooner you tame the monster, the better. Some key steps in that taming include

- **Create a wiki** *taxonomy.* This organizing principle is the first step in taming a monster wiki, which involves splitting the wiki functions into separate pages and webs. (See Chapter 8 for more on planning logical wiki taxonomies.)

- **Create a glossary area.** This area that includes term definitions is a key tool to ensure that all your wiki users speak the same language.

- **Create a strong list of standard pages.** *Standard pages* can include pages for participants, attachments, and chit-chat. Include standard pages in every wiki web to allow easy access to certain data and to create a predictable structure for the other webs, making it easier for users to navigate your wiki webs.

- **Prepare a pruning system that culls dead and unused pages after a certain period.** This culling process helps prevent confusion that occurs when people encounter pages that perhaps don't fit into the new mission of the wiki or those that were started or suggested but don't look like they will ever take off. Perhaps a quick e-mail notification to authors would jog their memories when it comes to removing or fixing dead links.

- **Consider hiring a wiki librarian.** A librarian can keep everything in its right place and act like a switchboard operator or referee, maintaining order in a cluttered environment.

Ending a wiki's life

Some wikis go gentle into that good night. Perhaps the wiki just wasn't meant to be, or maybe its department closed. Prepare yourself for expiring wikis by backing up wiki data and keeping it archived in a safe place. Shutting down a useful tool like a wiki is often heart wrenching, so be sure to think happy thoughts as you lock the backup disks away and shut off the wiki server.

Chapter 10

Choosing an Installed Wiki Engine

In This Chapter
▶ Understanding the basic wiki groups
▶ Deciding your wiki's purpose
▶ Comparing choices on the wiki menu
▶ Going on a wiki walkabout

*W*iki engines are the programs that run on Web servers that allow people to create, edit, and publish wiki pages. When you use a wiki, you use a wiki engine. The question, then, is who installs, runs, and maintains that engine? In most cases, that doesn't have to be you. In Chapter 5, we cover the easiest kind of wiki to use: a hosted wiki. With a hosted wiki, the people who run the hosted wiki take care of everything — installing the wiki, customizing it, backing it up, and maintaining the users and permissions — and you just sign up and use the wiki engine. Pretty darn easy.

For some people, though, a hosted wiki just won't do. For example, if you work for a company that's using its wiki to create or manage sensitive information, you might not trust a hosted wiki to keep that information safe. Or, if you plan on customizing your wiki heavily and making it do the advanced things we cover in Chapter 14, you want your own engine so that you can control absolutely everything about it. No matter the reason, after you decide that you need to run your own wiki engine, you have to make a decision: Which wiki engine is the best one for your needs?

Choosing software is never easy — sort of like deciding on a cellphone provider with a two-year contract. You try to do all the research to make sure that you make the right decision, but you never really know until you've used the cellphone for a while and gotten a few bills. Choosing a wiki engine often makes people nervous for the same reason. Instead of a contract, you implicitly have a time investment to learn about the wiki engine and then to work with it to see whether it meets your needs. Worry not. This chapter helps you create a short list of wiki engines that are most likely to meet your needs.

Evaluating Basic Wiki Groups

A huge part of successfully using wikis is understanding what you and the people you want to work with need from a wiki. A scout troop, for example, has different needs from a multinational corporation. Chapter 3 describes the different uses of a wiki. You might find that your needs fall into one of the categories listed there. If not, perhaps your use of a wiki will break new ground.

After you figure out what kind of wiki you need, your next steps are to

1. **Understand the capabilities of the various categories of wiki engines.**

   In this section, we give you a rundown of the wiki engine categories and detail when to use each.

2. **Determine the requirements for your wiki.**

   The "Assessing Your Wiki Requirements" section can help you determine wiki needs.

3. **Explore the capabilities of all the different wiki engines that are right for you.**

   The "Comparing Wiki Engines" and "Going on a Wiki Walkabout" sections can help you find the wiki engine that meets your wiki needs.

4. **Select the one with the best fit.**

More than 50 different wiki engines are available that are stable and reliable, and probably 25 more are in earlier stages of development. Each engine was created to meet a different set of needs and has a different set of features.

Most wiki engines are distributed as *open source,* meaning that they were created by developers who wanted to share their work with the rest of the world instead of selling it. Unlike commercial software, open source software is distributed without charge. (Yay! It's free.) The *source code* — the programming language files used to build the software — is also available free of charge. This open source model means that anyone with a good idea can pick up the source code and improve the software. Unfortunately, sometimes open source software doesn't come with all the documentation, installation scripts, and other support that makes software easier to use. (Boo! Extra work might be involved.)

To get a handle on what different wiki engines can do, we categorize the wiki engines into five basic groups, each matching a particular set of requirements:

✔ **Desktop wiki engines** run on your own computer and aren't accessible to other computers on your network or on the Internet. These can be an attractive way to store information for personal use. Sometimes people keep notes in wikis while they create content or organize information. Desktop wikis like TiddlyWiki, which creates an entire wiki within a Web page using Java, can keep track of information that is just for your own personal use, such as to-do lists and appointments. It comes as a single HTML file that you can save to your hard drive. (There are other options for creating shared wikis with TiddlyWiki.)

✔ **Hosted consumer wiki engines** are made to be as easy to use as possible. Commercial wiki providers such as Confluence Hosted (a hosted version of the Confluence wiki engine) and Google's JotSpot are easy to set up and use. So are free hosted wikis like WikiSpaces, seedwiki, PBwiki, or XWiki. All these wikis avoid the more gruesome installation and configuration challenges that you can encounter with some open source wikis.

The downside is that these wikis are hosted, which may not be acceptable, with limits to how they can be customized and extended. If all you want is a basic wiki, though — which can solve a lot of problems on its own — a hosted consumer wiki should be fine. If you think a hosted consumer wiki is what you need, take a trip to Chapter 5.

✔ **Industrial-strength wiki engines** are the state of the art in wiki technology. This category of wiki comes with features for security, integration with corporate computing environments, creation of complex documents, administration, spam prevention, and customization. TWiki.org and MediaWiki are two of the most powerful open source industrial strength wikis. Socialtext and Confluence are commercial examples. These wikis are used at some of the largest companies in the world including Google, Sun, Motorola, and others. The catch is that to use these wikis, you must have servers to host them as well as a system administrator to install, configure, and administer them.

✔ **Special-purpose wiki engines** apply the idea of wikis to specific needs. Here are some examples: Swiki is a search-oriented wiki. DokuWiki is designed to create documentation. MoinMoin has some great features that support the publication of complex documents. TikiWiki is focused on content management. When your need matches one of these special-purpose wikis, you'll feel like you're in heaven because all your needs are taken care of. Special-purpose wikis usually require that you have access to a server and know how to install, configure, and administer a wiki engine.

✔ **Development wiki engines** are designed to be platforms for development. TWiki has an architecture that allows it to be extended with plugins and add-ons that have been used by developers to create hundreds of special features. Kwiki and MoinMoin were created to be easily extensible. Development wiki engines allow you to take the basic functions of a wiki and then add new features that do anything you want. Development wiki engines are for the hackers among us who have the software development skills and want to put them to use building perfect solutions.

Given this list, you probably know right now which category is right for you. You are probably right, but don't be hasty. Keep an open mind. To choose the perfect wiki, you must analyze what you will be doing with your wiki. And who knows? You might discover that you actually need a different engine than you initially thought.

Assessing Your Wiki Requirements

The best way to decide which wiki engine to use is to first determine what you will use your wiki for — managing a work project, collaborating to write documentation, or sharing information on panda bears? Also think about who will contribute to the creation and maintenance of the wiki — experienced software developers or perhaps grandma, who got her first computer last Mother's Day? Then evaluate how each wiki engine could help. Open a new word processing file or get out a pad of paper. To begin creating a requirements document for your wiki, read this section and make notes about what your wiki is and will be.

The skill level of the user population

The right choice for a wiki engine depends largely on the skill levels of your users. For example, the wiki that Google uses (TWiki.org, an industrial-strength wiki) might or might not be the wiki engine for you. Google is full of brainiac engineers who learn new stuff pretty darned easily. Although your Cub Scout troop members might have bright parents, they might be a bit less adaptable or have less time or motivation to adapt to a new tool. Consumer wikis might work better for them. Here are the types of questions to help you define your user skill base:

- ✔ Are they experienced, every-day computer users, or are they beginners who aren't familiar with a browser? (If they can't use a browser, using a wiki would be a stretch.)

- ✔ If they are regular users of word processing programs, would the idea of wiki markup send them up a tree? Do they need WYSIWYG (What You See Is What You Get) editors?

- ✔ Can they understand camel case links? (For more on wiki markup and camel case linking, see Chapters 6 and 7.)

Don't just imagine the skills of new users. Sit them down in front of the wiki engines that you're considering and see how they do when they create and edit pages. You can discover a lot in just a few minutes, such as their ability to figure out how to move around the wiki as well as how comfortable they are with browsers in general. If you don't have access to the users of your wiki because you're putting it out in front of the general public, find stand-ins for who you expect to use the site.

The number of people who will add content

People who create and improve content provide the heartbeat of a wiki. In most wikis, for every person who edits a page, tens, hundreds, or even thousands of people might look at the page and use the information. The more contributors you have, the more you need to craft the experience to their needs — and the more you should lean toward an industrial-strength wiki.

The number of people who will view the content

Consider how many other people might be involved. Tens, hundreds, thousands, or even more? If a small number of people (10 to 20) are coming together in a casual way to work together (such as a scout troop), almost any wiki engine can handle that level of traffic, either as a hosted wiki or as a wiki engine running on a small server (like a desktop personal computer). In other words, a consumer wiki would do fine.

When you start reaching into the hundreds of potential wiki users, especially when they're all in the same organization or share the same information technology infrastructure, the more you enter the realm of the industrial strength wiki. Or if your wiki will face the public — for example, a wiki to be used by *American Idol* to create biographies of each candidate — you're likely going to have a ton of users. In that case, the wiki engine and servers you choose better be industrial strength — or *scalable,* as the engineers would say.

There are no J.D. Power and Associates ratings for wiki scalability and quality. However, you can answer questions about speed, reliability, and performance by looking at what sorts of sites use which wiki engines. Most wiki engines have Web pages listing sites using the engines. Most sites based on wikis say which wiki they use in the About section or in a Powered By link at the bottom of the page. MediaWiki, the wiki that runs Wikipedia, has lots of developers worried about making it reliable and speedy. For other wikis like WikiSpaces, the point is not scalability but ease of use. For more on scalability, see the later section, "Comparing Wiki Engines."

The wiki's security level

Some wiki engines come with a full-blown security system so that webs and pages can be protected from viewing by unauthorized eyes. On the other end of the spectrum, some wiki engine developers look down on the whole idea of security as a profoundly un-wiki idea. If you have some pages that are for some users but not others, you need an industrial-strength wiki. Think about what your security needs are before you go on a second date with a wiki engine.

The wiki's potential size

Some wiki engines handle a modest amount of content (fewer than 500 pages) rather well but then keel over and die when the number of pages gets too large (more than 5,000, for example). If your wiki will grow to tens of thousands of pages, sticking with industrial strength wiki engines makes sense.

Whether you need automation

A little history from Dan: When I started using my wiki, I never thought that I would end up automating anything. I just wanted pages that could be shared so I could write books. It didn't take long before I set up e-mail notifications to inform me when certain pages were changed. Then I set up reminders about when projects were due. Then I started mailing notes into the wiki that were automatically converted to wiki pages. Then I started keeping track of interviews and research in a wiki-style database that allowed me to search, sort, and write reports about pages that represented individual interviews and research documents.

Some people write advanced applications with wikis as a platform. If you're the kind of person who pushes technology to the limit to help you, consider a development wiki engine like TWiki or Kwiki that supports this sort of automation. (See Chapter 14 on structured wikis for a tour of the sort of tricks you can play.) Figure 10-1 shows a TWiki interview log page that was automatically generated from pages that were used like database records.

Interview Log

Add new

ID	Status	Interview Date	Name	Organization	Contact Info	Job Function, Web links, Comments
001	Invited	2006/01/16	Foo Test	Bar Corp	an@example.com 555-1212	test func, Site, Just a test
002	Interviewed	20060505	Jimmy Donal Wales	Wikipedia		founder, , Chapters 4, 5, 10 and 16
003	Accepted	2007/01/09	Matt Wiseley	Editme	Matt Wiseley <matt@editme.com> 781-771-5410	, , His pre-interview notes on our questions
004	Accepted	2007/01/08	Ken Tyler	Seed Wiki	ken@seedwiki.com	, , Pre-Interview notes from Ken
005	Interviewed	2007/01/09	James Byers	Wikispaces		, , Explains the history of WikiSpaces ? and his thoughts on wikis
006	Invited	2007/01/10	Sam Obio	Bluwiki		, , Explains his ides about Wikis and the story of BlueWiki ?
007	Interviewed	2007/01/12	Steven Marder	Swicki - a wiki-style search technology		, , Steven explains what Swicki is.

Figure 10-1:
This page was generated automatically.

Your technical expertise level

Consumer wiki engines are made to be easily installed and never have to be touched except for creating and editing pages. *Development* wiki engines are designed to be toolkits that allow developers to go wild creating new things, such as full-blown applications with workflow and document management. Industrial-strength wikis require care and feeding of the sort mentioned in Chapter 11. Can you handle the technical work yourself, or do you have access to people who can help you?

More from Dan: Although I did a fair amount of programming early in my career, I don't do much nowadays although I do heavily customize and extend my wikis through consultants who form an informal development department for me. All the people I work with are experts in Perl, TWiki, or both. If you want to push your wiki engine to the limit and develop custom applications, try to create the same sort of network for yourself. If you hang out with a bunch of PHP (PHP Hypertext Preprocessor) hackers, perhaps MediaWiki would be the best choice. There are Python wikis, Perl wikis, Java wikis, Ruby wikis, and all sorts of other wikis.

Choose your wiki engine so that getting the technical help will be easy. If you don't have access to technical skills because you don't have them or can't find them, stick with a hosted consumer wiki.

Your willingness to become a wiki champion

Although it's easy to dream about how a wiki can benefit an organization, bringing a wiki to life requires a lot of work. You must choose a wiki, get it running, seed it with content, and basically do all the things in this book related to creating and managing a wiki. If you want to change your organization through a wiki, you should seriously consider whether you have the passion — and most importantly, the time — to become the wiki champion who carries out all the tasks just mentioned. Don't fret if you're too busy to do the job. Perhaps someone else in your organization would be delighted to take on the role of wiki champion, so you can work together to create a wiki.

Comparing Wiki Engines

If you followed the earlier parts of this chapter, you have a handful of notes about what features and capabilities you need in a wiki. Feel proud of yourself.

You just lived up to the Socrates advice to "know thy wiki self." At least we think that's what he said. With these basics in mind — the parameters that your wiki engine must fit — you can start comparing wikis to choose the best one for your needs.

Making the safe choice

If you're not much of a do-it-yourselfer and you just want to make the safest choice, worry not. Table 10-1 lists the most obvious choices for various ways of using wikis.

Table 10-1	Safe Wiki Engine Choices for Various Uses
Wiki Purpose	*Safe Choice*
Publishing content, creating content in a group, creating a content-focused wiki	**MediaWiki** (www.mediawiki.org) The most popular wiki engine for content-focused wikis has many features for group collaboration and lots of documentation. **DokuWiki** (www.splitbrain.org/ projects/dokuwiki) A great choice if you're creating technical documentation or a user manual.
Creating advanced applications for collaboration and content management	**TWiki** (http://twiki.org) The most advanced structured wiki with many plug-ins to provide automation. Twiki.org also has a large, active developer community.
Creating a wiki in a company	**Confluence** from Atlassian (www.atlassian.com) **Socialtext** (www.socialtext.com) **TWiki** (http://twiki.org) All popular choices. All three provide support and professional services, which are must-haves for many IT departments.
Playing around	All the hosted wikis mentioned in Chapter 5 are great for playing around. **TiddlyWiki** (www.tiddlywiki.com) A wiki implemented in JavaScript in a downloadable page; the quickest way to have your own wiki that you can use even when you are not online.

Exploring the WikiMatrix

If you're a do-it-yourselfer and you want to perform your own analysis, here's some advice: "Know thy wiki engine." For a wiki comparison, visit WikiMatrix. org (www.wikimatrix.org), which was created by the German company CosmoCode. The WikiMatrix home page is shown in Figure 10-2.

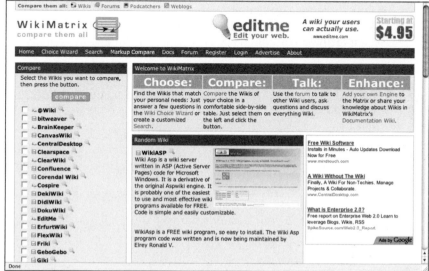

Figure 10-2: Compare wikis at WikiMatrix.

If you've ever tried to do side-by-side comparisons of software products, you can appreciate the great gift that WikiMatrix represents. Most of the time, getting an objective analysis of one software product compared with another is almost impossible. Software vendors frequently don't make accurate comparisons easy. Although you won't find barriers when gathering information about open source projects (which most wikis are based on), reading through Web sites and even source code to analyze what an open source project does can be hugely time-consuming.

The WikiMatrix home page

On the WikiMatrix home page shown in Figure 10-2, you can see a set of four main headings, each of which can be hugely helpful in your quest to understand wikis:

- ✔ **Choose:** The link under the Choose heading leads you to the Wiki Choice Wizard that asks you a series of questions and suggests wikis that can meet your needs.

- ✔ **Compare:** On the far left side of the page, the Compare button allows you to select any number of wikis and then create a page listing side-by-side comparisons of more than 40 different features that wikis have, such as which programming language they are based on, if they support WYSIWYG editing, and what database (if any) is used to store the wiki page files. (The Compare link in the center of the page just goes to Help text.)

✓ **Talk:** The link under the Talk heading leads to the forums where you can discuss your wiki needs and ask questions.

✓ **Enhance:** The first link under the Enhance heading leads to the page explaining how to add a wiki to the matrix. The second link leads to the Documentation Wiki of WikiMatrix, which is a storehouse of detailed information about many of the wikis included in the matrix.

The WikiMatrix Wiki Choice Wizard

A great way to start using WikiMatrix is to take a quick tour through the Wiki Choice Wizard to see the wikis that it suggests. This wizard asks such questions as

✓ Is a page history needed?

✓ Is WYSIWYG editing crucial?

✓ Do you prefer a hosted or installed solution?

✓ Do you need your own domain?

✓ Do you need corporate branding?

After answering these questions, you see a results page like the one shown in Figure 10-3.

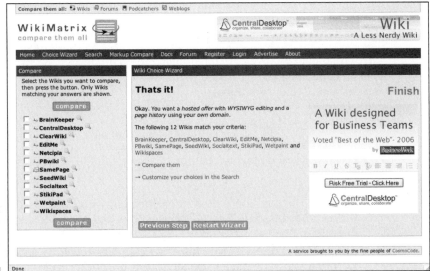

Figure 10-3: WikiMatrix helps you find wikis that meet your specific requirements.

You can jump right to a comparison by clicking the Compare button on the results page. Or to find out more about wikis that are suggested, click the Docs link to see a page similar to Figure 10-4.

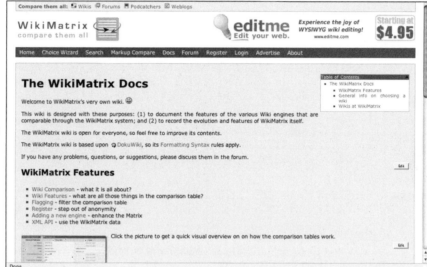

Figure 10-4: The WikiMatrix also serves as a storehouse of wiki documentation.

The WikiMatrix Docs page holds explanations of the features included in the comparison as well as a list of all the wikis in the WikiMatrix. For some of the wikis, extensive documentation is available on WikiMatrix. Just because a wiki doesn't have documentation on WikiMatrix doesn't mean that the documentation doesn't exist; it might exist at the home site of the wiki.

The WikiMatrix features list

The most valuable part of WikiMatrix could well be the WikiMatrix features list. Simply click the Wiki Features link in the page shown in Figure 10-4 to see the page shown in Figure 10-5.

For a great education in wiki features, such as page permissions and e-mail notification, read through the entries in this list. They explain in varying levels of detail the features that are supported by most wiki engines. For example

- ✔ **Text Files:** Click this link to find an excellent discussion of how wikis support text files as well as the advantages and disadvantages of using them to store wiki pages.

- ✔ **Host Blocking:** This entry explains how host blocking can be used as a last resort to stop a wiki vandal from harming a wiki.

- ✔ **Content Include Feature:** This entry explains how the Content Include feature allows one page to be all or part of another page.

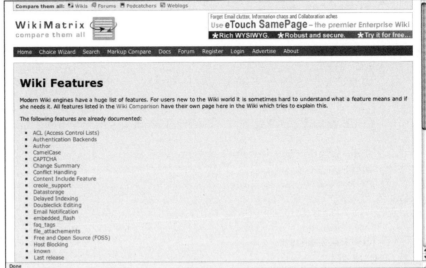

Figure 10-5:
Review the features list at WikiMatrix.

After you read through the feature list, you can make much more sense of the WikiMatrix Compare functionality. A few hours spent traveling between the features list and the Compare function should help you get the idea of what sort of choices you have in a wiki engine.

Keep your users in mind while you perform comparisons. You can easily get lost in the cool things that wikis can do and forget that the success of your wiki depends on getting a bunch of newcomers excited about learning to create and edit wiki pages.

When comparing wiki engines, take a minute to look at the discussion areas. You might see a post from someone who switched from one wiki engine to another — and the reason why.

Going on a Wiki Walkabout

The categories at the beginning of this chapter and the questions about your requirements will help you narrow down what sort of wiki you want to use. And time spent at WikiMatrix prepares you for afternoons wiled away blissfully thinking about wikis. However, in order to choose the right wiki, you must not only think about wikis, but you must use them and see how each wiki engine feels. That's why you need to go on a *wiki walkabout* — meaning that you must examine your short list of choices as closely as possible to see how well each wiki meets your requirements.

One of the reasons why WikiMatrix exists is so that information about wikis is easily available rather than cloistered and hoarded. Environments where you can play with wikis are also easy to find, either on each wiki engine site or on sites built from a particular wiki engine. You can thank the world of open source for all this easy access and openness. In the world of commercial software, getting access to the same level of information is much harder.

For someone choosing a wiki engine, the availability of wiki *sandboxes* — special areas on the sites for wiki engines that allow you to edit wiki pages — provide a perfect way to gain hands-on experience. Instead of having to read and analyze, you can play and discover what works for you.

You're not the only one who can play with a wiki. Invite others who are interested in your wiki to join you on your walkabout and see how they like each wiki engine.

Follow along as we take you on a sample wiki walkabout for a hypothetical project. In this example, we are choosing a wiki to create a policy and procedure manual for a bank. The initial requirements are

- ✔ **Security:** The users for this project are in a bank, which is supported by an IT (information technology) department that enforces heavy security on all computing resources.

- ✔ **Editability:** Users should be able to change and update the content.

- ✔ **Long page modification:** The first version of the manual was created using an open source wiki that presents wiki pages as one long page; experience shows that it is difficult to teach others to modify long wiki pages. A common wiki feature, called *section editing,* makes editing long pages much easier by allowing editing of just a portion of the page without having to edit the entire page.

- ✔ **PDF creation:** The wiki form of the content will serve as the means by which users access the document online. The policy and procedure manual will also be published and distributed as a PDF document. It would be great if the wiki engine had a feature to convert pages to PDFs or to export pages as plain HTML.

- ✔ **Easy installation/IT-compliant:** The solution should be easy to install and also acceptable to the IT department of the bank.

With all these factors in mind, we focus on industrial-strength and special-purpose wikis during our walkabout.

Points to ponder on your wiki walkabout

Your wiki walkabout will be different from ours. As you review and evaluate various wikis, keep the following points in mind:

- ✔ **Part of choosing a wiki is deciding when *not* to use a particular wiki.** Choosing a wiki can be like a multiple choice test: Narrow your answer by ruling out the ones that really aren't going to work for you. You're left with fewer choices to decide between, which will be an easier decision to make.

- ✔ **Rest assured that no wiki choice is always correct.** And don't be surprised if nothing seems very clear. With every wiki engine — just like with other types of software — some functionality will be missing, and you will have challenging problems to overcome.

- ✔ **Choosing a wiki engine is not irrevocable.** It's not even as bad as a cell-phone contract. You won't be locked in to your wiki engine, and you don't have to pay a fine to start over with another. You gotta start somewhere. Making a wiki engine choice and getting experience using a wiki is more important than agonizing over making the perfect choice.

- ✔ **You can test before making a commitment.** The great thing about wikis is that you can try one before you commit to it. If you want to test something like section editing, have at it. Usually, all the other features that you might want to use can be tested as well.

XWiki walkabout

A good wiki to begin with is XWiki, which is an industrial-strength, open source wiki that can be used in a hosted manner and has a huge amount of interesting features.

XWiki.com (www.xwiki.com) is a commercial, open source, hybrid company. Under this increasingly popular model, a group of people create a product as open source and then attempt to build a business by selling wiki development services and additional features. XWiki offers hosted wiki solutions for free and for a fee.

At the home page of XWiki.org, shown in Figure 10-6, you can get more details about the features. See how XWiki stacks up for our hypothetical bank wiki:

- ✔ **Security:** XWiki has a user-authentication system that allows control over page-access rights.
- ✔ **Editability:** XWiki supports WYSIWYG editing.

  ✔ **Long page modification:** XWiki doesn't support section editing, which allows editing of smaller sections of large pages.

  ✔ **PDF creation:** XWiki can create PDFs from pages and has a powerful templating system that controls the format of pages.

  ✔ **Easy installation/IT-compliant:** XWiki has all the advanced plumbing to fit into a large corporate IT environment, such as features to use existing user IDs and security.

One aspect of XWiki is a little worrisome: The product is based on Java, which is a language that most IT departments like; and it uses Java modules like Jakarta and Hibernate, which are also powerful and reliable software components. Although these are industrial-grade, open source components, installing XWiki at the bank might cause problems for the IT departments that are sometimes nervous about open source. The XWiki reliance on the MySQL open source database might also be hard to arrange at the bank.

After playing around with XWiki, we felt that the performance was slow and then we really started to think that the lack of section editing was a showstopper.

MoinMoin walkabout

At the MoinMoin wiki (`www.MoinMoin.WikiWikiWeb.de`), you might find a lot to like. The site is clear, clean, and readable, and it has a feature that allows a page to be shut off from editing. Other features include

  ✔ **Security:** MoinMoin has all the security features you would need.

  ✔ **Editability:** MoinMoin features a great WYSIWYG editor. In place of the traditional Edit button, you can substitute an Immutable Page indicator, meaning that certain pages can be shut off from editing.

  ✔ **Large page modification:** MoinMoin doesn't have section editing.

  ✔ **PDF creation:** MoinMoin has many advanced publishing features for converting pages into complex documents.

  ✔ **Easy installation/IT-compliant:** Like DokuWiki, MoinMoin stores pages in files, so a database isn't required. MoinMoin is written in the Python language. Python programmers tend to charge higher rates than PHP programmers and can be more difficult to find.

The MoinMoin wiki has an elegant architecture for macros and templates. Also, for each part of MoinMoin that is extensible, the site has a marketplace where extensions can be downloaded and examined. But at this point, you're really missing the lack of section editing.

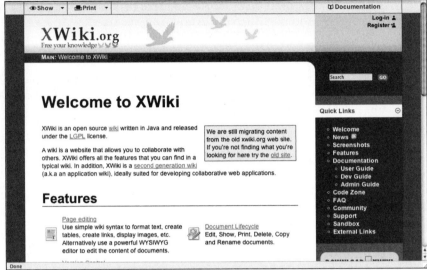

Figure 10-6:
XWiki is a
commercial,
open source
wiki.

TWiki walkabout

TWiki (http://twiki.org) is one of the most popular wikis used in the workplace. It is very extensible, with over 250 plug-ins at TWiki.org. The Web site lists many consultants that offer support and professional services for the open source wiki. TWiki has a long laundry list of features; the ones Dan is interested in include

- ✔ **Security:** TWiki has sophisticated access control features where you can define who can create, edit, and view content on a page level, web space level, or the whole site level. With LDAP (Lightweight Directory Access Protocol) integration, you can even restrict access based on LDAP groups.

- ✔ **Editability:** The user can choose between wiki markup editing and WYSIWYG editing.

- ✔ **Large page modification:** TWiki has good section editing, but the optional SectionalEditPlugin needs to be installed.

- ✔ **PDF creation:** TWiki has a number of extensions to export content into HTML and PDF. With the GenPDFAddOn, you get a PDF link on every page to generate a PDF file on-demand.

- ✔ **Easy installation/IT-compliant:** TWiki is relatively easy to install. It has a short list of required software; like DokuWiki and MoinMoin, TWiki does not require a database. TWiki is written in Perl.

TWiki has many advanced features to create composite documents. Variables can be defined to create text with dynamic content; pages can be included into a master document; it is even possible to pass parameters into included pages, which allows one to create reusable text fragments. A table of contents can be generated automatically, both on individual pages and across pages. The templating system makes it easy to create a set of pages that share a similar layout.

TWiki would be a possible choice for this wiki project, as it is for most of Dan's projects, but the fact that TWiki's more advanced features are not needed for this project caused Dan to continue his walkabout.

MediaWiki walkabout

MediaWiki (www.mediawiki.org/wiki/MediaWiki) is one of the best publishing wiki engines in existence. It powers Wikipedia and has a large developer community that focuses on scalability and ease of use as well as creating powerful tools for editing and managing a large community of editors, writers, and readers. MediaWiki has a lot of other great features, too:

- ✔ **Security:** MediaWiki has a good security model for public wikis, but it lacks fine-grained access control that's needed in a corporate environment.
- ✔ **Editability:** It offers excellent editing tools, including a WYSIWYG editor.
- ✔ **Large page modification:** MediaWiki has section editing.
- ✔ **PDF creation:** MediaWiki supports PDF creation.
- ✔ **Easy installation/IT-compliant:** MediaWiki is well regarded and installs easily, but it requires the MySQL database. MediaWiki is written mostly in PHP and another obscure language called OCaml, which might cause jitters.

MediaWiki would work in most ways, but we're nervous about asking the bank to install a database.

DokuWiki walkabout

DokuWiki (http://wiki.splitbrain.org/wiki:dokuwiki) is a clean and stripped-down wiki with the ability to edit portions of pages. Figure 10-7 shows the ultrabasic home page of DokuWiki.

Don't judge an open source project by its Web site. Excellent open source projects sometimes have bare-bones Web sites. A great Web site is usually a sign of quality, but there's no guarantee. Look at DokuWiki's features:

- ✔ **Security:** DokuWiki doesn't offer much in terms of security.
- ✔ **Editability:** The text editing is not WYSIWYG but is supplemented by buttons that make wiki markup much easier to use.

✔ **Large page modification:** The DokuWiki section-editing interface is quite natural and easy to use.

✔ **PDF creation:** DokuWiki doesn't support PDF creation, but its template system (although not advanced) — as well as the raw code that it uses — is simple and easy to understand. DokuWiki is written in PHP. Even if you're not a PHP expert, it's not too hard to figure out when you look at the code for the templates. You can also easily find PHP programmers.

✔ **Easy installation/IT-compliant:** DokuWiki has the ability to use an external user-registration database. Pages are not stored in a database. All its pages are stored in text files. For some purposes, this might be a problem — like if you want to search and sort through pages or do advanced application development — but this simplicity means that the bank might be more willing to install it because no database is required.

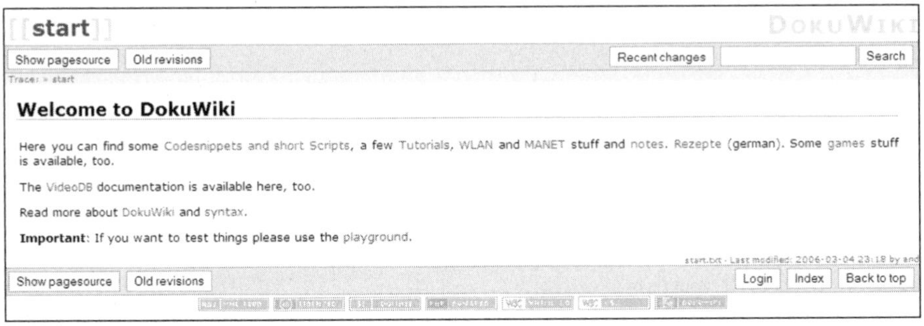

Figure 10-7: The DokuWiki home page.

When we went to the DokuWiki playground to enter text, the performance was fast, and the user interface was easy to understand, so not much training would be required. The automatic TOC and the search indexing are also excellent features that we weren't looking for but realized might be useful.

At the end of the walkabout, we decided to move forward with DokuWiki. We knew that we would have to spend some time to make DokuWiki work how we wanted, but the functionality it started with was sound. We also felt comfortable that we would easily be able to get help making DokuWiki work how we wanted and that it wouldn't be too hard to adapt DokuWiki given its simplicity.

Chapter 11

Getting Your Wiki Engine Up and Running

In This Chapter

▶ Getting your own wiki engine running

▶ Finding an Internet mechanic

▶ The basic requirements for getting started

▶ Getting help during installation

▶ Configuring the TWiki engine

*W*ikis are run by programs called *wiki engines.* For most of the history of wikis, getting a wiki engine running was much harder than most people could handle. That's why engineers had all the fun with wikis. They had the servers and advanced technical skills, allowing them to set up their own wiki engines in a snap. Today, hosted wikis (also known as *wiki farms*) allow many more people to get in the game. At a hosted wiki, a generic wiki engine is already set up and running on the farm. To get a hosted wiki up and running now takes only five or ten minutes and very little technical expertise.

Although hosted wikis have their place, many organizations and situations require their own wiki engine that is under their control and not shared in any way. The market has responded in a variety of ways to this demand. No longer do you need access to your own server to get your own wiki engine going. There are many ways to have a wiki that you can call your own.

Chapter 10 shows you how to select a wiki engine. This chapter helps you get your chosen wiki engine up and running. To give you an idea of what exactly is involved in installing and configuring a wiki, we tell you how to set up a TWiki engine, one of the most popular wiki engines. Although every engine is different, this chapter walks you through the basic steps of setting up pretty much any wiki engine that you might choose.

Finding a Home for Your Wiki

For many people, hosted wikis don't make sense for a variety of reasons. Perhaps the information on the wiki is sensitive. Or, the access to the wiki needs to be controlled. You might want to have the wiki tightly integrated with your work environment so you don't have to sign on separately to the wiki and keep track of an additional login account. Compliance regulations might forbid any sort of hosted arrangement.

Many people get started on a hosted wiki and then at some point want to customize more than the hosted environment allows. Hosted environments are always adding features to prevent this exodus, but it happens anyway, especially when you want to create structured wiki applications.

Whatever your reasons, if you want to host your own wiki, you must find a way to get your own wiki engine up and running on a server that you control. Of the many ways to make this happen, we recommend the following three as the most viable.

Hosting on a shared or dedicated server

If you're getting a wiki engine running on your own, the best plan is to find one of the many hosting providers on the Internet that sell access to shared or dedicated servers. One such site is www.wikihosting.net, which lists wiki-hosting offers. (See Figure 11-1.)

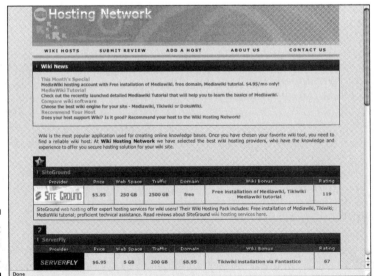

Figure 11-1:
Find hosted
wikis here.

Shared and dedicated servers differ in the following ways:

- ✔ **Shared server:** A *shared server* allows your Web site to run on a machine that hosts many other Web sites. You control your Web site but share the server space with other Web sites. If everything works well, none of the Web sites interfere with each other. Shared web hosting can run anywhere from $5 to $40 per month.

- ✔ **Dedicated server:** A *dedicated server* is one on which your Web site runs on a server exclusively. This is the model that Dan prefers for his wikis, though it is more expensive than using a shared server. Dedicated servers run anywhere from $100 to $300 per month, depending on the services offered and size of the machine being rented.

In either of these hosting methods, you might be able to install a wiki when you purchase your server. This is not usually the case, however, and you must find someone to help you who has the necessary skills and know-how — an *Internet mechanic,* if you will. After you find your mechanic, you grant the helper access to the server so that he or she can install your wiki.

For many small businesses or organizations that want to use advanced wikis, dedicated hosting can be a good choice. In larger organizations, though, this approach might not work because users must go outside the approved environment and must also remember a new username and password.

Hosting inside your organization

A second wiki-hosting choice is to use a computer inside your organization. Two reasons why wikis have flourished inside engineering organizations is that they have plenty of servers and that engineers know how to be their own Internet mechanics.

The rest of us aren't so lucky. If you try to set up a server on your own, you might run afoul of organizational policy. If you ask for a server to be set up, you might run into a lengthy bureaucratic process, or you might be forced to find financing in some budget. This is often harder than you'd like. Although complaining about red tape is easy, that crimson cord is usually in place to make sure that any server is properly supported, backed up, and maintained.

Contracting all-in-one hosting and consulting

The demand for wikis has become so great that the market has developed all sorts of services. Some dedicated and shared hosting providers give you a server with a wiki already installed. MediaWiki is probably the most common wiki engine used in this way. After you get started with such a wiki, though, you must perform maintenance and make updates to it on your own.

If you don't have access to your own Internet mechanic to handle advanced wiki configuration, consider looking for a hosting solution that provides professional wiki consulting as well. XWiki.com (`www.xwiki.com`) is a hosted wiki that truly offers all-in-one service. In addition to basic various hosted and self-run wiki services, you can hire XWiki.com consultants to help you get everything going and afterward on an as-needed basis.

Getting help requires money, of course, but XWiki (see Figure 11-2) has an impressive list of happy clients on its site. Fees to set up a wiki can run from several hundred dollars to several thousand dollars, based on how much customization you are seeking, whether there is existing content to convert, and the number of servers you will need to run your wiki.

Figure 11-2:
Find
consultants
at
XWiki.com.

Finding an Internet Mechanic

Most people are comfortable with flipping a compact disc into a computer and then clicking through the steps to install a word processor program or a photo database. Wikis don't run on your desktop computer, though. For a wiki engine to run properly, it must be installed on a Web server, which requires some knowledge of how Web servers work. Expertise is also required to set up the storehouse of wiki pages, configure account login settings for users, and so on. If installing a program on your desktop is like filling up the gas tank of your car, installing a wiki engine is like changing your own oil and spark plugs and resetting the ignition timing.

The technical challenges of running a wiki engine mean that you must make a choice:

- Take the time to master all the different aspects of Web hosting and system administration to get a wiki engine running.
- Find someone else to do it for you.

For most wiki owners, including Dan, the right answer is to find someone to help. You likely want someone with the following skills:

- **System administration:** Your Internet mechanic should know how to set up and run a server as well as be knowledgeable about system and network administration.

- **Internet administration:** The Internet mechanic should be knowledgeable about Web servers and the Internet in general.

- **Programming and database experience:** Programming skills are usually beneficial, as is having experience managing databases.

- **Security experience:** An understanding of Internet security and the changing threat-landscape is very important.

- **Backup and recovery expertise:** Wikis are often work repositories. As a result, they must be carefully backed up by someone who doesn't take chances. Losing your hard drive is nothing compared with the pain that you could feel when your entire wiki is lost or can be recovered only from month-old backups.

If you're serious about getting a wiki going, sit down and make a list of all of the people you know who are programmers and system administrators and anyone else who might be qualified. Web sites such as Guru.com (www.guru.com) or RentACoder (www.rentacoder.com) help you find freelance Internet mechanics. Although setting up a wiki does require special knowledge, an expert Internet mechanic can help you get a wiki engine running in just two to three hours.

All you really need to tell your Internet mechanic is

- Which wiki engine you want to set up
- Where he can download it from

Then, grant your mechanic access to the administrative account for the server that you're going to use for your wiki.

It helps if you get an Internet mechanic who is familiar with the wiki software you want to have installed. Some open source wikis list consultants on their Web sites. On TWiki.org, you can find this list at

```
http://twiki.org/cgi-bin/view/Codev/ConsultantsForHire
```

If you're setting up a wiki inside a company, your information technology (IT) department is the place to start. In some companies, getting help can be as easy as getting someone to throw a wiki on a development server so you can play with it. In other companies, it might mean a lengthy process of getting the wiki approved.

Here's another good resource for information about what it takes to be an Internet mechanic for wikis:

```
http://twiki.org/cgi-bin/view/TWiki/AdminSkillsAssumptions
```

This page at TWiki.org — the wiki shown in most of the examples in this chapter — lists the desirable attributes for a wiki Internet mechanic, as shown in Figure 11-3.

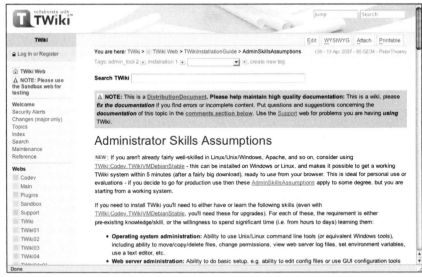

Figure 11-3: TWiki.org provides this handy reference to system administration skills.

Starting Your Wiki Engine

The first requirements for getting a wiki engine running are getting access to a server and (unless you have the expertise yourself) finding a qualified Internet mechanic to help you. At this point, we assume that you've done both these things. If you haven't, please refer to the earlier sections of this chapter. The following sections help you prepare for and configure a wiki engine.

Meeting system requirements

After you have a server and a mechanic lined up, the next step is to make sure that your server has everything you need. For TWiki (one of the more well-documented engines available), this is as simple as going to the Web page at

```
http://twiki.org/cgi-bin/view/TWiki/TWikiSystemRequirements
```

This page (as shown in Figure 11-4) lists the detailed system requirements for the TWiki engine.

Figure 11-4: The TWiki Web site lists system requirements for the TWiki engine.

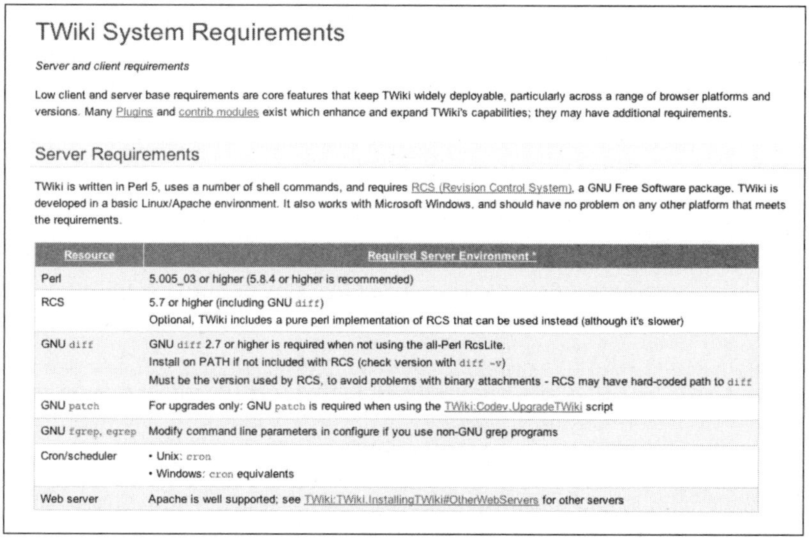

TWiki System Requirements

Server and client requirements

Low client and server base requirements are core features that keep TWiki widely deployable, particularly across a range of browser platforms and versions. Many Plugins and contrib modules exist which enhance and expand TWiki's capabilities; they may have additional requirements.

Server Requirements

TWiki is written in Perl 5, uses a number of shell commands, and requires RCS (Revision Control System), a GNU Free Software package. TWiki is developed in a basic Linux/Apache environment. It also works with Microsoft Windows, and should have no problem on any other platform that meets the requirements.

Resource	Required Server Environment *
Perl	5.005_03 or higher (5.8.4 or higher is recommended)
RCS	5.7 or higher (including GNU diff) Optional, TWiki includes a pure perl implementation of RCS that can be used instead (although it's slower)
GNU diff	GNU diff 2.7 or higher is required when not using the all-Perl RcsLite. Install on PATH if not included with RCS (check version with diff -v) Must be the version used by RCS, to avoid problems with binary attachments - RCS may have hard-coded path to diff
GNU patch	For upgrades only: GNU patch is required when using the TWiki:Codev.UpgradeTWiki script
GNU fgrep, egrep	Modify command line parameters in configure if you use non-GNU grep programs
Cron/scheduler	• Unix: cron • Windows: cron equivalents
Web server	Apache is well supported; see TWiki:TWiki.InstallingTWiki#OtherWebServers for other servers

In addition to hardware requirements for the server, TWiki also requires that certain software be installed. This is very typical of wiki engines and many other open source applications. Some of the open source programs that TWiki requires are

- ✓ **Perl:** This is the programming language used to write TWiki. TWiki came to life because Peter Thoeny, inspired by another wiki, started writing a new wiki in the Perl language. To make TWiki work, a version of the Perl language must be installed on your server. Version 4 of TWiki requires Perl Version 5.6.1 or higher. (The *or higher* means that newer versions [those with a higher version number] will also work.)

- ✓ **CPAN Modules:** CPAN, the *Comprehensive Perl Archive Network,* is a repository of thousands of these modules. CPAN modules are programs written in Perl that perform special functions. These modules are the software equivalent of an inventory of special-purpose, reusable parts. The developers of TWiki used these modules to save time, but it's crucial that all the required modules are installed; otherwise, TWiki won't work. The TWiki requirements page also lists optional CPAN modules that could be useful for special purposes.

- ✓ **Other software:** TWiki uses RCS (a version control system), GNU utilities for determining the differences between files and applying changes to the software, `grep` utilities for searching through text files, and the `cron` scheduling system for running programs repeatedly at predetermined times. (If you don't know terms like `grep` and `cron`, you might think that they're rude noises. Actually, they are Linux things.)

Besides required software, there is often also a *recommended* list of software. For TWiki, the recommended software for the operating system and Web server are

- ✓ **Linux:** This is the famous, open source operating system created by Linus Torvalds. *Linux* is a Unix-like operating system that runs on personal computers (PCs) and servers.

Linux isn't mentioned as a requirement on the TWiki system requirements page. The page says that TWiki is developed in a Linux/Apache environment and that it will also work in Microsoft Windows. In practice, however, unless you are an expert and want to fight a lot of technical battles, Linux is recommended. The installation will work smoothly on Linux, will be pretty easy in other flavors of Unix (such as Mac OS X), and will be more difficult on Microsoft Windows. Nevertheless, TWiki has been installed on many different operating systems, all the way from PDAs to mainframes.

✔ **Apache:** This is an open source Web server that accepts requests for pages from your browser and then sends back pages. TWiki communicates through the Web server.

TWiki has its own environment. This environment is the combination of the Web server, language, language modules, and utilities that TWiki needs to work. Every other open source wiki (and most of them are open source) has its own collection of requirements. Choosing a wiki that your Internet mechanic understands means choosing one that uses a set of components your mechanic already knows so that he or she won't have to start from scratch when learning about the wiki.

After you and your Internet mechanic create a system that meets all these requirements, the next step is to visit the TWiki Installation Guide at

```
http://twiki.org/cgi-bin/view/TWiki/TWikiInstallationGuide
```

The Installation Guide — as shown in Figure 11-5 — takes you through the step-by-step process of installing TWiki. Because TWiki is one of the most mature wiki engines, the installation and configuration process is highly automated and contains a lot of fill-in-the-blanks procedures. Other, more bare-bones wikis, such as DokuWiki and Kwiki, require more fiddling with complicated settings contained in parameter files.

Figure 11-5:
Visit the
Installation
Guide at
TWiki for
guidance.

TWiki Installation Guide

Installation instructions for the TWiki 4.0 production release.

TWiki should be fine with any web server and OS that meet the system requirements. The following installation instructions are written for experienced system administrators; please review the AdminSkillsAssumptions before you install TWiki. If you need help, ask a question in the TWiki:Support web or on TWiki:Codev.TWikiIRC (irc.freenode.net, channel #twiki)

> **Hint:** TWiki.TWiki.InstallingTWiki on TWiki.org has supplemental documentation that help you install TWiki on different platforms, environments and web hosting sites.

Basic Installation

1. **Download** the TWiki distribution from http://TWiki.org/download.html.
2. **Make a directory** for the installation and **unpack the distribution** in it.
3. **Make sure** the user that runs CGI scripts on your system can read and write all files in the distribution.
   Detailed instructions on file permissions are beyond the scope of this guide, but in general:
   ○ During installation and configuration, the CGI user needs to be able to read and write *everything* in the distribution,
   ○ Once installation and configuration is complete, the CGI user needs write access to everything under the `data` and `pub` directories and to `lib/LocalSite.cfg`. *Everything else* should be read-only.
   ○ Everybody else should be denied access to everything, always.
4. **Make sure** Perl 5 and the Perl CGI library are installed on your system.
   The default location of Perl is `/usr/bin/perl`. **If it's somewhere else**, change the path to Perl in the first line of each script in the `twiki/bin` directory.
   > Some systems require a special extension on perl scripts (e.g. `.cgi` or `.pl`). If necessary, rename all files in `twiki/bin` (i.e. rename `view` to `view.pl` etc). If you do this, make sure you set the `ScriptSuffix` option in `configure` (Step 6).
5. **Create the file** `/twiki/bin/LocalLib.cfg`.
   There is a template for this file in `/twiki/bin/LocalLib.cfg.txt`.
   The file must contain a setting for `$twikiLibPath`, which must point to the absolute file path of your `twiki/lib` e.g. `/home/httpd/twiki/lib`.
   > If you need to install additional CPAN modules, but can't update the main Perl installation files on the server, you can set `$CPANBASE` to point to your personal CPAN install. Don't forget that the webserver user has to be able to read those files as well.
6. **Configure the webserver** so you can execute the `bin/configure` script from your browser.

Finding installation help

No matter what your skill or experience level, when you install TWiki or any other wiki engine, you will have questions. TWiki.org has many ways to find answers, including

- ✔ **Installation Guide:** Read the Installation Guide carefully before you start installing so that you understand the configuration process. When you start installing, though, you might have questions that are not answered in the guide. The guide refers to other parts of the detailed and extensive TWiki documentation. To view the documentation guide, visit http:// twiki.org and click the Documentation link in the left navigation bar.

- ✔ **Support Web:** This is the second help stop for most users. Here, you can look through other questions that people have asked and also add your own questions. At TWiki.org, the Support Web is found at

  ```
  http://twiki.org/cgi-bin/view/Support/WebHome
  ```

- ✔ **IRC:** You can often find wiki help using *IRC* (Internet Relay Chat), which is an open source precursor to the instant messaging (IM) programs that are so popular. IRC is an early version of IM that is used quite a bit in open source communities. IRC allows you to join the equivalent of a chat room and then ask questions to experts who might be hanging out in the chat room, waiting to help. Instructions for downloading the TWiki IRC software are on the TWiki Support Web.

- ✔ **Mailing lists:** Usually, open source projects have one electronic mailing list for the developers and another list for the users. These mailing lists can be used to keep track of developments and to see the kinds of questions being asked and answered. You, of course, can ask your own questions on these mailing lists. At TWiki.org, the mailing lists are primarily for development and system administrators. The lists are listed at

  ```
  http://twiki.org/cgi-bin/view/Codev/TWikiMailingLists
  ```

Observe certain ethics and protocols when asking questions in open source communities. For example, if you spend but a few minutes trying to figure something out and then start asking basic questions that are already answered in documentation, don't be surprised if the responses to your inquiries are a little frosty. However, if you precede your questions with a description of all the information you found to help solve your problem and detailed explanations that show you did your homework, you'll likely get a rapid and helpful response.

If you're installing another open source wiki, you'll probably find support options similar to the ones listed here, especially for projects that have been around a few years. For commercial wikis, you'll find some of the same support sources that we just mentioned as well as others, such as telephone- or IM-based support.

Downloading and unpacking binaries

When your wiki server environment is ready, your Internet mechanic is all revved up, and you know how to get questions answered, let the installation process begin.

The first step is to download the wiki engine software from the Web site. At TWiki.org (like most open source projects), you'll find a link to download the binaries — the *distribution* — of the software, prominently placed on the home page. Figure 11-6 shows the TWiki.org home page with the Download link at the top-right.

Figure 11-6: The Download link at TWiki.org is easy to spot.

The download page has a lot of information about the current release, such as what new features have been added and other ways in which TWiki might have changed. To download the software, follow these steps:

1. **Click the TWiki Release link.**

   The download page for the current release version of TWiki appears.

2. **Click either the Zip or the Tgz link in the box marked Download TWiki, as shown in Figure 11-7. (Read about these formats in the nearby sidebar, "ZIP and TGZ.")**

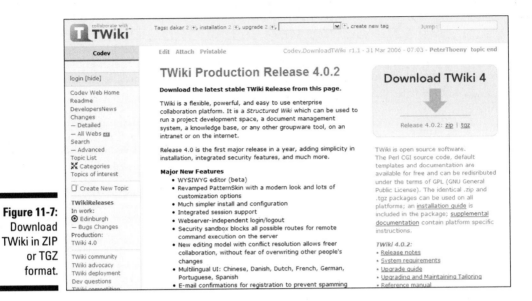

Figure 11-7:
Download
TWiki in ZIP
or TGZ
format.

3. **Go refill your coffee cup while the download commences.**

4. **When the download is complete, double-click on the ZIP or the TGZ file to unzip it.**

   After the download is complete and you unzipped the files, you're ready to connect to the wiki's Web server and begin the actual installation process.

Connecting to the Web server

Downloading and unpacking the binaries for the wiki engine is pretty easy. The next step — connecting to the Web server that will host the wiki — is a lot trickier. After that's done, though, the rest of the TWiki installation is pretty much downhill. By *connecting*, we mean that you tell the Web server that when a request for a URL comes in the View program in TWiki, binaries should run and display the pages requested by the URL. A typical URL might look like this:

```
www.mysite.com/twiki/bin/view
```

Here's where you start putting a lot of things together. The view program is a Perl 5 program that uses all the CPAN modules, the utilities, and the RCS repository to perform the functions of the TWiki engine. So far, so good.

ZIP and TGZ

ZIP and TGZ file formats are two ways how TWiki binaries are compressed. ZIP is popular on Windows PCs. TGZ is a form of compression used on Linux and other Unix operating systems. Your Internet mechanic will know which one to use.

However, telling you exactly how to configure your Web server correctly so that it connects the URL to the TWiki binary is beyond the scope of this book. The TWiki documentation doesn't even explain it because it can vary in so many ways, depending on what sort of Web server you use and what version you use. This step is where you really need your Internet mechanic.

What should happen is something like this:

1. When the Internet mechanic gets to the connecting step, he or she will stroke his beard (or curl her hair) and mumble in a knowing way.

2. The mechanic follows the instructions in the Basic Installation section of the TWiki Installation Guide.

3. After performing the basic installation, the Internet mechanic goes to the `http.conf` file on the server and makes a few changes to connect the wiki's URL to the right directory in the file system.

4. The mechanic enters a URL into a browser.

   The TWiki engine spits out the configure page described in the next section.

This is an exciting moment. Often, the process doesn't work the first time you do it (for example, because permissions in the file system are set wrong or because the Web server needed to be restarted), but eventually it does. After you see the configure page delivered from TWiki, you're almost done.

Running the configure script

The *configure script* is the basic script that controls configuration of your wiki. In most Linux-style installations, you have to run this script at the command line. Because TWiki is more evolved, you can configure your wiki by using a browser. (We still call this section "Running the configure script" so that you can impress any geeky friends you might have by saying, "And then I ran the configure script.") To configure your wiki, enter this URL in a Web browser:

```
www.mysite.com/twiki/bin/configure
```

The page that appears lists the current configuration settings for your wiki, as shown in Figure 11-8. Use this page to finish the configuration and installation process.

The TWiki configure page sets a high standard for ease of use that is rare in open source software. With other wiki engines, you might find yourself editing parameter files or changing variables in programming language files. This is how it starts out for most open source software; after a while, though, someone takes on the task of making configuration easier. The TWiki configure page represents just such an effort.

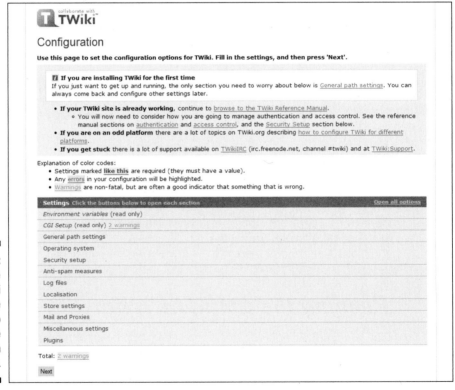

Figure 11-8:
Use the TWiki configure page to finish the installation process.

To configure your wiki, review each section of the configure page and adjust settings as needed. The sections are

 ✔ **General Path Settings:** These variables tell TWiki where all the wiki's moving parts are located. The settings here tell TWiki the external URL — for example, www.*mysite.com*/twiki — for accessing TWiki from a Web browser, the directory in which scripts are stored, and the locations of other important files.

 ✔ **Operating System:** This section contains settings that tell TWiki under which operating system it is running. This should rarely have to be changed.

 ✔ **Security Setup:** Here you set how sessions are managed, what security mechanisms are used, and how passwords are handled. This section is a good one to discuss in detail with your Internet mechanic to make sure that your system is secure. The sort of issues that arise in these settings include

   • *LDAP integration if TWiki is using existing usernames*

     LDAP is the Lightweight Directory Access Protocol. What it means to you is not entering usernames twice.

   • *How internal usernames are managed*

   • *How usernames are mapped to the TWiki usernames*

 ✔ **Anti-Spam Measures:** This section controls anti-spam settings on your wiki and rarely needs to be changed.

 ✔ **Log Files:** Another seldom changed section, this specifies the location of wiki log files. The *log files* are where TWiki keeps track of what happens with the wiki, such as registering users or accessing, saving, renaming, or deleting wiki pages.

 ✔ **Localisation:** Modify this section if languages other than English are supported by your TWiki engine.

 ✔ **Store Settings:** This section lets you choose the kind of repository in which your wiki pages will be stored. RCS (a version control system) is the typical choice although other options, such as using the file system or a database, are possible.

 ✔ **Mail and Proxies:** TWiki has an excellent integration with mail. Alerts of various kinds can be sent when pages change or when project management deadline entries expire.

✔ **Miscellaneous Settings:** This section controls a general mishmash of TWiki settings, such as the default names for various pages and the length of time that pages remain locked for editing before they expire.

✔ **Plugins:** These settings list which plug-ins are installed and enabled. *Plug-ins* are extensions to TWiki that provide support for calendars, spreadsheets, editable tables, and other such items inside TWiki pages.

After making changes to the configuration settings, click Next and then save your changes using the triple-top-secret password that your Internet mechanic set for you. You are ready to start making wiki pages and letting the magic happen.

Chapter 12

Managing Wikis

Congratulations! If you're reading this chapter, you probably already have a successful wiki. Like a weekend gardener going pro, or a home cook applying to gourmet school, you're ready to start thinking about managing your pet project in ways that go against — but actually work with — the loosey-goosey way you've been doing things thus far. You're ready to bring that nasty business term *management* to the organic beauty of your wiki. This doesn't mean that you've sold out to The Man or that you're no longer an indie wiki-creator. It simply means that your wiki has grown from a simple page to a complex ecosystem of competing interests and multifaceted concepts. And that's good news, right?

Mostly. The bad news is that problems can arise because, like any project, wikis tend to take on a life of their own as they grow. New people add content willy-nilly. And their contributions, albeit valuable, are filling up corners of the wiki you never expected to become populated. Old users resent the new users and vice versa. You might have multiple users who just plain disagree and are changing pages back and forth like a ping-pong ball. Other conflicts might pop up that you never expected.

Here's more good news: You can fix these hiccups by stepping in as the *wiki manager* — tactfully removing and reorganizing content and interposing in edit wars with a diplomatic flair — and lead the community to create a process for resolving disputes. This chapter shows you how to strike the necessary balance to ensure that your wiki remains a manicured haven of organization and collaboration and doesn't become an unkempt garden.

Wiki Maintenance: Pruning, Training, and Making Changes

A wiki is like a garden. It must be seeded, tended, and maintained over months and years. Eventually the wiki grows and overflows its original, stated boundaries. It is led in different directions, changing as it mutates and grows. It's time to step in, grab some pruning shears, and get to work to keep the wiki garden from becoming overgrown.

An overgrown wiki is almost useless. Wikis use the Internet's HTML protocol to its best advantage, creating a linked set of "pages" or "cards" that are organized in a coherent and useful manner. But what if things get out of hand? In the worst case, an overgrown wiki means you can't find what you need. You don't know what is on the wiki and what isn't. The taxonomy might break down, leaving you with 1,000 pages linked from one section's home page. (See Chapter 8 for more on creating logical wiki taxonomies.) The following sections show you how to cut back the mess and train your fellow wiki-teers to keep things clear.

Before we get started, here's an overview of the kinds of tasks that you, as a wiki manager, will do and train others to do:

- ✔ **Decide what goes where and what should just plain go.** You'll reorganize, delete, break long pages into multiple pages, and just generally help create an optimal structure.

- ✔ **Train others to do likewise.** When wiki-teers ask you to do *XYZ* on the wiki, teach them how to do it themselves.

- ✔ **Evaluate changes.** Are the changes coming in valid contributions (or even semivalid), or are they the work of a spammer or vandal? You have to keep an eye out for this, and most wiki engines let you receive a summary of the changes via e-mail or an RSS (really simple syndication) feed. Changes that just plain shouldn't be there must be rolled back.

- ✔ **Refactor the wiki, adding structure as necessary.** Reorganizing can lead to adding some structure, using templates for example.

- ✔ **Do all those routine tasks that wikis require.** In this chapter, we lay it all out in terms of daily, weekly, monthly, and yearly tasks, from daily backups to team meetings to evaluating and celebrating the wiki on its birthday.

Deciding what to cut and what to keep

An important goal of wiki management is deciding what to remove and what to keep. Although your wiki team might value everything it created, the difference between a usable wiki and a mess is sometimes unnecessary or poorly organized content. Often, fixing the problem is merely a matter of finding the right home for a few misplaced pages.

Another problem is wikis that might look like empty flower beds, waiting for content. Deciding what goes into these beds is one facet of the wiki manager's job. Encourage your team members to be bold, asking them to fill in the sparse spots and prune the dense spots. By encouraging your team to help in the pruning process, you ensure that their delicate sensibilities aren't insulted by overindulgent page removal.

The deletion of data also depends on your office or community data retention policy. Even if no data retention policy exists governing your wiki, backups and version control systems that allow you to roll back to a previous version are still important. (See the section, "Rolling back changes," later in this chapter.) Here are two ways to handle deleted or modified data:

✔ **Change markups:** *Change markups* are special HTML styles that show changes to pages. You can use the <s> HTML tag (which strikes-through text) to show deleted content, and adds tiny "change" tags to modified or added text that users can roll over to view changes. Chapter 13 describes the change-tracking features offered by WikiSpaces.

✔ **Prune:** Unwanted content should be pruned from your wiki on a regular basis. When deciding what to prune, use this checklist:

   1. *Check with the author.*

      If a page looks aged, does the author know? Can the author tell you more about it? More importantly, can the author do something about it? For example, the Confluence wiki engine lists the author and the last editor at the top of the page. TWiki lists the last editor, but you'll have to look through the history to find the original author.

   2. *Check the date.*

      Is the page out of data compared with the rest of the content? Is it still active? Is it still being visited? Archive or repurpose the page if you don't expect visitors. Check with the author first to see whether the page is ready to slip into wiki obscurity.

3. *Check the content.*

Has the topic been covered elsewhere, making this page redundant and a candidate for deletion? Is it simply an administrative page created to maintain a template? (If so, keep it in a housekeeping section of the wiki, if you must keep it at all.)

4. *Check the links.*

Is this page a dead end? How can your users find the page? Does it come off a main page, or is it orphaned somewhere in the taxonomy? What other pages should this page link to?

5. *Check the word count.*

How long is this page? An overly long page suggests that it might be better broken into smaller sub-pages. If it's too short, could you add it to another topic rather than leave it as a standalone page?

Training your troops

A good wiki needs good people. A wiki without contributors who write content is just a hard disk. Your wiki also needs editors — also known as *gardeners* — to make corrections. Your initial passion and efforts are for naught if your merry band of wiki-teers gives up during the extensive management stage. That's where the roles of manager and wiki champion become crucial.

Training your crack team of wiki-teers is important both at the initial stages of the wiki as well as during regular intervals in the wiki's life cycle. Wiki training usually happens on the job and as needed; you probably won't conduct formal training courses. Instead, you should copy the sort of approach taken by Wikipedia, which has a community area where the roles and policies are clearly explained, as you can see later in this chapter.

Your training will have to address the fact that people take on new roles as they get more and more involved with a wiki. Read about the wiki life cycle that we mention in Chapter 1. As your wiki grows, create a page that describes what each role does:

- ✔ **Contributors** (or writers) as well as **editors** (or gardeners) need to know whether any style should be followed when creating new pages or whether policies exist as to what sort of content is appropriate.

- ✔ **Managers** need access to perform special functions as well as access to descriptions of the maintenance tasks that should be performed.

- ✔ **Champions** need a copy of this book and any reminders distilled from it to help make the wiki succeed.

Seeding the mysterious flame of community wikis

The Mysterious Flame of Queen Loana, a book by cult favorite and erudite scholar Umberto Eco's book, is considered one of the densest — and richest — novels ever to grace the page. There are thousands of literary and cultural references throughout, and it would take an army of grad students to unpack them. As a result, it has taken on a reputation as a scholarly curiosity.

Luckily, there are wikis. A group of Eco fans got together to write about the book and bring to light all the references and allusions. The result is a chapter-by-chapter wiki (as shown in the figure here), full of cross-references, outside links, and scholarship as diligent as Eco's.

The way that this wiki grew is a lesson in wiki gardening. At first, a wiki page was created on one chapter, and then it was corrected and embellished until it was pretty much complete. Nothing much would happen until someone expanded the wiki to cover a new set of pages. The expansions would then get corrected and fixed by the community. The lesson is that the gardener might need to take the lead and create new flower beds so that the community can do the work of weeding them and filling them out.

If your wiki becomes stale, attempt to seed new content and add new kinds of pages. Writing about music? Add pages for each song on an album and flesh out those pages with cross-links and obsessively cataloged information. Keep things fresh. Expand from your original mission and add applicable information. Build another Wikipedia or even improve Wikipedia by adding your own hard-fought information.

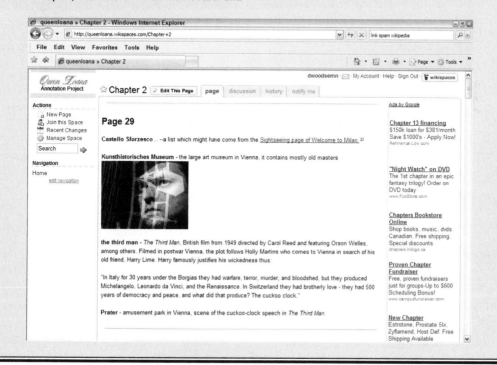

Wikis are usually self-organizing. A small group of people acts as a management committee, but these people rarely tell each other what to do. The training documentation on most wikis is not a law to be enforced but is, rather, a guideline that shows how someone else approached the task. As time goes on, these guidelines might become well established and seem like laws — but they don't start out that way.

Wikipedia has excellent models for such training content, as shown in Figure 12-1. This and other pages can be found at

en.wikipedia.org/wiki/Wikipedia:How_to_edit_a_page

en.wikipedia.org/wiki/Wikipedia:Manual_of_Style

en.wikipedia.org/wiki/Wikipedia:Guide_to_layout

Figure 12-1: Basic instructions are an important part of any wiki.

Many wikis that use MediaWiki (the wiki engine on which Wikipedia is based) link to these pages as a way to provide training resources. After your wiki gains steam, though, your community will probably need its own pages to express local policies and habits. In addition to posting help pages, some other good training measures include the following:

✔ **Conduct meetings during the wiki's growth and maintenance phases.**
Meetings offer a sense of ownership and responsibility to the members.

✔ **Hold a wiki roundtable to review content,** spending a few hours going
through documents and assessing their values.

✔ **Publish a monthly wiki newsletter.** Mention your pruning efforts in the
newsletter, thereby encouraging others to proactively prune as well.

✔ **Compare your wiki with other successful wikis,** such as Wikipedia.
Point out differences to your wiki's members. Visit `http://en.`
`Wikipedia.org/wiki/Wikipedia` to read about Wikipedia's history
and see how it compares with your own.

✔ **Treat the wiki as a project,** not just a one-off team effort. This develops
a sense of buy-in and purpose.

The training should help people to train others not only in basic wiki skills,
such as text formatting and creating links, but also in the wiki mindset and
the values of wikis. Your trainees should become evangelists for putting wikis
to work where they will succeed.

Rolling back changes

A good wiki tracks page versions so that you can easily roll back unwanted
changes. This is one of the most important features of a wiki because it
allows you to safely encourage users to be bold. A roll-back feature makes it
easy to undo boldness when that boldness is ill advised. To roll back changes
on your wiki, follow these basic steps:

1. **Determine whether changes need to be rolled back.**

   In most wikis, someone involved in running the wiki goes on a regular
   change patrol to examine recent changes and see whether they make
   sense.

   The Recent Changes feature of most wikis, as explained in Chapter 2, is the
   best way to run a change patrol. When you click the Recent Changes link,
   you see all the pages that have been changed. You can then go to each
   page and use the versioning feature to see exactly what was changed.

2. **Click the History tab or link on a page that you want to roll back.**

   Versioning makes rolling back changes pretty easy, and each wiki engine
   handles versioning a bit differently. This chapter uses WikiSpaces as an
   example, but most other wiki engines work pretty much the same way.
   When you click that the History tab, you see a page listing all of the versions of the page, as shown in Figure 12-2.

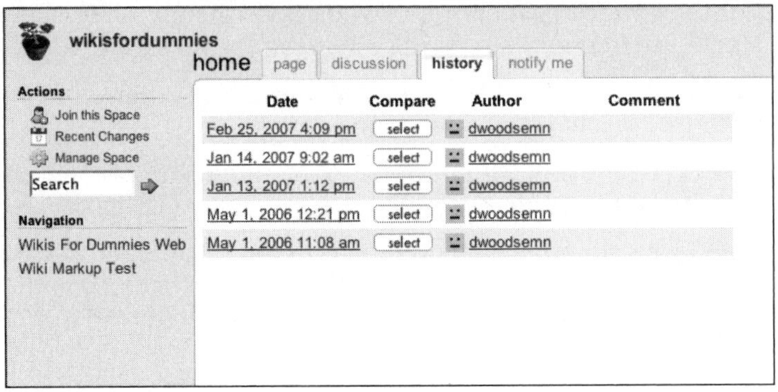

Figure 12-2:
The history
page of
WikiSpaces
shows a list
of versions.

3. **Click the link for the most recent version and see what has been changed.**

The page that appears shows the changes made to that page compared with the most recent prior version. Figure 12-3 shows how the differences are highlighted. Additions are shown in light green. Deletions are shown in light red. Some wiki engines show the old and new versions side by side.

Figure 12-3:
The
changes
from one
version to
the next can
be
displayed.

4. **To roll back the changes, click the Revert to This Version link at the top of the page.**

The page reverts to the earlier version.

Avoiding wiki spam

Spamdexing is another name for commercially oriented vandalism. Spamdexers put advertisements or promotional links in wiki content designed to promote their products or to increase their page rank so they appear higher on search engines. Rolling back spam changes is the most basic way to combat spam, but there is often a long-term battle between the spammers and the spammees with constantly changing tactics. If your site starts to get spammed on a regular basis, read through these sites for the most current ways of combating spamdexing. Then, consult your Internet mechanic for help in implementing them:

- ✔ `en.wikipedia.org/wiki/Link_spam`: Antispam advice straight from the granddaddy of wikis

- ✔ `www.structuredwikis.com/peter_2006-08-06.html`: Peter Thoeny's survey of wiki-related spam resources

Refactoring your wiki

Refactoring means restructuring. This term is often applied to computer code, but it also applies to design: taking something that's awkward and turning it into something elegant; or changing it to make it work better.

Wikis are filled with content, much of which is text. You can refactor text in the ways that we describe earlier in this chapter: pruning, breaking large pages into smaller ones, and changing the structure.

More uniform structuring calls for a different type of refactoring that might involve code, as we describe in Chapter 14. Here is a brief introduction to using templates to structure wiki content.

Reinventing the wheel every time you create a new page makes no sense. Certain pages in your wiki start to take on similar forms and eventually become standardized in a template. Many wikis also have a way to put the same content on many different pages without creating new versions of that content. Keeping on top of when new templates or new reusable content must be created is an important task in managing a wiki.

How Wikipedia fixes itself

Wikipedia is a wonderful resource, but it's also a target for vandals. Too, the temptation to add two (or three) cents worth of gibberish is often too great to resist. Great and small topics are often vandalized, leading to messy pages and real problems.

Despite this, Wikipedia is self healing because of its large community. First, a thriving band of people are on change patrol at Wikipedia. When a user — or moderator — discovers a problematic page, the administrators can automatically roll back a page to its original state very quickly. If one user makes lots of nasty changes, all changes made by a single user can be rolled back in one command, and the vandalism is taken care of. In other words, Wikipedia is great at playing defense. Wikipedia's change patrol is so active that many times, ridiculous changes are rolled back in a few minutes.

In the world of word processing, a *template* is a shell document that you fill in. In the world of MediaWiki — the wiki engine that runs Wikipedia — *template* often means a link to some standard text that might be included in many different pages. See Chapters 6 and 8 for more on using MediaWiki-style templates. For the purposes of this chapter, a template is an empty page with a structure that you can fill in.

Templates simplify tasks and solve problems in many ways, including

✔ Templates can simply be instructions for how to create standard pages. For example, the Baseball Reference Bullpen page shown in Figure 12-4 lists the basic sections that should be included on each page.

✔ Templates are indispensable when deciding what goes where in your wiki taxonomy. By creating a set of pages — and templates — that users can expect to see, you ensure that they follow the proper formats and do self pruning.

✔ Templates help standardize information. When you're looking to collect certain information from every member of the Lost in Space fan club — such as age, favorite character, and the like — providing a template through which users can enter this information helps you get what you're looking for. Such standardization won't happen on its own, leaving you to wonder whether certain readers (like you) prefer the Robot to Dr. Smith.

Chapter 14 provides details about creating your own wiki templates. With a little simple code, you can create templates that guide users to enter similar information. For example, a list of contact information is much easier to compile automatically if everyone enters the same information in the Contact form. (Chapter 14 also covers wiki magic like this.)

Figure 12-4:
Sometimes
a template
is simply a
set of
instructions
for creating
pages.

Grinding through Routine Administrative Tasks

If you ever have to write a wiki management job description, please leave out the florid, community-oriented prose we use in this chapter. Write something like, "Informational manager needed to create and maintain an asynchronous content management system based around the wiki framework." Then, list a few requirements:

- An ability to herd cats
- An understanding of library sciences and templating
- A love of language in all its forms

Then, when your new hire comes in, hand over the following lists of daily, weekly, monthly, and yearly tasks that are key to wiki maintenance.

Daily tasks

Daily tasks should be performed to ensure the integrity of the wiki. You won't have to do them all every day. By paying attention to these tasks each day, though, you can see what needs to be done. (After all, if someone wants to use your wiki, you don't want to make him wait for a week to get access!) Daily tasks should include

- **Managing users:** Fix user registrations, reset passwords, rename user accounts, lock user accounts, and remove user accounts. You might need your Internet mechanic to train you on how to do this or set up an interface through which you can do it. This depends both on the wiki engine and on your level of expertise in system administration.

- **Rolling back problematic modifications:** Because anyone can change a wiki, sometimes people add inappropriate or whacky content. You have to watch your wiki.

- **Backing up the wiki or making sure that it's backed up:** Backups are covered in Chapter 13.

Weekly tasks

Some tasks don't need to be done every day. They can be performed more infrequently, but they shouldn't be ignored. Here are some tasks to attend to weekly to keep your wiki humming:

- **Manage groups.** Create groups, add/remove users to/from groups, and set read/write access restrictions based on groups.

- **Suggest new ways of using the wiki.** Send out helpful hints such as: "Did you know you can automate the meeting minutes? Here's how." Or, "You can use a spreadsheet formula to calculate the total. Do this. . . ."

- **Look for old pages that might have become obsolete.** Send obsolete pages to the contributor for repair.

- **Ensure that front page links are active and usable.** Do this by visiting the home page of each department and following the taxonomy down one level.

Monthly tasks

Once per month, take a step back and really assess how your wiki is doing. Monthly wiki tasks include the following:

✔ **Assess the current business, organizational, or community structure.** Has it changed? Do you need to change the wiki to reflect these changes?

✔ **Check the taxonomy.** Have your users created new pages that don't fit into existing categories? Do new categories need to be created?

✔ **Look for new forms of standardized information.** Is the same sort of information showing up on many pages? Should that information be standardized. Should templates to encourage use of this new standardized information be added to the main template repository?

✔ **Look for pages with heavy use.** The pages that are edited the most are probably extremely useful. But just like high-traffic areas in your home, you have to clean them out and organize them so they continue to be useful and pleasant. They may grow too long and become overgrown with irrelevant information that makes a useful page less useful. Edit and trim them as necessary, perhaps breaking one page into several.

✔ **Look for old pages for deletion or repurposing.** Check with the page's creator to see whether it's still useful information that just needs to be updated. If not, delete or repurpose it.

✔ **Check for new wikis and create them as needed.** Is a department's wiki getting too complex? They might be ready for their own web, and you can create it for them. Better yet, train someone in that department to watch over the new web and help you out.

✔ **Produce a wiki e-mail newsletter.** Send interesting links to your team and encourage them to use the wiki more next month. By keeping the wiki on their radar, you ensure its growth and development.

Yearly tasks

Some tasks need to occur only once yearly. These often involve meetings, assessing the big picture, and having face-time with your team. Do not be afraid of the team! They are here to help. Annual tasks to conduct with your team include the following:

✔ **Decide whether the wiki is working.** How is the team using the wiki? Should resources be spent next year to maintain it? Is it valuable? Decide what makes it valuable and worth the resources (in both time and money) that you're spending on it.

✔ **Create a list of wiki best practices.** Have each team member describe his experiences with the wiki and distill those insights into a best practices document. Is someone in accounting using the wiki to plan lunch? Suggest that the marketing team try the same. Is the wiki becoming too cumbersome? Figure out how other departments prevented this problem.

✔ **Reassess the current crop of wiki management systems.** Could your roll backs and backups be made easier with new hardware or software? What does your wiki need to thrive? Are there new plug-ins that provide functionality you'd like to try out? (See Chapter 14 for more about plug-ins; chat up some wiki administrators to find out about the latest hardware and software.)

✔ **Reassert the wiki's importance through memos, interpretive dance, or by buying a Happy Birthday, Wiki cake.** Celebrate the wiki, recognize those who have contributed to the wiki, and show others you're excited about it. Your excitement might just rub off on more members of the team.

Chapter 13

Protecting Your Wiki

. . . .

In This Chapter

▶ Understanding threats to your wiki

▶ Running your own change patrol

▶ Controlling editing access

▶ Preparing for and recovering from disaster

. . . .

*T*he whole idea of protecting a wiki seems like a contradiction. Aren't wikis supposed to be open and free? Isn't the idea of wikis to avoid putting up barriers while encouraging everyone to share and participate?

To be sure, wikis are all about openness and sharing, but you must face facts. If your wiki is out in the open, always remember that the Internet has some bad neighborhoods. A small number of people with malice in their hearts will vandalize anything that they can for no good reason. Malice isn't the only danger, though. Even if your wiki is within the boundaries of a trusted community, people make mistakes. In their zeal to share and contribute, vast portions of your wiki could be erased by a naive and well-meaning beginner — or even a seasoned user who is in a hurry or having a bad day.

The solution to wiki security is not to erect barriers and undo the ease of use and free expression that make wikis what they are. More than a decade of experience has evolved into a prudent approach to wiki protection as a three-fold defense:

✔ **Be able to roll back damage.** Many wikis come with a *reversion capability* — that is, you can revert a page to an earlier version of itself. Being able to keep an eye on what edits are made (through a change-tracking feature) will help in this department.

✔ **Selectively erect barriers that protect certain types of content.** If you're not cool with letting all people come to your wiki and edit to their heart's content, you can restrict editing privileges to those who have member accounts. You can even restrict viewing rights in some cases.

✔ **Back up the wiki's content.** The best offense is a good defense, and there's no better defense than making regular backups of your wiki.

This chapter reviews the mechanisms and practices that have become standard ways to protect your wiki while keeping it free and open.

Evaluating Threats to Your Wiki

Don't get the wrong impression: Most of the time, wikis are used properly. Wikis are seeded with content. People learn how to use them. More content is created. Goals are achieved. Hooray for your wiki!

The more successful your wiki becomes, though — whether you're inside a company with a project management wiki or out on the high seas of the Internet with a content-focused wiki about a TV show — the more you should be ready to deal with the threats described in the following sections.

Vandalism

Wikipedia is probably the most vandalized wiki on the planet. Any regular visitor to the site will occasionally notice erroneously deleted pages or stupid changes that are meant to be clever. Spammers put advertising messages in wiki pages. People seeking to improve their ranking in search engines put links from wiki pages to their sites.

As part of the process of running Wikipedia, volunteers regularly staff the *Change Patrol*. They use the ability of wikis to report recent changes as a way to create to-do lists. People on the Change Patrol look over changes made to pages and roll back those that are just plain vandalism. The community of people who maintains Wikipedia has all sorts of fancy tools that can roll back all the changes made by a user in one command. This makes it easy to quickly undo changes made by some jerk.

If your wiki is open to collaboration, it is open to vandalism. There is really no recourse but to have your own version of the Change Patrol and to get good at using the tools described in this chapter to manage your wiki.

Passion

The *Los Angeles Times* created an experimental wiki called *Wikitorials*. This experiment quickly showed that wikis don't resolve conflicts that exist in the real world. Instead, wikis generally just reflect those conflicts. If you have a wiki page that brings out the passion people have about an issue, that page or set of pages might have to be managed differently. Figure 13-1 shows just a few of the warnings that appear on the discussion section of the Wikipedia page about abortion.

Figure 13-1:
This
discussion
section
requires
many
warnings.

The warnings in Figure 13-1 attempt to handle the passion that people have on the subject by explaining to potential contributors that content on the discussion section of the page should be about how to improve the page — not about debating the issue of abortion.

Wikipedia also limits editing of the article section of the abortion page, as shown in Figure 13-2. If you are unregistered or newly registered, you can't edit the page. Instead, you are referred to the discussion page — the one with all the warnings shown in Figure 13-1. You can request that these restrictions be waived by clicking the Request Unprotection link (in the box with the padlock) shown in Figure 13-2.

These restrictions stop people from going ballistic on the page in the heat of the moment. If you want to edit the abortion page, be prepared to back up your request to edit the page with a detailed rationale for why the edits are both unbiased and needed. This policy (of protecting certain pages from edits) was born of much experience and seems to work. This tactic might work for controversial pages on your site as well.

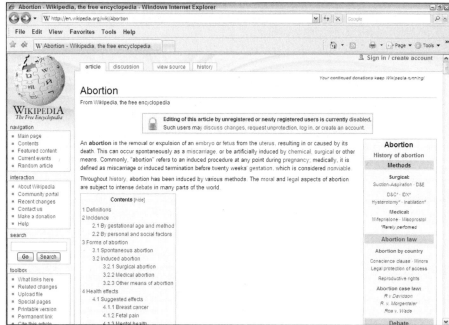

Figure 13-2:
Wikipedia
restricts
changes on
the abortion
article page.

Enthusiasm

Wiki culture recommends bold action. Don't be afraid to change things. Do it. Get involved. Understandably, the price of this attitude is that sometimes people get carried away and make changes all over the place, even in places where their contribution is not terribly valuable. Enthusiasm can also lead people to make changes that don't take into account the style of the wiki or its editorial practices. Damage done through enthusiasm is not as black-and-white as vandalism, but you will know it when you see it. Usually, finding a bunch of problematic changes from a user who wants to get involved can be an opportunity for training, eventually creating a strong player for the community.

Mistakes

Because wikis work through browsers, which are not quite as reliable or easy to use as most word processors, pages are frequently marred by editing mistakes. Sometimes just a few slip-ups on the keyboard can cause a whole page of content to disappear. Or perhaps your cat jumps on your keyboard and makes a statement while you have a page in editing mode. These mistakes can make you quite grateful for the version control feature of wikis that lets you go back to and restore previous versions. (We explain how to do this later in the chapter.)

System failure

Because wiki engines are pretty simple programs, most of the time, they work fine just as intended. However, software does fail, servers crash, and disk drives go bad. Like every other sort of computer-based resource, wikis must be protected from system failure based on the importance of the wiki. At the very minimum, the wiki must be backed up. In addition to this, you might want to have some other server waiting in the wings to restore the data so that you can keep working while your original wiki server is repaired.

Running Your Own Change Patrol

So, it happened. You went to your wiki and were shocked to find that someone added a huge picture of a kitten wearing a sunbonnet on your front page. The Help section was changed to a recipe for buttermilk pancakes. All over the site, you found links to sites about crochet patterns. Clearly, something weird is afoot. What are you going to do?

Clearly, your wiki needs a Change Patrol. This patrol might be a cadre of trusted and willing wiki members, or it might be a task that you have to do yourself. Whoever staffs your Change Patrol, the following sections describe what they (or you) need to do. We use a wikispaces.com wiki (`http://wikisfordummies.wikispaces.com`) to show the general steps involved, but most other wikis work in a similar manner.

Rolling back changes

The first order of business in dealing with unwanted changes is to get this junk off of your wiki. The great news is that almost every wiki engine has an easy way to go back to previous versions of pages.

As we wrote *Wikis For Dummies,* we added some links to the page shown in Figure 13-3 to see how they would be formatted. The figure shows two entries at the bottom of the page that were put in to see how wikispaces.com handled WikiWord links and links to external sites. Now it's time for those links to come out.

These two lines are no longer needed.

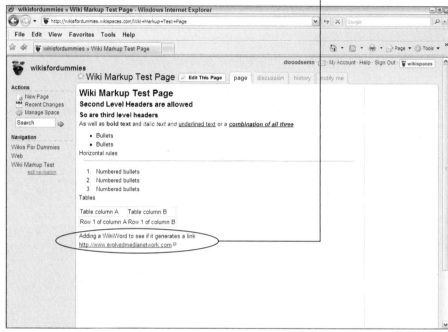

Figure 13-3:
This Wiki Markup Test Page has two experimental lines at the bottom.

Across the top of the page in Figure 13-3 are several tabs:

- ✔ **Page:** Shows the content of the page
- ✔ **Discussion:** Shows a page for making comments about the page
- ✔ **History:** Shows the version history of the page
- ✔ **Notify Me:** Helps you keep track of changes on the page

Click the History tab to open the page shown in Figure 13-4. The History page shows a list of all the versions of the page, descending by date. At the top of the list is the most recent version of the page, which is the version displayed on the Page tab. As you go down the list, you find older and older versions of the pages, each of which was the starting point for the version higher on the list.

To compare any two versions, click the Select button under Compare next to one version, and then click Compare next to another version. The page in Figure 13-5 appears, highlighting changes in one of two ways:

- ✔ **Green text:** Green text was inserted in the newer version.
- ✔ **Red text:** Red text was deleted in the newer version.

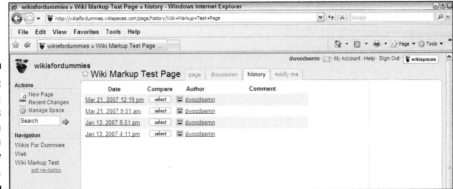

Figure 13-4:
Review a
page's
revision
history on
the History
tab.

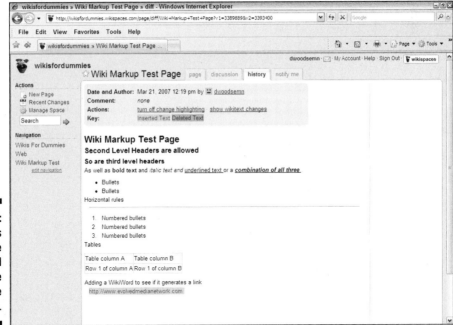

Figure 13-5:
Changes
are
highlighted
with the
Compare
feature.

Text that isn't highlighted is part of both the newer and older versions. If
you're investigating un-highlighted text, click the History tab again and compare two older versions until you find the version in which the offending text
was added. To revert to a specific version, follow these steps:

1. **Click the History tab to return to the History page; refer to Figure 13-4.**

2. **Click the date of the version to which you want to revert.**

3. **When you see a screen like the one shown in Figure 13-6, click the Revert to This Version link in the Actions section near the top of the screen.**

   Note: The Revert to This Version link doesn't appear at the top of the screen when using the Compare feature.

4. **(Optional) In the confirmation screen shown in Figure 13-7, add a descriptive comment, if desired.**

   You might say who reverted the page and why. If you leave the Comment box empty, the History page still displays the date and time of the version to which you reverted.

5. **Click the Revert button.**

   The earlier version becomes the current version of the page. Check out the page's History tab to see that your revert action is noted in the comments, as shown in Figure 13-8. Even if it seems like a lot of steps to revert to an earlier page version, reverting takes only a minute or so.

Click this link to revert
to an earlier version of a page.

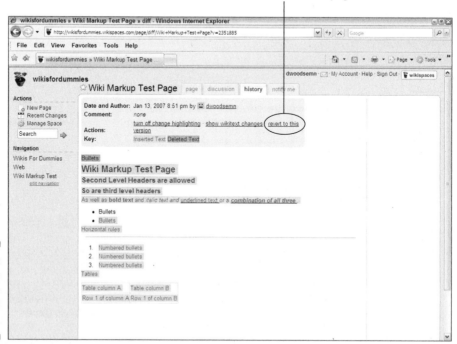

Figure 13-6:
Revert to
restore the
displayed
version.

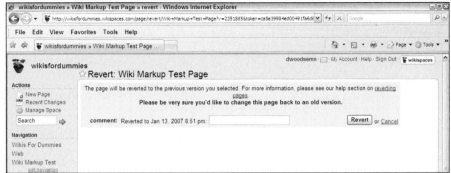

Figure 13-7:
Confirm that
you want to
revert to a
previous
version.

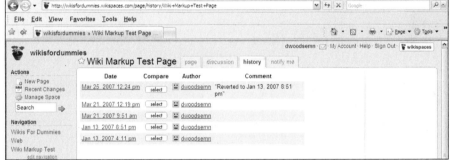

Figure 13-8:
The version
History tab
notes your
revert
action.

Some wiki engines don't have a Revert to This Version feature. In those wikis, you have to go to the version you want to restore, select and copy the text of the page, edit the current version, and replace the current text by pasting in the text from the version to be restored.

Tracking recent changes

Knowing how to roll back changes is the first basic skill in running a Change Patrol. The second is being efficient at checking changes to the wiki. Two mechanisms offered by most wikis make change review quite easy:

✔ **Recent Changes page:** Like the wikispaces.com examples shown here, most wikis have a Recent Changes link in the left-hand navigation, as shown in Figure 13-9. Click that link to see a list of all recent changes to the wiki, as shown in Figure 13-9.

The Recent Changes page is the to-do list for the Change Patrol. How often you check it depends on the wiki's activity level. Once weekly might be good enough for some wikis; others might need a daily check. For the busiest wikis, the Change Patrol works continuously so that vandalism and mistakes are removed minutes after they are made.

✔ **E-mail Notifications:** Most wikis support automatic e-mail notification of changes to pages, and this is another good friend of the Change Patrol. This feature allows you to sign up and be notified by e-mail when someone makes a change to a page. Click the Notify Me tab on any page to see the page shown in Figure 13-10.

Click this link to see recent changes.

Figure 13-9:
Regularly
review all
recent
changes to
your wiki.

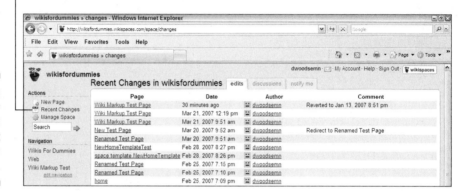

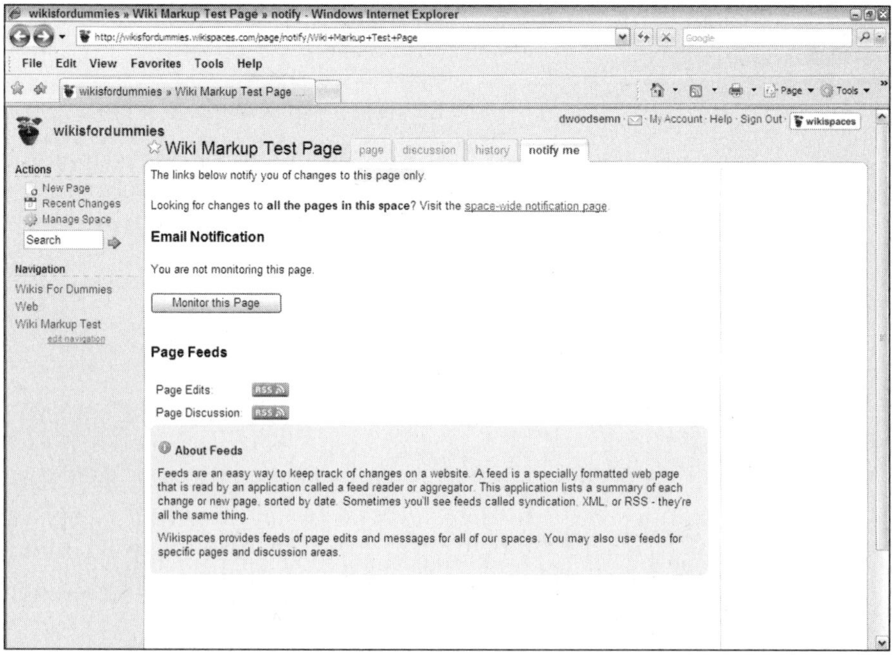

Figure 13-10:
Use this
page to set
up e-mail
notifications.

The notifications page allows you to sign up to monitor a page. If you click the Monitor This Page button, an e-mail will be sent to you every time someone changes the page. You can also sign up for *RSS* (really simple syndication) *feeds,* which are streams of updates that can be accessed through programs (RSS readers).

wikispaces.com also allows you to sign up to be notified when *any* page on the site is changed, a feature that is common for other wikis. This feature is especially handy to the Change Patrols on lower-traffic wikis.

Controlling Editing Access

Another strategy for protecting your wiki is to limit the number of people who are allowed to edit pages. Although this strategy seemingly contradicts some of the general principles of wikis, it actually makes sense in many cases. As we show earlier in this chapter, Wikipedia uses this strategy for some of its most controversial pages.

Most wiki engines offer some way to control access. Some wiki engines, such as wikispaces.com, control access at the level of the wiki. A wiki can either be edited by anyone or only by those who have been invited and have their own accounts on the wiki. Other wikis, such as TWiki.org, MediaWiki, JotSpot, and EditMe.com, have more finely grained control.

To see how access control works at wikispaces.com, click the Manage Space link under Actions in the left-side navigation area. Then click Members and Permissions to see a page like the one shown in Figure 13-11. At the top of the page, wikispaces.com lets you choose one of three modes:

- **Public:** Anyone can view or edit any page.
- **Protected:** Only those invited to have a member account can edit pages, but anyone can view pages.
- **Private:** This setting restricts viewing and editing to those who are members of the space. At wikispaces.com, this feature is available only by paying a subscription fee.

The bottom part of the page shown in Figure 13-11 lists member accounts and also includes a tool to invite new members to sign up for the wiki. Simply enter an e-mail address and then click Add Member to invite a new member to your wiki.

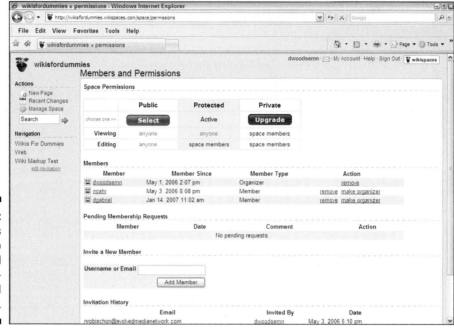

Figure 13-11:
Most wikis
allow you to
control
member-
ships and
permissions.

Some wikis offer more advanced access control methods. These often include

- ✔ Grouping users and then assigning permissions by group
- ✔ Grouping pages and assigning groups of users permissions to create, read, update, or delete the pages

Other advanced mechanisms for controlling access include blocking individual users from making changes or stopping specific IP addresses from making changes or viewing the wiki. These more advanced mechanisms might require getting a hand from your Internet mechanic. Effectively using the mechanisms of access control means that you have less to do on your Change Patrol.

Preparing for Disaster

One of the things that people don't realize when they set up a wiki is that they have gone into the business of data center operations. Even if you're using a hosted wiki, you still need to take responsibility for making sure that you're protected if something bad happens, and access to your wiki is cut off.

Backing up your wiki

Perhaps the biggest sense of comfort you can get when managing your wiki is knowing that you have a complete backup of all the pages on your wiki. Many hosted wikis make this extremely easy. wikispaces.com has one of the best systems. On the left side of a wikispaces.com page, click the Manage Spaces link (under Actions) to open the page shown in Figure 13-12. This page has four buttons dedicated to backups:

- ✔ **Backup Space: Windows .zip:** This compresses all the wiki markup text for each page into a Windows ZIP archive.

- ✔ **Backup Space: Unix .tgz:** This compresses all the wiki markup text for each page into a Unix TGZ archive.

- ✔ **Export Space as HTML: Windows .zip:** This creates an HTML version of your space and compresses it in a Windows ZIP compressed archive.

- ✔ **Export Space as HTML: Unix .tgz:** This creates an HTML version of your space and compresses it in a Unix TGZ compressed archive.

If you use these options, you can save the resulting file wherever you want. It's best to keep two copies: one on your local computer and one on removable media in case of hard drive failure. To restore your wiki from the markup text form of the backup, you have to re-create the pages one at a time and then copy and paste the markup text into each page. The HTML backup preserves the content and makes it possible to view the pages on a Web server or on your personal computer, but it is harder to re-create your wiki from them. Some commercial wikis (such as Confluence) provide more sophisticated support for restoring your wiki.

This sort of backup is a quick way to capture almost all the information stored in your wiki. Some things might be missing from these backups (such as discussion threads and version histories), but saving the core content is a great start on a full backup.

Of course, if you host your own wiki engine, you'll need to have someone in charge of making backups. Proficiency in creating systematic and complete backups is one very important qualification for an Internet mechanic, as described in Chapter 11.

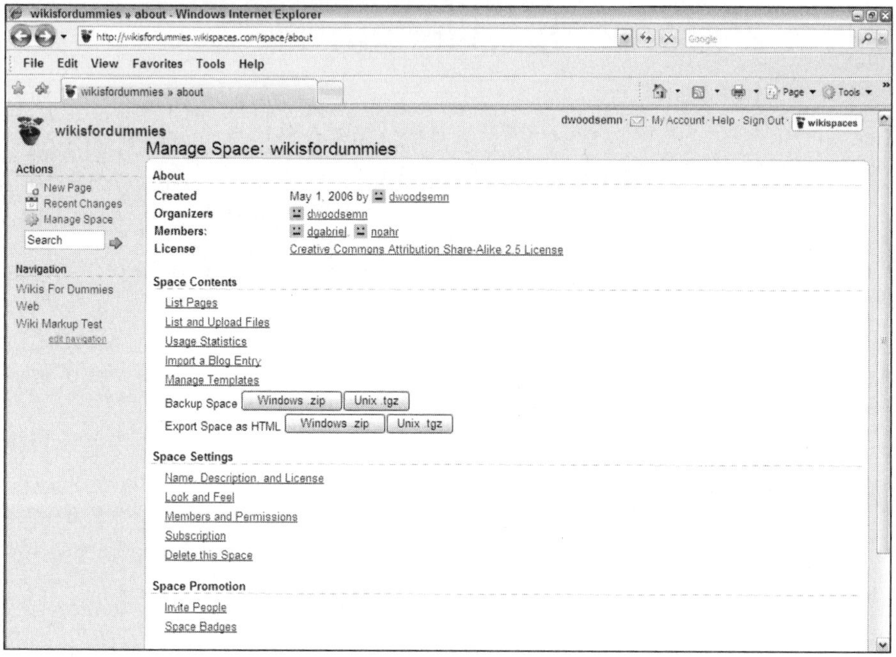

Figure 13-12:
Back up
your wiki.

Finding a new home for your wiki

When a wiki becomes important to you, the thought of living without it is a horror. If your business or organization relies on a wiki as part of its everyday work, plan for how you would restore your wiki to operation if some catastrophic event destroyed the facility currently hosting the wiki. This could take the form of working out the details to move your wiki to another hosting provider or having some other backup server available. In any case, make sure that you have a plan for moving your wiki.

Chapter 14

Creating Applications Using Structured Wikis

In This Chapter

▶ Understanding structured wikis

▶ Adding a search function to your wiki

▶ Using variables, templates, and forms to create applications

▶ Enhancing your wiki pages with plug-ins

*W*hen you sit down to explore wikis, you likely don't want to delve into complex variables, search terms, and forms. You want to make a cool wiki for you and your office mates, get a big promotion for being proactive, and retire on the beach in Maui, forever branded in corporate history as "the guy/gal who made us wiki-tastic." Right? Right.

But now you face the prospect of building something more with your wiki. Will you stand on that precipice, elated and excited at the possibilities? Or will you shy away and read a different book on, say, cooking or gardening? You, it seems, are the decider.

So you make the leap and decide to add those advanced features that everyone has been asking for to your wiki. Good. We begin by talking about *structured wikis.* Structured wikis originated in the brain of Peter Thoeny, the co-author of this book. Peter's vision was that by using simple components to add structure to wiki pages, and then adding plug-ins and basic programming mechanisms, wikis could be transformed into simple applications. Structured wikis are almost too complex for this book, but this chapter provides a good foundation. We start by showing you the basic concepts behind structured wikis, and then we show you how to make structured wikis perform specific tasks such as searching, taking input from forms, and enhancing your wiki with plug-ins. You're so close to doing some cool wiki things that you can probably taste it. If not, try licking this book. Go ahead, we'll wait.

Note: Our examples throughout this chapter use TWiki, which is a structured Wiki application that offers many cool features. Another example of a structured wiki is JotSpot, but that engine is currently closed to outside users because it was purchased by Google. TWiki is available for download and testing at `http://twiki.org`. Downloading and installing TWiki is covered in Chapter 11. You can safely test most of the examples described here using the TWiki sandbox at

```
http://twiki.org/cgi-bin/view/Sandbox/WebHome
```

Reviewing Structured Wiki Basics

Structured wikis are a hybrid of two different concepts: wikis and databases. A wiki is like a whiteboard — an open slate waiting for information. A *database* is a structured system for organizing data. If a wiki is like a hippie, a database is a square. As we all know, hippies rarely hang with squares. However, wikis and databases can work together with very little effort. In this section, we not only introduce you to the wild world of databases, but also discuss the important decision you face about whether you need structure in your wiki or not. We also talk about how you can easily include variables as well as functions in your wiki. This might sound technical, but don't worry — we take a step by step (not to mention fun) approach you can follow along with.

To structure or not: That is the question

How much structure should you add to content? It depends. Typically, you want to start simple and add structure only as needed. The organic and free-form nature of wikis is the essence of effective collaboration. That is, it's better to start wiki pages without giving too much thought to structure. Watch how the teams are using the wiki. If you discover a usage pattern where things are done repetitively in a similar way, it's time to create a wiki application that structures the content. Forms-based wiki applications with queries and reports help automate the daily workflow of the teams.

Consider this example. A call center has a simple wiki page with a status board listing who is on-call at what time. This could be in the form of a bulleted list or a table. While you're maintaining the status board, look for a usage pattern. There is a fixed list of support engineers and a fixed list of time slots. You can now build a simple application that automates the task of changing the status board: You can pick a person and time by simply clicking a button instead of typing a new name and time. Discovering patterns and adding structure is typically done a little at a time. You recognize a pattern, and you create a structure that makes a task or process easier for wiki users.

You then improve on that structure based on feedback from users, repeating those steps until you (and the users) are happy with the way it works. Figure 14-1 shows the final iteration of a status board. When you edit the table, you get pick lists to select a new time and person. This example uses the EditTablePlugin, described later in this chapter.

Figure 14-1:
Edit the status board table to pick a new person and time.

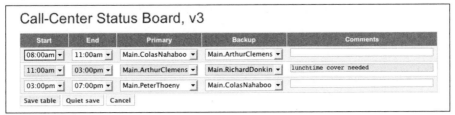

Using wiki variables

Before you can do much with structured wikis, you need to understand how variables work. A *variable* is an item that can assume any given value or set of values. Take, for example, the oath that starts out like this:

```
"I, (STATE YOUR NAME), do solemnly swear..."
```

(*STATE YOUR NAME*) is a variable because it will be replaced with an actual name; what that name is depends on who is taking the oath.

Wiki variables are used in dynamic portions of a page that allow you to create tables of contents, insert the time and date, and keep track of pages with ease. Wiki variables can also insert little graphics into your workspace. The syntax for wiki variables is %*VARIABLE*%. (Note that variables are enclosed between percent signs.) This is the same syntax used in PHP and many scripting languages. To see how variables work in wiki markup, open a wiki page for editing (see Chapter 6 for more on editing wiki markup) and enter the following:

```
---+ Fun Times
%U% %BR%
%N% %BR%
%X% %BR%

   * Set FUNTIMES = Yes, Absolutely!

Are we having fun on %DATE%? %BR%
%FUNTIMES%
```

Save this markup on your page and view the result, as shown in Figure 14-2. The following describes what is happening:

✔ `%U%`, `%N%`, and `%X%`: These variables show the Updated, New, and Alert icons, respectively. These are predefined variables in TWiki that refer to specific graphic files. The graphic files can be changed, if you wish.

✔ `%BR%`: This variable generates the HTML break (`<br />`) tag, which inserts a manual line break.

✔ `* Set FUNTIMES = Yes, Absolutely!`: This line creates a new variable. We set a variable called `FUNTIMES` to `Yes, Absolutely!`.

✔ `%DATE%`: A sentence includes another predefined variable, `%DATE%`, which shows today's date.

✔ `%FUNTIMES%`: This displays the `%FUNTIMES%` variable that was defined two lines earlier.

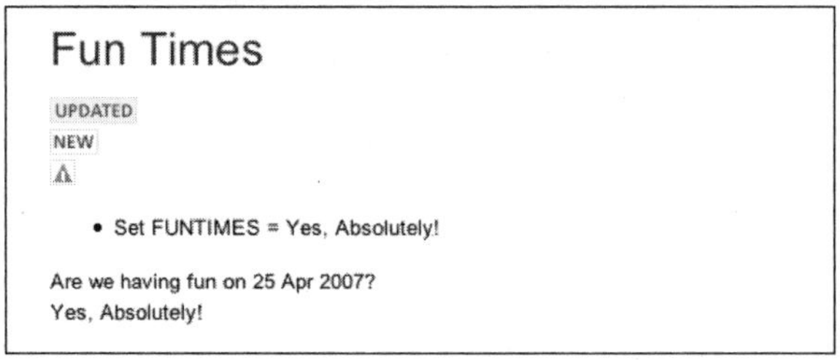

Figure 14-2:
Variables can be used to fill in data automatically.

Fun Times

UPDATED
NEW
⚠

• Set FUNTIMES = Yes, Absolutely!

Are we having fun on 25 Apr 2007?
Yes, Absolutely!

Although this is a trivial example, you can easily use these dynamic variables to create keys and other data for your database.

Performing functions with variables

Some wiki variables are also *functions,* which produce varying results depending on what parameters you pass into them. For example, `%GMTIME{"$hour:$min:$sec"}%` spits out the time formatted as 12:01:23. This variable takes parameters, processes them, and spits out a result.

Notice how parameters, such as hour, are prefaced with a dollar sign like this `$hour`. The parameters are enclosed in curly brackets. This function tells the wiki engine to return the current hour, minute, and second. You'll see other parameters with obvious names like `$year`, `$mo`, and `$day`. Funky, right? For another example, look at this long, ugly HTML code:

```
<input type="hidden" name="topic"
          value="BookT%GMTIME{"$year$mo$day$hour$min$sec"}%" />
```

This sets the key to this book as BookT plus the current time in year, month, day, hour, minute, and second. If this code runs at 1:30:25 p.m. on March 01, 2007, the result looks like this:

```
20070301133025
```

From this you can tell that the $hours parameter is using a 24-hour military clock (13 for the hour instead of 01).

Some favorites from the wiki variables vault

Hey, cool cats and kittens, want to take a look at some blasts from the future? How about rocking and rolling your own wiki to the break of dawn with the hip, wiki TWiki variables shown in Table 14-1?

Table 14-1	Some TWiki Variables
Name	*Description*
%BR%	Line break.
%BULLET%	Bullet.
%BB%	Line break and bullet combined.
%BB2%	Indented line break and bullet.
%RED% text %ENDCOLOR%	Colors the text between %RED% and %END-COLOR% red. Try different colors. A nice GREEN, maybe? Or MAROON?
%H%	Help icon.
%I%	Idea icon.
%N%	New icon.
%Q%	Question icon.
%U%	Updated icon.
%T%	Tip icon.
%X%	Alert icon.
%Y%	Yes icon.

Table 14-1 *(continued)*

Name	Description
`%ICON{"name"}%`	Adds a small documentation graphic (such as `edittopic`, `group`, `home`, `person`, `save`, `viewtopic`) or icon of common attachment types (such as `doc`, `gif`, `html`, `mp3`, `pdf`, `ppt`, `txt`).
`%DATE%`	Today's date in day/month/year format: for example, 03 Jun 2007.
`%DISPLAYTIME{"format"}%`	The format can include anything from `$year` to `$sec`. Hours (`$hour`) are in military time.
`%INCLUDE{"page"}%`	Adds the content of another page to the current page. Useful to create a big manual.
`%SPACEOUT{ "%TOPIC%" }%`	No, this isn't something to do with mind-altering substances. This variable takes the name — or any text in camel case — and spaces it out. For example, if the name of the topic is BabeRuthsUndies, this variable returns `Babe Ruths Undies`.
`%TOC%`	Generates a table of contents based on headings.
`%TOPIC%`	The name of the current topic; it gets linked automatically if it is a WikiWord.
`%URLPARAM{"name"}%`	Returns the value of a URL parameter. For example, if you append `?lunch=Sushi` to the URL of a topic, `%URLPARAM{"lunch"}%` returns `Sushi`.
`%WEB%`	The name of the current TWiki web.

Many more variables are available. For a complete list, check out

`http://twiki.org/cgi-bin/view/TWiki/TWikiVariables`

Searching Your Wiki

Suppose you want to find all mentions of the words *fun times* in your wiki. The %SEARCH% variable can be used to search your wiki and return results. Edit any page or create a brand-new page and add this code to see the %SEARCH% variable in action:

```
%SEARCH{"fun times" scope="text" nosearch="on"
        nototal="on" header="| *Topic: * | *Summary: *
        |" format="| $topic | $summary |"}%
```

Now save the page. You should see a table of search results, as shown in Figure 14-3. How did this happen?

Figure 14-3:
Use the
%SEARCH%
variable to
search your
wiki.

The preceding code sample gives the variable %SEARCH% a few parameters. Look at the code, one piece at a time:

- -"fun times": This is the search text. Search is not case sensitive by default, so it's okay to enter all-lowercase text. If you enter **"fun"**, the engine will search for the word *fun* as well as words containing the fragment *fun-*, such as *function* or *funky*. It will also find words with *fun* in the middle, such as the extremely fun word *profundity*.

- scope="text": This shows where to search. Setting the scope to "topic" searches topic names only. Other options are "text" (to search in the topic text) and "all" (to search topic text and names).

✔ nosearch="on": This parameter hides the search string, making the table pretty.

✔ nototal="on": This hides the total number of results returned, which is another prettification maneuver.

✔ header="| *Topic: * | *Summary: * |": This is what the header of the search result looks like. It is a table row with two header cells: Topic and Summary.

✔ format="| $topic | $summary |": This defines how each search result is formatted. Here, the row will show the topic name in one cell and the summary in another cell.

You can use the %SEARCH% variable to automatically generate a table of contents for your wiki. Imagine creating a page in your Beatles wiki dedicated to Ringo. Enter the following wiki markup:

```
%SEARCH{"Ringo" scope="all" nosearch="on" nototal="on"
        header="|*Topic:* | *Summary:* |"
        format="| $topic | $summary |"}%
```

This search brings up all the topics containing the word *Ringo,* allowing your intrepid users to dynamically check for Ringo mentions in your wiki. If you add another Ringo page, a new Ringo mention pops up in the search results. And if you delete a Ringo page, Ringo goes away, just like Pete Best.

Templating Your Wiki

Do you ever feel like a lot of the work that you do on your wiki is redundant? Do you repeat yourself? Do you keep doing the same thing over and over? If so, you probably need some templates for your wiki. Templates simplify wiki page creation because they contain basic elements shared by most pages, and all you have to do is fill in some unique data. Templates can provide a predefined method of representing data, or they can serve as containers for automated data entry.

Templates can be used to quickly create new pages with set contents. For example, suppose you wanted to create BeatlesGuitar entries detailing the Beatles' various guitars. Although each guitar page will have unique data, they share certain data categories and the basic layout.

A template-based application has these components:

- ✔ A **base topic,** which typically contains

  - *A form* to create new topics based on a template

  - *A search* showing all topics that were created based on a template topic

- ✔ A **template topic,** upon which new entries are based

Creating a base topic

You have to start somewhere. In the case of using forms with your wiki, you start by creating a new topic. The process takes just four easy steps:

1. **Click Create New Topic in the left bar.**

   Refer to Figure 14-3 to see this link.

   A Create New Topic page appears.

2. **Name the new topic BeatlesGuitarPage and click Create This Topic (there's no need to specify a topic parent or a template).**

3. **Enter the following content in the edit box:**

   ```
   ---+ The Beatles Guitar Page


   New topics are based on BeatlesGuitarTemplate.
   ```

4. **Save the topic.**

   A question mark link appears after BeatlesGuitarTemplate. This is an indication that the template topic does not yet exist.

Creating a basic template

After you have your base topic, the next step is to create the new template topic. Just follow these steps:

1. **Click the question mark after BeatlesGuitarTemplate.**

2. **In the new page's editing window, enter the following:**

   ```
   ---+!! Guitar Name
   ```

```
   * Played By:
   * Owned By:
   * Played On: (Albums)
   * Played At: (Concerts)




-- %WIKIUSERNAME% - %DATE%
```

You now have a straightforward template.

3. **Save the template with the name BeatlesGuitarTemplate.**

   The template looks like the page shown in Figure 14-4.

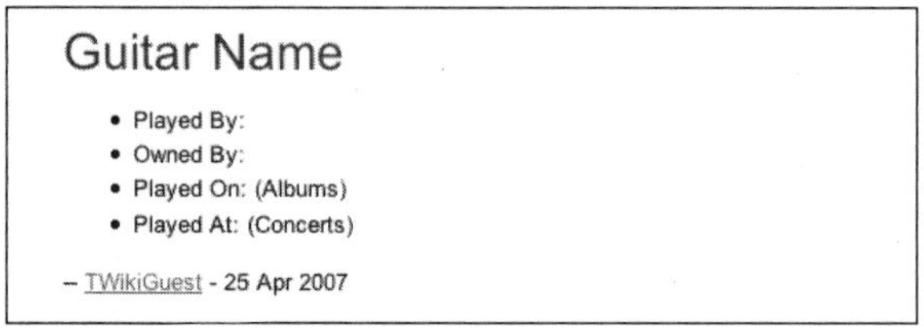

Figure 14-4:
Templates
simplify
page
creation.

> ### Guitar Name
>
> - Played By:
> - Owned By:
> - Played On: (Albums)
> - Played At: (Concerts)
>
> — TWikiGuest - 25 Apr 2007

Making new pages from templates

Templates make it easy to quickly create new pages. In the previous section, we show you how to create a basic template for pages about guitars used by The Beatles. To create a new page based on this template, follow these steps:

1. **Click the Create New Topic link located in the sidebar.**

   You see a form.

2. **In the Topic Name field, enter** BeatlesGuitars1.

3. **From the Topic Parent list, select the BeatlesGuitarPage base topic you created earlier.**

4. **From the Use Template list, select the BeatlesGuitarTemplate template topic.**

5. **Click the Create This Topic button.**

6. **Replace the Guitar name heading with the name of the guitar.**

7. **Enter some text in the Played By, Owned By, Played On, and Played At fields.**

8. **Click Save to save the topic.**

Repeat these steps to create additional pages like this, incrementing the number at the end of the page name each time: BeatlesGuitars2, BeatlesGuitars3, and so on. Now you know how to create new entries based on a template. Later, we show you how to simplify the page-creation process. First, though, we show you how to find the pages just created.

Finding pages created from a template

In addition to making it easy to create new pages, templates also simplify the process of finding similar pages and generating tables of contents for those pages. Use the *bread crumbs* (the links at the top of the page that show the path you have taken through the wiki) to go back to the BeatlesGuitarPage base topic. To build a table of all pages created based on the BeatlesGuitarTemplate topic, edit the BeatlesGuitarPage topic and enter the following:

```
%SEARCH{"BeatlesGuitars" scope="topic" nosearch="on"
        nototal="on"
        header="| *Topic:* | *Summary:* |"
        format="| $topic | $summary |"}%
```

When you save the topic, you see a table listing all pages with *BeatlesGuitars* in the name, as shown in Figure 14-5. Simply click a page name to view that page.

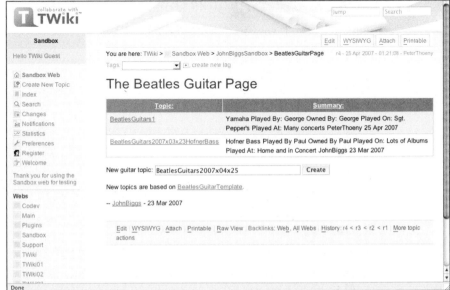

Figure 14-5: Search for all files created from a specific template.

Simplifying page creation

In the previous section, we show you how to create a new page from a template by using the Create New Topic link located in the sidebar. Using an HTML form is a much easier way to create new pages from templates. Edit the BeatlesGuitarPage base topic again and add the markup shown in Listing 14-1.

Listing 14-1: Using an HTML Form to Create a New Page from a Template

```
<form name="new" action="%SCRIPTURLPATH{edit}%/%WEB%/">
New guitar topic:
    <input type="text" name="topic"
            value="BeatlesGuitars%SERVERTIME{$yearx$mox$day}%" size="36" />
    <input type="hidden" name="templatetopic" value="BeatlesGuitarTemplate" />
    <input type="hidden" name="topicparent" value="%TOPIC%" />
    <input type="hidden" name="onlywikiname" value="on" />
    <input type="hidden" name="onlynewtopic" value="on" />
    <input type="submit" class="twikiSubmit" value="Create" />

New topics are based on BeatlesGuitarTemplate.
</form>
```

Save the page. This basic HTML form creates a text entry box like the New Guitar Topic text entry box in Figure 14-5. The form asks for a name which will become the name of a new page when you click Create.

The form has a visible input field named `topic`. It specifies the name of the topic you are going to create. The form field value is defined as

```
BeatlesGuitars%SERVERTIME{$yearx$mox$day}%
```

It contains a variable that generates a topic name based on a date, such as `BeatlesGuitars2007x04x24`.

The form also contains several hidden input fields and a submit field:

- `templatetopic`: This value specifies the template to be used when creating the new topic (`BeatlesGuitarTemplate`, in this example).

- `topicparent`: This value specifies the parent of the new topic. The value is set to the variable `%TOPIC%`, which expands to the current topic name `BeatlesGuitarPage`.

- `onlywikiname`: If set, the form rejects any topic name that is not a WikiWord.

> ✔ onlynewtopic: If set, the form rejects any topic name that is already taken, preventing you from overwriting existing topics.
>
> ✔ submit: This input produces the Create button, which submits the form data to the wiki engine.

Forms can do much more than create pages, as we show you in the following section of this chapter.

Adding Forms to Your Wiki

Forms are a natural extension of wiki templates. They provide a way for users to add content in a structured way. After you structure your content, you can run meaningful queries on it. Forms are, in many ways, the marriage of wikis and databases. They enable users without programming experience to create wiki applications, such as to-do lists, project trackers, inventory systems, and more.

A *form-based* wiki application consists of a set of topics that have the same type of form attached to the topics. This set of topics represents a database table. The form is custom designed for each application and might contain edit fields, radio buttons, pick lists, date fields, and other widgets. A custom query can pull content from the set of topics and display the form fields in table format.

Building a form-based application using TWiki is a seven-step process, as described in the following sections. The basic steps are

1. Create a home page for the database.

2. Define the form.

3. Enable the form for a wiki web.

4. Create a template topic.

5. Add the form to the template topic.

6. Build an HTML form to create new topics based on the template topic.

7. Build a formatted search to list topics that share the same form.

Creating a database home page

The first step in building a form-based wiki application is to create a new home page for the database. In this example, we show you how to create a database of Beatles fans: Collect the fans' names, their favorite Beatle, their Super Fan status, and their Beatles' story (how they became enamored with the Fab Four). Create a new page and enter the following markup:

```
---+!! Beatles Fan Forum

   * BeatlesFanForm
   * BeatlesFanTemplate
```

After saving this page, `BeatlesFanForm` and `BeatlesFanTemplate` become subtopics. These two subtopics are key to creating a database of fans.

Defining a form

After you create a database home page, you're ready to start building the form. Continuing with our running example; do the following:

1. **Click the question mark after `BeatlesFanForm` to create the form definition topic.**

   In TWiki and most other wikis, links are automatically created for words in camel case: for example, BeatlesFanForm. If the link points to a page that does not yet exist, you may see a question mark after the word. Every wiki engine is a little different, but TWiki uses the question mark. For more on camel case and wiki links, see Chapter 7.

2. **When an edit window for a new page opens, enter the following markup:**

```
---+!! Beatles Fan Form
| *Name* | *Type* | *Size * | *Values* | *Tooltip message* |
| FanName | text | 40 | | The Fan's Name |
| FavoriteBeatle | select | 10 | , John, Paul, Ringo, George, Yoko,
         Mick | Favorite Beatle |
| SuperFan | radio | 2 | yes, no | Is this fan a Super Fan? |
| FanStory | text | 100 | | How they came to love the Beatles |


See also: BeatlesFan, BeatlesFanTemplate
```

3. **Save the page.**

   Something that looks like Figure 14-6 appears.

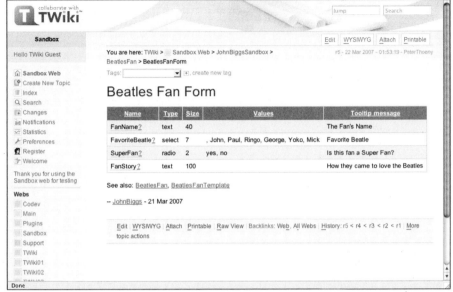

Figure 14-6:
This form
definition
defines the
form.

So what is this mess? What you see here is a form definition. The rows in the *Form definitions* table shown in Figure 14-6 define the fields of our simple database: FanName, FavoriteBeatle, SuperFan, and FanStory. Each field needs to be defined as follows:

✔ Name: As the name implies, this column contains the name of each form field.

✔ Type: This column defines the type of the form field. Types include

- text: A single-line text entry box
- select: A pull-down menu with specific selectable options
- checkbox: Check boxes (surprise!)
- radio: Mutually exclusive radio buttons
- label: Read-only text
- date: A text field with a date picker
- textarea: A multiline text box

✔ Size: This column specifies the size of the data field. For example, the FanName text box will be 40 characters long, and the FanStory text area will be 100 characters long. For type select, it is the vertical size of the select box.

✔ `Values`: The `select` input type requires defined values. In the example here, we added a few possible values for selection, including *Mick* for those folks who might have stumbled upon the wrong fan club.

✔ `Tooltip message`: This is what shows up next to the mouse pointer when you scroll over a column name. This is a good place for short helpful tips or comments.

Enabling a form

After you define a form, you must enable it for a web on your wiki. In TWiki, you start by telling the wiki engine that you created a new form using the WebPreferences page. Follow these steps:

1. **Click the Preferences link in the left-hand navigation area of your wiki.**

2. **Scroll down to locate the WEBFORMS setting.**

   You should see a list of topics with names ending in `Form`.

3. **Edit this page to add `BeatlesFanForm` to the WEBFORMS setting.**

   Don't worry. You won't bust anything.

4. **Save the WebPreferences page.**

   It will look like Figure 14-7.

Figure 14-7: Add your form to the WEBFORMS variable.

Creating a template topic

After creating your form, you're ready to create a template topic. Later, we show you how to create a form that uses this topic as a template. Each time someone creates a new Beatles fan entry, it will be based on this template topic.

To create a template topic, follow these steps:

1. **Return to the BeatlesFan home page created earlier in this chapter.**

2. **Click the question mark next to BeatlesFanTemplate.**

   A new topic is created.

3. **Enter the following markup:**

```
---+!! Beatles Fan: %FORMFIELD{FanName}%


Rock out, Beatles Fans. Back to other BeatlesFans



---++ Feedback


%COMMENT%


-- %WIKIUSERNAME% - %DATE%
```

4. **Don't save the page yet!**

   If you're curious, the markup you entered will render as shown in Figure 14-8. This markup serves as a placeholder for new topics that are created based on this template.

In the following section, you'll take this template to the next level by adding a form.

Figure 14-8: Enter some placeholder text for your template.

Adding a form to the template topic

In the previous section, we show you how to create a basic template and enter some placeholder text. Earlier in the chapter (in the "Defining a form" section), we show you how to create a form definition. Now, you're ready to put the two together:

1. **Click the Replace Form button to display a list of enabled forms, as shown in Figure 14-9.**

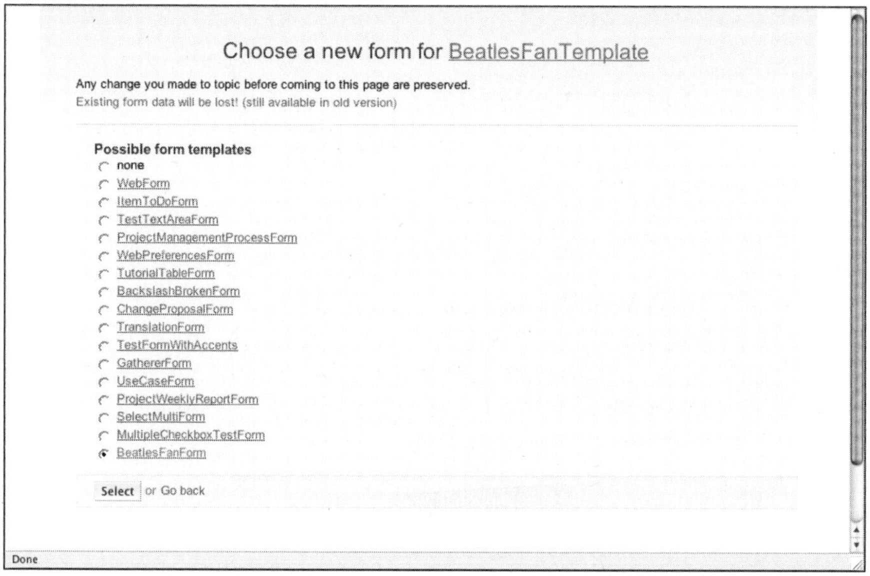

Figure 14-9: Choose a form to add to your template.

2. **Choose BeatlesFanForm and then click Select.**

   This puts you back into edit mode, where you will see the form attached to the topic just below the edit box.

3. **Don't enter any data at this point — simply save the topic.**

Building an HTML form for topic creation

You're almost ready to take your form-based wiki application live and let people use it. But how will users get started? Starting with a simple HTML form, as shown in Figure 14-10, guides users down the right path.

Figure 14-10:
Fans can
quickly add
a new page
with this
form.

> # Beatles Fan Forum
>
> • New Beatles fan: [BeatlesFan1001_____] [Create]

1. **Return to the database home page created earlier in this chapter.**

   Its markup looks like this:

   ```
   ---+!! Beatles Fan Forum


      * BeatlesFanForm
      * BeatlesFanTemplate
   ```

2. **Edit the page and add the following markup to the end:**

   ```
   <form name="new" action="%SCRIPTURLPATH{edit}%/%WEB%/">
      * New Beatles fan:
      <input type="text" name="topic" value="BeatlesFan1001" size="26" />
      <input type="hidden" name="templatetopic" value="BeatlesFanTemplate"
         />
      <input type="hidden" name="topicparent" value="%TOPIC%" />
      <input type="hidden" name="onlywikiname" value="on" />
      <input type="hidden" name="onlynewtopic" value="on" />
      <input type="submit" class="twikiSubmit" value="Create" />
   </form>
   ```

   The input field with the name `templatetopic` tells the form what template to use — in this case, `BeatlesFanTemplate` — when the user clicks Create to create a new topic.

3. **Save the page.**

   You'll see that a default topic name (`BeatlesFan1001`) is already entered in the text box, as shown in Figure 14-10. You may change the `BeatlesFan` number to another number and test the form by clicking Create. A form like the one in Figure 14-11 appears.

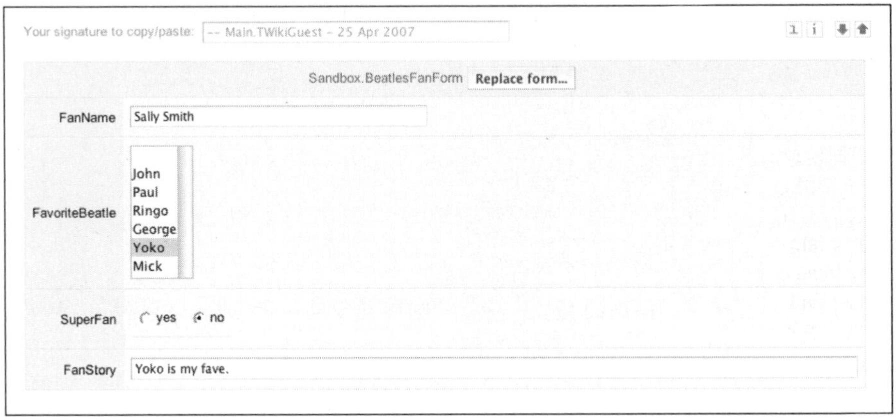

Figure 14-11:
This form is
the result of
all your hard
work.

Building a formatted topic list

Perhaps the most important benefit of both templates and forms is *standard-ization*. If you let people enter whatever text they want, chances are you won't get the same kinds of information from everyone. Standardization means collecting the information you want in a structured way. Templates standardize pages, and forms standardize the data that you collect from users. And with standardized data, you can easily build a formatted search to list related topics. In the previous sections of this chapter, we show you how to build a form to collect data from Beatles fans. You can easily build a for-matted list of all the topic pages created by this form. Open the BeatlesFans home page for editing and add the following markup:

```
%SEARCH{"BeatlesFan[0-9]" type="regex" scope="topic"
        nosearch="on" nototal="on"
        header="| *Topic:* | *Summary:* |"
        format="| $topic | $summary |"}%
```

The type="regex" parameter enables a so-called *regular expression* search. The actual search string is BeatlesFan[0-9]. It basically means that the engine searches for BeatlesFan, followed by any number. When you save the page, the result looks like Figure 14-12. Every time a user loads the BeatlesFans home page, a search is performed, and an updated topics list is displayed.

Beatles Fan Forum

Topic:	Summary:
BeatlesFan1001	Beatles Fan: Rock out, Beatles Fans. Back to other BeatlesFans Feedback JohnBiggs 21 Mar 2007
BeatlesFan1002	Beatles Fan: Rock out, Beatles Fans. Back to other BeatlesFans Feedback JohnBiggs 21 Mar 2007
BeatlesFan1003	Beatles Fan: Rock out, Beatles Fans. Back to other BeatlesFans Feedback PeterThoeny 22 Mar 2007
BeatlesFan1004	Beatles Fan: Rock out, Beatles Fans. Back to other BeatlesFans Feedback PeterThoeny 22 Mar 2007
BeatlesFan1005	Beatles Fan: Rock out, Beatles Fans. Back to other BeatlesFans Feedback PeterThoeny 22 Mar 2007

Figure 14-12:
The topics list updates every time a user visits the page.

Improving the topic list

Although functional, the forms and topic list generated in the previous sections are not yet very user friendly. Several things can be improved:

✔ The search that generates the topic list just shows the linked topic with summary. We would like to add other data such as fan names or favorite Beatles.

✔ We do not want the user to have to type the next free number each time a new entry is created.

✔ It would be nicer to simply fill out a form on the BeatlesFan home page with all details, click Create, and return to the home page with an updated list.

Spice things up a bit. Use the $formfield()$ variable in the format parameter of the search. This is an odd variable that has direct access to form items. Edit the BeatlesFan home page and replace the %SEARCH variable and HTML form with the markup shown in Listing 14-2.

Listing 14-2: Improving the Beatles Fan Form

```
---+!! Beatles Fan Forum

%SEARCH{"BeatlesFan[0-9]" type="regex" scope="topic"
        excludetopic="BeatlesFanTemplate" nosearch="on"
        nototal="on"
        header="| *Entry* | *Fan Name* | *Favorite
        Beatle* | *Super Fan* | *Fan Story* |"
```

(continued)

Listing 14-2 *(continued)*

```
        format="|   [[$topic][
        %PUBURL%/%TWIKIWEB%/TWikiDocGraphics/viewtopic.
        gif ]]  | $formfield(FanName) |
        $formfield(FavoriteBeatle) |
        $formfield(SuperFan) | $formfield(FanStory)
        |"}%

<form name="new" action="%SCRIPTURLPATH{save}%/%WEB%/">
| *Add New Beatles Fan* ||
| Fan Name: | <input type="text" name="FanName" value=""
        size="60" /> |
| Favorite Beatle: | <select name="FavoriteBeatle"
        size="6"> <option>John</option>
        <option>Paul</option> <option>Ringo</option>
        <option>George</option> <option>Yoko</option>
        <option>Mick</option> </select> |
| Super Fan: | <input type="radio" name="SuperFan"
        value="yes" /> yes, <input type="radio"
        name="SuperFan" value="no" checked="checked" />
        no |
| Fan Story: | <input type="text" name="FanStory" value=""
        size="60" /> |
| | <input type="submit" class="twikiSubmit"
        value="Create" /> |
    <input type="hidden" name="topic"
        value="BeatlesFanAUTOINC1001" />
    <input type="hidden" name="templatetopic"
        value="BeatlesFanTemplate" />
    <input type="hidden" name="topicparent"
        value="%TOPIC%" />
    <input type="hidden" name="onlywikiname" value="on"
        />
    <input type="hidden" name="onlynewtopic" value="on"
        />
    <input type="hidden" name="redirectto"
        value="%TOPIC%" />
</form>

For administrator only:

    * BeatlesFanForm
    * BeatlesFanTemplate
```

Notice that the HTML form has a hidden field named `topic` with the value `BeatlesFanAUTOINC1001`. `AUTOINC1001` is a special keyword telling TWiki to look for the next free number starting with 1001. By using this keyword, you can auto-generate the topic names.

After you save the topic, you see a table listing all Beatles fans and a form to add a new entry, as shown in Figure 14-13.

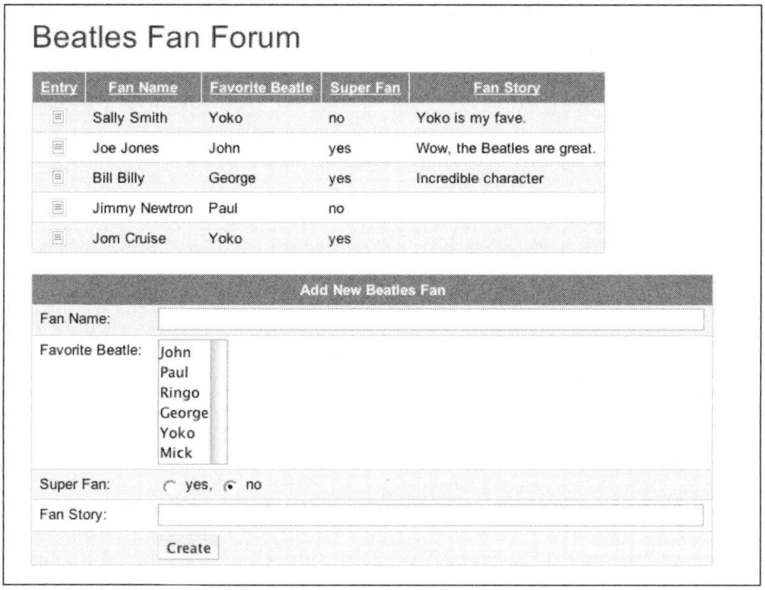

Figure 14-13:
The Beatles fan input form has been greatly improved.

This is an example of a truly powerful TWiki application made with our simple form and template pages. Feel free to experiment with the markup to see how you can apply it to other uses.

Adding Wiki Plug-Ins

Much of a wiki's power comes from its simplicity. But there may come times when you want more features than those provided by your wiki's basic feature set. Some wiki engines (such as TWiki) support cool plug-ins that quickly and easily expand the wiki's power. You might be familiar with Web browser plug-ins such as Flash or QuickTime that allow your Web browser to do more than just browse HTML pages. Wiki plug-ins work in a similar manner, but they are installed on the wiki server, not in your browser. The next couple of sections show you a few TWiki plug-ins to whet your palate.

CommentPlugin

CommentPlugin is preinstalled in the TWiki engine, so it's ready to be used right away. (We use it in this chapter; refer to Figure 14-8.) This plug-in allows you to add content to a topic quickly without an edit/save cycle. For example, if you're writing a design document in the wiki and would like to solicit feedback, you can do that by adding this at the bottom of the design document:

```
%COMMENT%
```

This single line of markup shows a comment box with an Add Comment button. Users can quickly leave comments.

CommentPlugin has many ready-made templates to capture content in a variety of formats, such as bulleted lists and tables. You can even define your own input form and output format. The CommentPlugin topic located in the TWiki web explains all the details and features of this cool plug-in.

SpreadSheetPlugin

Like CommentPlugin, SpreadSheetPlugin is preinstalled with the TWiki engine and is ready to use. It allows you to add spreadsheet syntax to tables. For example, you can create a table like this:

```
| *Region:* | *Sales:* |
| Northeast |   320 |
| Northwest |   580 |
| South |   240 |
| Europe |   610 |
| Asia |   220 |
| Total: |   %CALC{"$SUM( $ABOVE() )"}% |
```

When you save this page, the `%CALC{"SUM( $ABOVE() )"}%` markup is replaced with the sum of the preceding cells. The operation in this case is `$SUM`. (Note that if you want to right-justify the numbers, as we did for the sales column, you'll need two spaces after the vertical bar.) Other available operations include

- `$INT`: Rounds a number to nearest integer
- `$LOWER`: Converts a string of text to lowercase
- `$MAX`: Returns the biggest value of a list of numbers
- `$RAND`: Returns a random number

There are many more functions — over 70 in total. The SpreadSheetPlugin topic in the TWiki web documents all functions of this versatile plug-in.

Unlike spreadsheet programs, you are not confined to tables; you can add functions anywhere in the topic text. For example, you can use $IF to output text only if certain conditions are true. Here's an example. You might want to display a cross-reference to another topic. To avoid confusing your readers, though, you want to make sure that the topic exists first — thus, avoiding the problem of automatically generating something like See ThisUnusableLink. If you want to show a link to another topic only if that topic exists, you would use the following markup:

```
%CALC{"IF( $EXISTS(Sandbox.DiscussionTopic), See
         Sandbox.DiscussionTopic)"}%
```

EditTablePlugin

Wouldn't it be nice to be able to edit just one table instead of a whole topic? You can do that with the EditTablePlugin, which is another preinstalled, ready-to-use TWiki plug-in. To try it, type the following:

```
%EDITTABLE{}%
| *Tasks* | *Status* |
| Give flowers | Done |
| Buy digital camera | On Hold |
```

This plug-in displays an Edit button below the table. (It's worth typing this markup to see the button!) When the user clicks Edit, an editable spread-sheet appears. You can also add some structure to the editable table with this markup:

```
%EDITTABLE{ format="| text, 30 | date, 10,
           %SERVERTIME{"$year-$mo-$day"}%, %Y-%m-%d |
           select, 1, New, In Progress, On Hold, Done |
           text, 20 |" }%
| *Tasks* | *Completion Date* | *Status* | *Notes* |
| Give flowers | 2007-03-20 | Done | none |
| Buy digital camera | 2007-03-30 | On Hold | none |
```

When the user clicks Edit under this table, the editable fields include date pickers and pull-down menus, as shown in Figure 14-14. See the EditTablePlugin topic at TWiki for more on using this helpful plug-in.

Figure 14-14:
The
EditTable-
Plugin adds
advanced
features to
editable
tables.

InterwikiPlugin

Wouldn't it be nice to simply type **ISBN:978-0-470-04399-8**, **Wikipedia: Switzerland**, and **Google:alphorn**, and have it linked automagically to a book description, a Wikipedia article, and a Google search, respectively? That is exactly what the pre-installed InterwikiPlugin does. You can also add your own rules, such as `Bug:12345`, to link to your bug-tracking database. For more on this plug-in, visit the InterwikiPlugin topic in the TWiki web.

TWikiDrawPlugin

This plug-in isn't preinstalled, but it's worth the effort! You can add a Java-based drawing editor to your wiki, as shown in Figure 14-15, by using TWikiDrawPlugin. Simply add the variable `%DRAWING{name}%` to any page, replacing *name* with any name you like. When the page is saved, an empty drawing appears. When you click the drawing, a Java applet editor appears like the one shown in Figure 14-15. You can draw many different shapes, and you can even link shapes to other pages. When you click the Save button, the drawing is attached to the topic. For more on the TWikiDrawPlugin, see its topic page in the TWiki web after downloading and installing from TWiki.org.

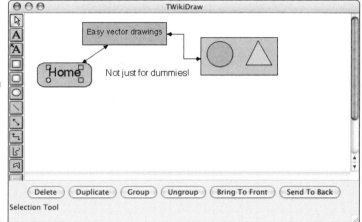

Figure 14-15:
Add a
drawing
editor to
your wiki
with
TWikiDraw-
Plugin.

Finding more plug-ins

Many more useful plug-ins are available on TWiki.org. To see what's available, check out

```
http://twiki.org/cgi-bin/view/Plugins/PluginPackage
```

A few noteworthy plug-ins include

- **ActionTrackerPlugin:** Track action items, run queries, and notify people of pending action items
- **BlackListPlugin:** Utility to keep malicious users away from a public TWiki site
- **CalendarPlugin:** Monthly calendar for teams
- **ChartPlugin:** Embed charts into wiki pages
- **DatabasePlugin:** Secure read and write access to data in an SQL database
- **HeadlinesPlugin:** Embed RSS (really simple syndication) news feeds into wiki pages
- **ImagePlugin:** Control the display and alignment of images using an easy syntax
- **SectionalEditPlugin:** Edit sections of a topic, one at a time
- **TreePlugin:** Dynamic generation of TWiki topic trees
- **TwistyPlugin:** Twisty section JavaScript library to open and close content dynamically
- **TagMePlugin:** Tag wiki content collectively to find content by keywords

Part IV
The Part of Tens

In this part . . .

This part summarizes key information about wikis that gets to the heart of what wikis are all about and how to put them to work. We explain essential wiki attitudes so you know how to think in a wiki-way. We also present the common roles that people play so you can walk the wiki-walk in the style that suits your personality. We conclude with some tips on how to put wikis to work in your office and then take you on a tour of some exotic wikis.

Chapter 15

Ten Essential Wiki Attitudes

*T*he mechanisms of wikis are so simple. After you understand them, it's hard to fathom how such a small set of functions could have such a large effect. Of course, the simplicity and ease of use of wikis is a big part of the success of the concept. However, another part of the story might be more important: Over and over, groups of people who use the simple mechanisms of wikis become more productive because new attitudes crop up. When faced with a wiki, people make new assumptions that lead to new ways of working and creating huge benefits for millions of people. Here are the ten wiki attitudes that we think are most important.

Shared Authorship

"Look at this great article I wrote," is a natural thing for any author to say, but it's also a statement that doesn't reflect the wiki attitude of shared authorship. Comparatively, "Look at this great article that *we* created," is a statement that reflects how most people involved in a wiki feel about the content that was created. This genuine feeling of shared authorship and ownership of the content is something that is profoundly unnatural at first because we're all trained that writing is a solitary process, reflecting only the contents of our own minds. When you get involved in a thriving wiki, though, this attitude can fade away and leave you with a sense of collective pride in having helped create something that is much larger than any one person could do alone.

Easier Is Better

When you compare wikis with most word processing programs or content management systems, you see how easy and simple wikis really are. Wikis have only a fraction of the functions of more complicated systems, but less functionality leads to way more content because wikis remove the barriers to involvement. Making everything as easy as possible is an essential wiki attitude.

Throw It Up There

Wikis are lifeless unless someone takes action by creating and posting content, but we're all sometimes afraid to publish. What if my article isn't any good? What if it's wrong? What if somebody doesn't like it and says something mean about it? Just toss those fears in the trash can, friend. Throwing content up there to see what happens is an essential wiki attitude. Don't worry whether it is bad or wrong or provocative. Other people on the wiki will let you know soon enough, and they will probably be pretty nice about it.

Unfinished Is Okay

One common barrier that prevents people from putting content on a wiki deserves special mention. Frequently, people don't feel comfortable putting up a piece of content until it's "done." On wikis, content is never "done." Even if you think it is done, it ain't done. After you post something, the community will probably make it better. So why wait until you are done to get help from others? Posting unfinished content is a key wiki attitude, one that reflects that Japanese concept of *wabi-sabi:* the beauty of imperfect, impermanent, and incomplete things. As soon as you have a good start on an idea, outline, or draft, get it on the wiki and see how other brains react to it.

Bold Is Beautiful

Do not be shy. Do not be afraid of offending somebody by changing his content. Do not be worried what others will think. To be bold, to take action, to make corrections, to get involved, and to make it happen are wiki attitudes that get people involved and give a wiki a sense of motion. Without bold community members, nothing happens on a wiki, and it withers and dies.

Set an Example

When people are new to a wiki, they don't know all the necessary wiki attitudes. They don't know that they should be bold, post unfinished content, and adopt all the other wiki attitudes. How will they know? How will they learn? You will teach them. Set an example to others who are new to a wiki. If someone sends you an e-mail that should instead be on the wiki, post it for her and tell her. Direct her to content you have posted. People become part of a wiki community by imitating others. Be an example for others to imitate. Take the message to them.

Let It Happen

Say that you are one of the *cognoscenti* for your wiki. You were there when it was founded. You helped write some of the early content and recruited others to join the fun. Now new kids are joining the party, and you have been setting an example for them. But wait, they aren't doing it just the way you did. They have new ideas and are starting to write pages that seem a bit strange and to change some of the things you wrote long ago. Yes, you must be bold and unafraid to disagree. However, in your position of respect as a wiki champion, you should not be too quick to quash the energy of the newly hatched community members. Letting it all happen is a good policy.

Structure Can Wait

After you become a wiki expert, you will see just how much you can do with each page of your wiki. You can add tables. You can e-mail content. You can put in forms and treat pages like databases. The problem with all these powerful ways to craft wiki pages is that they are at war with the simplicity that makes wikis succeed in the first place. When people try to edit a page with a lot of structured wiki elements, they can get scared. Remember that adding structure to wikis can wait. Don't be too hasty to introduce advanced wiki elements until you are absolutely sure that they will provide a big payoff and not chase people away.

We Don't Need No Stinkin' Rules

Structure of wiki pages is not the only thing that can wait. After a community gets going, powerful urges emerge in the founders to direct the work of others. When you look closely at communities in advanced stages, such as Wikipedia, you find quite a bit of structure to the processes that run the site. Well-defined roles exist as well as governance processes for resolving disputes and making policy decisions. Remember that structure should emerge from the bottom up — not be inflicted from the top down.

Follow the Community

This last attitude applies to those who would be wiki champions and brings together the spirit of many of the attitudes expressed in this chapter. Even if you're the person who started the wiki, don't act like that gives you special rights to be the boss. Linus Torvalds, the creator of Linux, is a master of understatement in his leadership of the Linux development community. When eager programmers would ask him, "What can I do to get involved with Linux?" or "What part of Linux should I work on?" his answer would usually be, "Let me know when you find out."

In suppressing the urge to give people direction, even to those who wanted it, Torvalds strengthened the community he founded by allowing each individual to find his or her own way to the right activity. If he himself directed them, they might end up doing the wrong thing and bowing out. So, if you are lucky enough to create a useful wiki, don't be the boss. Rather, be just another member and follow the community where it goes.

Chapter 16

Ten Roles People Play When Using Wikis

*W*hen wikis succeed, they do so to a large degree because they meet the needs of so many different kinds of people. With a wiki, whatever your inclination, there is always a way for everyone to chip in and add his and her special talent or knowledge to the mix. If you look at any successful wiki community, whether it be Wikipedia or an internal wiki inside a company, you will find many different people playing many roles. This chapter is a catalog of those roles that might suggest new ways of having fun with wikis other than those that have already occurred to you.

Reader/Researcher

The most common role that most of us play when interacting with wikis is that of a *reader* or *researcher*. We want to find out something, so we use our favorite search engine and are directed to a wiki. Much of the time, people who find information this way don't know that they're using a wiki. They just see a nicely formatted page with the information they seek. This is as it should be. The content of a wiki is always more important than the form.

After you see a page, though, knowing that it is part of a wiki and was created by people in a self-organizing community, you might be ready to put yourself and your knowledge out there and become a contributor.

Contributor

Contributors to wikis are those of us who have something to say or have knowledge that we're burning to share. Contributors read wiki pages and click that Edit button to make them better. Contributors start new pages and do their best to fill them out. Contributors make comments on pages in wikis that have discussions attached to pages. What contributors inevitably find is that other people created those pages or are reading them. It doesn't take long after you are a wiki contributor to start meeting and interacting with other people who are drawn to the same pages that you are.

Evangelist

The excitement of learning, sharing, and creating knowledge as well as collaborating to get work done often leads readers and contributors to want to spread the word — to become *wiki evangelists*. For public wikis, this can mean something as simple as linking from other Web sites or blogs to pages on the wikis. For wikis inside the boundaries of companies or other organizations, it can mean helping to make others aware of what is on the wiki and how that content can be used to help them do their work. Most people who use a wiki regularly become evangelists because they start bringing others into the wiki or driving people to the content they have helped create.

Editorial Quality Maven

A wiki is only as good as the information on it. With an active wiki, tens, hundreds, or thousands of people might contribute content. Some contributions will be better than others. Some will be brilliant, and others will be sloppy or just plain wrong. In most successful wikis, a *quality control patrol* springs up. This patrol is staffed by people who care about the quality of the information on the wiki and who know how to use the Recent Changes button to good effect. The quality control patrollers look at changes made to the wiki and examine them to make sure that they are accurate and meet the standards of the other content on the wiki.

Administrator

When wikis get active, all sorts of maintenance tasks spring up. New users must be given accounts. Special tasks such as archiving old content or performing bulk changes must be performed. New wikis must be set up and old wikis must be taken down. Permissions to who can see which wiki must be changed. New extensions to wiki functionality must be installed and brought into production. *Administrators* are the equivalent of the auto mechanics of wikis who make all this happen.

Operations and Hosting Engineer

Wiki engines run on servers. A slow wiki or one that is unreliable isn't likely to be successful. It's not uncommon for a wiki to fall into disuse after just one major outage shakes the confidence of the community of users. When a wiki becomes popular, the server should be enhanced to keep pace. *Operations and hosting engineers* — who keep the servers on wiki engines humming along — are key players in a wiki community.

Wiki Engine Developer

Wiki engine developers are the programmers who create the wiki engine in the first place and who continue to develop it by adding functionality. Developers can also help by tailoring the wiki to meet the needs of the community. When wikis are used to support communication, project management, and work flows in organizations large and small, the bells and whistles that many wikis offer become invaluable. In addition to the basic functions of a wiki, features such as calendars, alerting mechanisms, task tracking, meeting minutes, easy commenting, and simple work flow systems can amplify productivity immensely.

Policy and Process Contributor

Wiki communities not only have computer plumbing, but they have social plumbing, too. In most active wikis, natural disagreements (that people in most communities have) soon express themselves in the context of the wiki. If disputes are not handled in a fair manner that satisfies everyone involved, people might be driven away from the wiki, possibly decreasing its value. *Policy and process contributors,* the people who worry about setting up policies and processes (often by example but sometimes formally), play a crucial role in keeping a wiki running. The larger the wiki is and the more people involved, the more important this role becomes.

Critic

Not everyone likes working with wikis. Not everyone likes the communities that form around them. *Critics* look at wikis from the outside and point out where they fail and how they fall short of their stated mission. This can be a valuable service to those who want to make wikis work as well as they possibly can.

Champion/Founder

The *wiki champion* or *founder* is the person who fought the battles needed to get the wiki up and running, recruited the initial participants, seeded the content, found servers to use, set up the software, and did whatever it took to get the wiki going. In almost every wiki community, the champion or founder plays a special role and provides the crucial energy to keep the community moving forward and the cool head to resolve disputes.

Chapter 17

Ten Ways How Wikis Work at the Office

*W*hen wikis take root in the workplace, they are usually started by one person or a small team for a single project. Months later, those wiki pioneers discover that someone else in the organization is also using a wiki on a different project. Then a third team in a satellite office turns out to be using another one. It's possible that none of these teams is using the same wiki — for example, one team uses TWiki while another is happy with MediaWiki. Still, by and large, they use each wiki for the same basic purposes and to achieve similar goals.

This chapter is about those ten most commonly used functions of wikis among groups who are working within an organization to maximize efficiency, minimize duplicated effort, make collaboration easier, and achieve a common goal.

Shared Repository

Take a moment to remember how a business without a wiki stores information. For example, Kip in Accounting has a document on his hard drive that would help you finish an expense report. And Parker-Lulu in HR sent the latest update to the holiday leave regulations via e-mail — now which folder did you put it in? Josiah, the Marketing lead from your own team, has the only copy of your most recently edited pitch, and he's on vacation. You get the point: A huge amount of important information is stored on individual hard drives and spread across an organization. Using intranets sometimes alleviates these problems, but they are rarely used to the extent that a wiki is.

Wikis can store, manage, and organize information in a way that moves vital data off the hard drive and into a shared space. Wikis are as flexible as a desktop file and folder system, and you can search them by keyword. Wikis can contain every type of file you have access to. Better yet, if you move the documents from files right into wiki pages, people can write directly into the wiki itself. All the information is accessible all the time. It is the one source of information for an entire office.

There are lots of advantages converting documents stored in word processing files into a wiki (aside from helping to avoid the *Where did I put that?* syndrome described here). Documents that reside in wiki pages can be used to contain the sort of information that changes all the time, which can avoid creating a new set of printed or electronic documents for each revision, which can be costly and time consuming. By placing them on a wiki — not as attachment files but rather as text that can be edited on the wiki itself — they become living, breathing documents. Procedures can be changed as they evolve. Policies can be updated soon after they are determined. What's more, sections of each manual can be organized and tagged. That way, the person reading the manual doesn't have to wade through pages of useless material in order to find that one tiny piece of information that is relevant to his query.

Reducing "To All" E-Mail

To: All

From: Kip in Accounting

Subject: 23rd Floor Refrigerator

Would whoever ate my Frogurt please replace it?

Sincerely,

The Kipster

Sometimes, you will come across an e-mail that everyone in a company should read. Unfortunately, the entire company usually has to read e-mail that they really shouldn't. By moving this sort of communication onto the wiki, people at the office can be more productive and in control of their time.

Lots of wikis include the ability to create newsfeeds or alerts that appear whenever a person logs on. By using this mechanism, you can ensure that people are made aware of important updates without forcing them to actively check a news page. Now, please replace that Frogurt.

Simple Databases

Wiki pages are ultimately flexible. Although most of the time, you think of them as documents, there is no reason you can't use them for simple databases. For example, say you're doing some hiring, and you sorted through 100 candidates to get to the 20 whom you want to interview. To make a simple database, just create an index page and link to 20 pages, one for each candidate. Then, during the interview process, everyone can post their notes about each candidate to see what others said. This simple technique can be used to quickly create databases to track contracts, nondisclosure agreements, the software installed on computers — whatever you want. Because wiki pages are so easy to create, almost any one can whip up a simple database. Comparatively, using a database program to create equivalent databases is much harder to create and to share.

Knowledge Management

After many years of dedicated service, Kip is taking his Frogurt and leaving the company to pursue his dream of becoming an acrobat in Cirque du Soleil. You have just weeks to find his replacement and get Kip to transfer all his knowledge to that new person. This happens all the time, and it shouldn't.

Now, imagine that Kip had been using the wiki as a shared e-mail repository, as a place to put the accounting department's policy and procedure manuals, and also as a way to organize and manage projects and contacts. Instead of having to transfer all the data in his head, the new accounting chief would have an entire library of information to page through and learn from.

The longer a wiki is used by a company, the more valuable it becomes.

Training

Training goes hand-in-hand with knowledge management. Kip, being the wiki champion that he was, created a training guide that he used whenever a new employee joined his number-crunching staff. Because it existed on the wiki, it was easy to update with new information, such as phone numbers, policies, and procedures. Now when Kip leaves the company, instead of passing along a dusty and outdated training manual, his replacement can work from a wiki that has grown along with the changes in the company.

Intranet

Replacing a corporate intranet with a wiki mostly benefits the IT staff. Because a wiki is accessed through a Web browser and does not require any customization of the user's desktop, far fewer Help Desk calls are needed. Intranets are also notoriously prone to crashing, with hiccups that slow a user's machine to a crawl. Because wikis use Internet protocols, they are often more stable than office-wide networks. Users often confuse the folders on their own desktop with those that exist on an intranet. This leads to duplicated or conflicting documents when users save files locally and then make changes. This is much less likely to occur on a wiki because the content does not sit on the user's desktop, and it is easier to keep track of updates and changes in a given document or project area.

Web Publishing

Because wikis are Web based, they do a great job of acting like Web sites. A wiki can be used as an internal and secure Web for employees to use for accessing everything from departmental contacts to holiday schedules. And it can also be used as a way to reach customers on the other side of the firewall. DokuWiki, TiddlyWiki, and TWiki all have built-in support for publishing Web pages and syndicated RSS (really simple syndication) feeds.

RSS feeds can be used in the following ways:

- An internal Web site to keep employees abreast of industry news
- Externally as a way to avail customers of the latest news about the company

User Documentation

User-generated content has become an Internet buzz-phrase. In a nutshell, it refers to Web sites that encourage visitors to create text, images, or sounds for the enjoyment of other visitors. This creates a never-ending cycle of (sometimes) entertaining content. The same principle can be applied to documentation as well. Instead of having one set of answers, created internally and disseminated to the outside world, you could have instructions created by the very customers who use your products.

Generally, your task is to create the *stubs* — sample sections that invite visitors to add content — that get the user-generated documentation started. However, keeping that material updated is much more easily done by the customer who uses the product in ways that you might not have predicted. This shortens the time between updates to documentation of a product, often giving the customer a greater sense of ownership. User-generated documentation is not perfect for every type of company. When it works, though, it can be a powerful tool.

Shared Spreadsheets

Until now, spreadsheets have existed only as a document that had to be traded to be updated. However, with wikis, a single spreadsheet can be made accessible to multiple users at any given time. Instead of copies proliferating across individual hard drives and an intranet, the calculations live in one place. Every version as well as each change can be viewed or rolled back as necessary. TWiki, wikiCalc, and ZippApp all provide the functionality necessary to create shared spreadsheets.

Project Management

At their root, all wikis are project management spaces. The preceding nine entries, used together or in different combinations, make up a project management toolbox. And unlike project management solutions that you buy off the shelf, wikis are flexible and open to almost limitless customization.

Chapter 18

Ten Innovative Wikis

*T*he explosion in popularity of wikis has led to a kind of collective breeding experiment. Every genetic variation of a wiki is being tested. Here's one such fruit fly-like formula: Wikipedia + television = "The TV IV, the online compendium of television knowledge that anyone can edit" (http://tviv.org). Dozens of other such oddities exist. Many other variants involve the cross breeding of wikis with technologies or programming languages, such as the Microsoft Robotics Studio wiki (http://channel9.msdn.com/wiki/default.aspx/Channel9.MSRoboticsStudio).

In this chapter, we introduce you to ten notable wikis. Some represent worthy wikis that we just didn't have time or space to cover elsewhere in the book. Others are oddities that are fascinating in their own right. They have been chosen either because they offer a technological innovation or because they present wiki functionality in a pleasing combination that is worthy of attention.

TiddlyWiki

www.tiddlywiki.com

The wikis that grab the most attention today are the big, public ones used by millions of people. It's easy to forget that wikis evolved from one man's desire to create a killer, personal filing system. TiddlyWiki is, in many ways, a return to the roots of wiki. And it's so much fun to use that, after you understand it, you won't be able to stop playing with it.

TiddlyWiki is a wiki for your personal computer. You access it through a Web browser, and it looks just like a Web site. However, TiddlyWiki excels mostly as a mechanism for scribbling personal notes (known as *Tiddlers*) and keeping those notes organized, hyperlinked, and tagged with keywords. Tiddlers are not intended for use with big chunks of content. Even TiddlyWiki's creator, Jeremy Ruston, says that it's best suited for *MicroContent* — fragments of text, pictures, or other material that is smaller than a full page. TiddlyWiki is good for lots of other things, too. It can

- Replace Stickies or small text files that clutter your desktop
- Be used as a regularly updated to-do list
- Become a personal glossary or encyclopedia
- Serve as a phone book

And, last but not least, your TiddlyWiki can be put online and used as a blog or personal Web site. Just follow the instructions found in the Help section.

wetpaint

www.wetpaint.com

wetpaint is a hosted wiki that combines features of wikis, blogs, and forums to create rich Web sites quickly and without a lot of technical knowledge. The sites created by wetpaint are created from one of 24 different skins, each designed by someone who knows what they are doing. (A *skin* is a template that changes the look and feel of a wiki.) Comments can be added to wetpaint pages, but individual pages can be locked. Check out http://booklust.wetpaint.com for an example of what wetpaint can do. wetpaint sites are free, but advertisements are placed on the pages. Go to www.wetpaint.com to start a site.

Central Desktop

www.centraldesktop.com

Central Desktop takes the spirit of wikis and applies it to the problem of getting people to work together efficiently in business. The creators of Central Desktop use the concepts and mechanisms of wikis, but they fearlessly added features and embedded applications for discussions, blogs, file managers, task lists, milestone management, and calendars. Central Desktop has

WYSIWYG (What You See Is What You Get) editing and the ability to control page access. Central Desktop is free for limited use, but a variety of subscription plans are available for increased number of users and more disk space.

StikiPad

www.stikipad.com

StikiPad is a hosted wiki that offers task lists, discussions, file attachments, and innovative features like integration with Google maps and mobile access, something that is rarely addressed by other wikis. StikiPad is created by using the Ruby language. StikiPad wikis are free, but upgrades provide more space, advanced features, and technical support. To create a wiki on StikiPad, go to www.stikipad.com.

wikiCalc

www.softwaregarden.com/wkcalpha

Spreadsheets are among the essential items found on almost every PC. When the co-creator of the first electronic spreadsheet (Dan Bricklin) became interested in wikis, he immediately applied it to his area of expertise. The result is wikiCalc.

wikiCalc takes the power of a spreadsheet — the ability to format data or text and calculate data in a tabular layout — and combines it with the collaborative flexibility of a wiki. At the time of this writing, wikiCalc is so new that it's still in the *alpha* stage, which means that it's untested and might have bugs that still need to be worked out. Don't let that stop you from downloading and installing the program, though, which is available for both Mac and Windows platforms. wikiCalc can be run *locally* (on your own hard drive) or *remotely* (you install it on a server and make it accessible to the outside world via the Web). If you're a beginner, try running wikiCalc locally at first. Just download the application and run the install program to get started.

wikiCalc is not the only wiki that you can use for creating spreadsheets. TWiki (along with several others) lets you create tables that can be edited collaboratively online. None of the spreadsheets we have encountered, though, are as easy to get up and running as wikiCalc.

Another powerful feature of wikiCalc is that you can easily publish your spreadsheet online in a variety of ways. When you tell wikiCalc to publish a spreadsheet, it automatically converts the spreadsheet to HTML (the language used by Web sites) for you.

WikiTree

```
www.wikitree.org
```

Anyone who has put together a family tree will recognize some distinct phases to the process:

- **Phase One:** Sketch out the historical dates of every family member you can think of.

- **Phase Two:** Contact everyone on the list you made in Phase One, ask them to fill in the gaps, and see whether they have any details on family members who aren't listed.

- **Phase Three:** Trace family connections to be led to people who you've never met before, live in some faraway place, share your last name, and just might share your genealogy.

This enormously rewarding process enhances family bonds but essentially takes place in isolation. WikiTree is going to change family research forever.

WikiTree is an attempt to create a family tree of everyone who has ever lived. And it does so by automating the process of creating bloodline trees and making them accessible to everyone. Creating a new tree is completely free.

WikiTree is still in its infancy. Volunteers are hard at work improving the graphics and functionality of the entries. If you want to help a budding wiki grow, WikiTree is a great place to set down roots. Look for the Treehouse link in the left navigation bar to see how to pitch in.

WikiTimeScale

```
www.wikitimescale.org
```

The presentation of content can sometimes be as important as the information itself, WikiTimeScale is a case in point: It is a wiki that shows historical events through a graphical interface. The default home (shown in Figure 18-1 page is a graph showing empires, epochs, and great people. Underneath the graph is a Zoom feature; go ahead and click +25% to zoom in on the graph a bit.

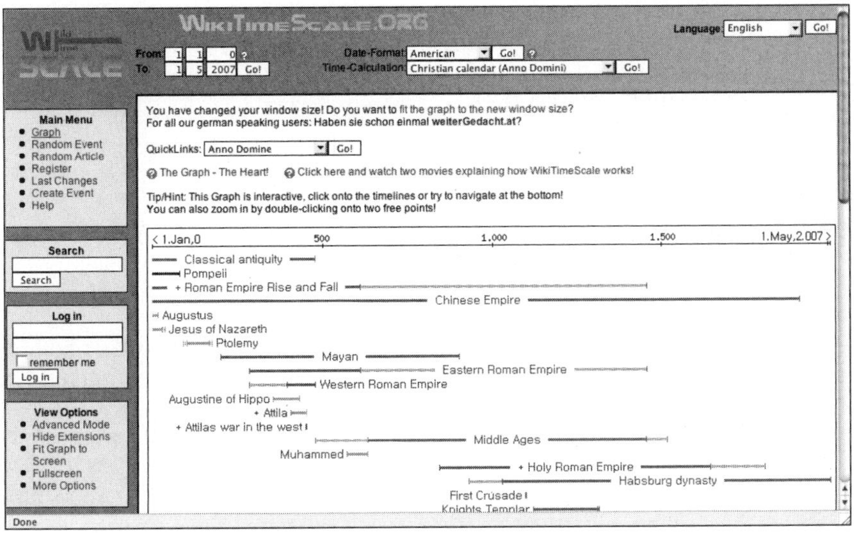

Figure 18-1:
The
WikiTime-
Scale home
page.

You can sort the WikiTimeScale page so that it shows only wars or empires, for example, by clicking the More View Options link in the left navigation bar. You can also adjust the scale and size of the graph.

WikiTimeScale is still a stub, with much work to be done before it becomes a truly useful tool. (For more on stubs, see Chapter 4.) Right now, for example, there are relatively few U.S. Presidents included on the scale (likely because the WikiTimeScale project was created by a Dutchman). If you're looking for a wiki to make your mark on, this one offers an excellent opportunity.

WikiTimeScale is also available for personal and private use. You can download the underlying code for the scale by clicking the Open Source link on the navigation bar.

Swicki

    http://swicki.eurekster.com

Swicki is a fascinating combination of wikis, search, and community collaboration intended to improve the way people find information. When you put a *swiki* in your site, a tag cloud interface displays that shows words with font sizes based on how popular they were as search terms. This tag cloud is created based on what users of your site are searching for. Then, when search results are displayed, user behavior is monitored, and users can vote on which search results are most useful. The search results page also allows questions to be asked and answered. Swicki intends to extend personal publishing on the Web by allowing anyone to publish a community-powered search engine that produces only the targeted search results that you and your community want.

Kwiki

www.kwiki.org

Kwiki is Perl-based implementation of a wiki, created by Brian Ingerson, that is designed to be easily extensible. Pretty much everything in Kwiki is a plug-in. (A *plug-in* is a bit of code to perform a small function that fits neatly in with all the other bits of code in a program.) This architecture makes it easy to add new functionality to make Kwiki do whatever you want it to do. If you have Perl skills and want to explore the possibilities of what wikis can do, go directly to www.kwiki.org.

FlexWiki

www.flexwiki.com

The wiki world was taken by surprise when David Ornstein created FlexWiki, based on the Microsoft .NET technology, and released it as part of the company's shared source initiative. FlexWiki is unique not only because of its foundations in Microsoft but also because it's the only wiki that implements the WikiTalk language, which is a descendant of *SmallTalk,* a pioneering object-oriented language. FlexWiki is used on the Microsoft Channel 9 community Web site.

Index

• *J* •

• *K* •

• Q •

• R •

• X •

• Z •